RACHAEL RAY

CLASSIC

30-MINUTE MEALS

CLASSIC

RACHAEL RAY

30-MINUTE MEALS

LAKE ISLE PRESS

All recipes in this book are reprinted from previously published books by Rachael Ray, namely, *30-Minute Meals*, *The Open House Cookbook*, *Comfort Foods*, *Veggie Meals*, *30-Minute Meals 2*, *Get Togethers*, *Cooking Rocks!*, and *Cooking 'Round the Clock*.

Published by:
Lake Isle Press, Inc.
16 West 32nd Street, Suite 10-B
New York, NY 10001
(212) 273-0796
E-mail: lakeisle@earthlink.net

Distributed to the trade by:
National Book Network, Inc.
4501 Forbes Boulevard, Suite 200
Lanham, MD 20706
1(800) 462-6420
www.nbnbooks.com

Library of Congress Control Number: 2006930190

ISBN-13: 978-1-891105-30-2

ISBN-10: 1-891105-30-2

Complete list of photo credits: see page 342

Book and cover design: Ellen Swandiak

Editors: Pimpila Thanaporn, Katherine Trimble

This book is available at special sales discounts for bulk purchases as premiums or special editions, including customized covers. For more information, contact the publisher at (212) 273-0796 or by e-mail, lakeisle@earthlink.net

First edition

Printed in China

10 9 8 7 6

To new fans and new friends

DON'T MEASURE WITH INSTRUMENTS, USE YOUR HANDS. You're not baking or conducting experiments for the government— just feel your way through.

Measuring Rachael's Way

HANDFUL
about 3 tablespoons

PALMFUL
about 2 tablespoons

HALF A PALMFUL
you do the math

A PINCH
about 1/4 teaspoon

A FEW GOOD PINCHES
about 1 teaspoon

ONCE AROUND THE PAN
about 1 tablespoon of liquid

TWICE AROUND THE PAN
more math: about 2 tablespoons,
3 or 4 would be 1/4 cup

Introduction

You know me, I like the oldies but goodies. This collection of recipes, taken from my earlier books, puts my best, classic recipes all in a single volume. Perfect for any occasion, it can be your go-to source any night of the week. Had a busy day at work? Turn to the EVERYDAY section for casual, hearty meals you can get on the table in no time. Company coming? The menus in the PARTIES section will show off your good taste. And for that special someone, DATE NIGHTS are sure to please. For a fun, family activity, try the recipes in KID CHEFS, a special section on cooking with children. It's the perfect way to inspire confidence in young ones. And remember, a great dinner with your family is just 30 minutes away!

Rachael Ray

TABLE OF CONTENTS

RACHAEL RAY
CLASSIC
30-MINUTE MEALS

RACHAEL RAY

CLASSIC
30-MINUTE MEALS

EVERYDAY

30-MINUTE MEALS
MENU

PIZZA WITH PIZZAZZ

1

entree
PUTTANESCA
PIZZA: TOMATO,
OLIVE, CAPER,
AND ANCHOVY

2

suggested side
GREEN SALAD

Puttanesca is a pasta sauce named for streetwalkers, or ladies of the night, as it is spicy, fast, and easy to make. This pizza packs the same strong flavor as the pasta dish, and it's quicker to make than it is to call Domino's. A perforated pizza pan can be bought for $6 to $12 in most supermarkets. I recommend the small investment for anyone who likes crisp crust.

MAKES 2 SERVINGS

Puttanesca Pizza: Tomato, Olive, Caper, and Anchovy

2 cloves garlic, minced

1/8 teaspoon (a pinch) crushed red pepper flakes

2 tablespoons extra-virgin olive oil (evoo) (twice around the pan)

2 anchovy fillets

1 can (14 ounces) tomatoes, drained and diced

One 12-inch thin-crust Boboli pizza shell

2 tablespoons chopped fresh flat-leaf parsley (a palmful)

2 tablespoons capers, drained (available in international foods aisle)

1/4 cup pitted Kalamata olives, drained and coarsely chopped (available in international aisle)

1/2 cup grated blended Italian cheeses

Preheat oven to 425°F.

In a small skillet over medium heat, sauté garlic and crushed red pepper flakes in evoo until the garlic begins to sizzle. Add anchovy fillets, and use the back of a wooden spoon to help melt the anchovies into the evoo. Once dissolved, the anchovies' taste will mellow and serve only to give the sauce a nutty flavor and provide natural salt in the finished pizza. Add tomatoes, and stir to coat evenly with flavored oil. Remove from heat.

Place the pizza crust on a pizza pan. Sprinkle evenly with tomato mixture, spreading ito the edges of the pizza shell. Add the parsley, capers, and olives in the same manner. Run your fingers through the cheese in the sack to fluff it up. Cover the pie with a light layer of the cheese right out to the edges. Some of the colors of the toppings should still peek through; too much cheese will result in a soggy pie.

Place pie in oven directly on center rack or on perforated pizza pan. Cook the pie at least 8 minutes before checking on it and no more than 12 minutes altogether. The cheese should begin to brown and the edges should be crisp when you remove the pizza from the oven. Serve with a green salad for a complete meal. ★

30-MINUTE MEALS
MENU

OPEN
SESAME

1

entree
SESAME
NOODLES

2

suggested side
FRUIT OR A
CHUNKED
VEGETABLE
SALAD

A paste made from ground sesame seeds, tahini can be found in the international or whole/natural food aisles of your local market.

★ ★ ★ ☆

MAKES 4 LUNCH OR LIGHT SUPPER SERVINGS

Sesame Noodles

Salt, to taste

1 pound cappellini (angel hair pasta)

1/4 cup low-sodium soy sauce

2 tablespoons tahini (see Note)

2 tablespoons (twice around the bowl) toasted sesame oil (available in Asian foods aisle)

2 pinches cayenne pepper

2 cloves garlic, minced

1 inch gingerroot, peeled and grated, or 2 pinches ground ginger

3 scallions, thinly sliced on an angle

1 large carrot, grated

Toasted sesame seeds, for garnish

Crushed red pepper flakes, for garnish

Put a pot of water over high heat to boil. When it comes to a boil, add salt and pasta. Cook pasta according to package directions, until al dente.

Meanwhile, combine soy sauce, tahini, sesame oil, cayenne, garlic, and gingerroot in a bowl. Whisk until smooth.

Drain pasta and run it under cold water until noodles are chilled. Drain the cooled noodles well—give them several good, strong shakes.

Dump noodles into a big bowl with the sauce and combine until noodles are evenly coated. Add veggies and toss to combine; dump noodles onto a serving dish. Garnish with sesame seed sprinkles and a little crushed red pepper. Serve with fruit or a chunked vegetable salad. ★

14

MAKES 4 SERVINGS

Southwestern Chicken and Black Bean Burritos

4 boneless, skinless chicken breasts

1 teaspoon ground cumin

1 teaspoon chili powder

A couple shakes cayenne pepper sauce, such as Frank's Red Hot or Tabasco

1 tablespoon extra-virgin olive oil (evoo) or corn oil (once around the pan)

1/2 medium Spanish onion, chopped

2 cloves garlic, minced

1 can (15 ounces) black beans, drained and rinsed

3 tablespoons (a couple of glugs) smoky barbecue sauce

Kosher salt and freshly ground black pepper, to taste

1 heart of romaine, shredded

6 scallions, thinly sliced

2 tomatoes, seeded and chopped

4 large flour tortillas (10 to 12 inches), flavored or plain

Rub chicken with cumin, chili powder, and cayenne sauce. Heat a griddle pan to high. Cook chicken breasts 4 minutes on each side and remove from heat.

While chicken is cooking, heat a skillet over medium-high heat. Go once around the pan with oil. Cook onions and garlic until onions are soft, about 5 minutes. Add beans and barbecue sauce. Chop cooked chicken breasts and drop into barbecued beans. Heat mixture through. Season with salt and pepper.

Place a tortilla on a plate and pile chicken and beans in center. Top with lettuce, scallions, and tomatoes. Wrap, roll, and repeat with remaining tortillas and filling. Serve with chips and salsa. ★

SPICE IT UP!

1

entree
SOUTHWESTERN CHICKEN AND BLACK BEAN BURRITOS

2

suggested sides
CHIPS AND SALSA

30-MINUTE MEALS
MENU

BIG FLAVOR
TAKE-OUT

1

entree
CURRY IN A
HURRY WITH
JASMINE RICE

2

suggested side
WARM FLAT
BREAD

No coconut milk, lower in fat, big flavor. Curry is actually a blend of several spices. In addition to curry powder, curry pastes are available in grocery stores on the international foods aisle. I prefer using the paste for texture and taste.

✪ ✪ ✪ ✪
MAKES 4 SERVINGS

Curry in a Hurry with Jasmine Rice

Jasmine rice

4 pieces boneless, skinless chicken breasts or thighs or combination of both, cut into chunks

All-purpose flour, for dusting

2 tablespoons peanut or sesame oil (twice around the pan)

1 yellow medium Spanish onion, peeled, halved, and cut into 1/4-inch strips

1 piece fresh gingerroot, about 2 inches, peeled and grated

3 cloves garlic, minced

1 can (15 ounces) no-fat, low-sodium chicken broth

3 tablespoons mild curry paste

A handful (about 1/4 cup packed) golden raisins

2 to 3 tablespoons mango chutney (found in condiment aisle) OR 1/4 cup mincemeat (found in baking goods aisle)

Coarse salt, to taste

Toppings: Spanish peanuts, Chopped cilantro, Mango chutney, Chopped scallions, Orange segments, Edible flowers, Coconut flakes, Pineapple chunks

Make rice, following the directions on the box for 4 to 6 servings. The rice will take longer than the dish to prepare.

Dust chicken lightly with flour. In a large skillet over medium-high heat, brown the chicken for 4 minutes on each side in the peanut or sesame oil. Remove chicken from pan and set aside.

Add onion, gingerroot, and garlic to pan. Sauté until the onion is tender, about 3 minutes. Add broth and scrape up all of the good junk stuck to the bottom of the pan. Add curry paste and raisins. Return chicken to the pan. Heat through to a boil. Give the pan a good shake. Reduce heat to medium low. Stir in chutney to thicken and sweeten. Simmer 5 to 10 minutes to desired thickness.

Serve with suggested toppings, white or jasmine rice, and warm flat bread, such as lavosh or pita. ★

✪ ✪ ✪ ✪

MAKES 4 SERVINGS

Blue Moon Burgers

1 pound lean ground beef

4 shakes Worcestershire sauce

Kosher salt and freshly ground black pepper, to taste

1/4 pound blue cheese, cut into 4 pieces

1/4 cup dry red wine

4 crusty rolls or toasted sourdough bread

Sliced red onion, for garnish

Romaine lettuce, for garnish

Season beef with Worcestershire and black pepper. Take a quarter of the beef in your hand. Nest some blue cheese in the meat and form a patty around the filling. Repeat with the rest of the meat and cheese, keeping the burgers no more than 3/4 inch thick.

Pour the wine into a shallow dish. Turn each burger in wine and let rest while you heat a nonstick griddle to medium hot. Cook burgers 4 minutes on each side. Check the internal temperature with a thermometer if you have one; 160°F is medium. Salt the burgers to your taste. Place burgers on rolls or bread and top with red onion and romaine. Serve with fancy chips, such as Yukon Gold Onion and Garlic Chips by Terra brand, and a green salad. ★

30-MINUTE MEALS

MENU

A BETTER BURGER

1

entree
BLUE MOON BURGERS

2

suggested side
FANCY CHIPS AND A GREEN SALAD

30-MINUTE MEALS
MENU

TACO BAR

1

entree
SPICY CHICKEN
TACOS

2

suggested side
CHUNKED
VEGETABLE
SALAD OR
GREEN SALAD

MAKES 5 SERVINGS

Spicy Chicken Tacos

1 tablespoon extra-virgin olive oil (evoo) (once around the pan)
1 & 1/2 pounds boneless, skinless chicken breasts, cut into small cubes
1 small onion, chopped
1 clove garlic, minced
1 cup tomato puree
2 teaspoons chili powder (1/3 palmful)
1 teaspoon ground cumin
A handful coarsely chopped Spanish olives stuffed with pimientos
A handful golden raisins
Coarse salt, to taste
8 jumbo corn taco shells or 8 flour tortillas for soft tacos

TOPPINGS:
• Shredded cheeses (smoked cheddar, Monterey Jack, or pepper Jack)
• Diced avocado
• Diced tomatoes
• Chopped scallion
• Shredded lettuce

Heat a big skillet over medium heat; add evoo, and brown chicken. Add onion and garlic and cook another couple of minutes to soften onion. Dump in tomato puree, chili powder, cumin, olives, raisins, and salt. Bring to a bubble, reduce heat to low, and simmer until ready to serve. Warm taco shells or flour tortillas in oven according to package directions. Scoop filling into shells and top at the table. Serve with a chunked vegetable or green salad. ★

Spicy Chicken Tacos

30-MINUTE MEALS
MENU

ITALIAN
COMFORT

1

entree
EMMANUEL
NINI'S
CAPONATA

▬▬ ▬▬ ▬▬ ▬▬

2

suggested sides
CRUSTY BREAD
OR PASTA

▬▬ ▬▬ ▬▬ ▬▬

Many recipes for caponata include sugar and/or vinegar; this is not one of them. My gran'pa Emmanuel said that the sweet and sour come out of the ingredients naturally, the sweet from the red peppers, onions, and raisins, the sour from the capers, eggplant, and parsley. If your grandparents put vinegar and/or sugar in, please make them happy and add some.

✪ ✪ ✪ ✪
MAKES 6 SERVINGS

Emmanuel Nini's Caponata

3 cloves garlic, minced

1/2 teaspoon crushed red pepper (1 to 2 pinches)

3 tablespoons extra-virgin olive oil (evoo) (two or three times around the pan)

1 palmful golden raisins (about 1/4 cup packed)

1 red bell pepper, chopped

1 green bell pepper, chopped

1 medium Spanish onion, chopped

1 medium eggplant, chopped (peeled or skin-on)

1 celery heart, chopped

1/4 pound green and black olives, pitted

3 tablespoons capers

Kosher salt, to taste

1 can (32 ounces) diced tomatoes

1 can (13 ounces) crushed tomatoes

A handful chopped fresh flat-leaf parsley

3 ounces pine nuts (pignoli), toasted in oven until golden

In a deep skillet or pot over medium heat, sauté garlic and crushed red pepper in evoo until garlic sizzles. Add raisins, peppers, onion, eggplant, celery, olives, capers, and salt. Cover pan and cook the vegetables, stirring occasionally, until eggplant begins to break down, 7 to 10 minutes.

Add tomatoes and parsley. Heat through. Turn off heat. Serve caponata hot or cold with bread, or tossed with pasta. Sprinkle with toasted pine nuts when ready to eat. ★

✪ ✪ ✪ ✪
MAKES 6 SERVINGS

My Sister Ria's Lazy Chicken, or My Lazy Sister Ria's Chicken

Balsamic vinegar

1 & 1/2 pounds boneless, skinless chicken breast cutlets (thinly sliced or pounded breast meat)

2 tablespoons extra-virgin olive oil (evoo)

2 medium white-skinned potatoes, thinly sliced

1 medium white onion, halved and thinly sliced

Montreal Steak Seasoning by McCormick or coarse salt and freshly ground black pepper, to taste

1/2 cup (a couple glugs) white wine or chicken broth

1 small zucchini, thinly sliced

1 can (28 ounces) crushed tomatoes

10 leaves fresh basil, torn or coarsely chopped

2 sprigs fresh oregano, leaves stripped from stem and chopped

1/2 to 2/3 cup shredded Italian cheese of your choice (provolone, mozzarella, Asiago)

Rub a little splash of balsamic vinegar into each chicken breast. Heat 1 tablespoon evoo (once around the pan) in a deep skillet over medium-high heat. Brown chicken for 2 minutes on each side. Remove chicken.

Add 1 tablespoon evoo (once around the pan) to pan. Add a layer of thin-sliced potatoes and onion. Sprinkle the potatoes and onion with Montreal Seasoning or coarse salt and black pepper. Let potatoes and onions cook, turning occasionally but maintaining a thin layer, until they begin to brown all over. Add a little broth or wine to pan. Spread a thin layer of zucchini across the pan on top of the potatoes and onion and sprinkle with a touch more Montreal Seasoning or coarse salt and pepper. Top with a layer of chicken breast. Dump the crushed tomatoes evenly over the top. Sprinkle with chopped herbs. Cover and cook until chicken is cooked through and potatoes are tender, 10 to 12 minutes.

Sprinkle with the shredded Italian cheeses. Place pan under the broiler for a minute until cheese melts and begins to brown. Serve directly from the hot pan at the table, with a green salad on the side. ★

30-MINUTE MEALS
MENU

IT RUNS IN THE FAMILY

1
entree
MY SISTER RIA'S LAZY CHICKEN, OR MY LAZY SISTER RIA'S CHICKEN

2
suggested side
GREEN SALAD

A spicy pork chili served up in bowls and topped with corn cakes—a Cajun not-pot-pie.

✪ ✪ ✪ ✪
MAKES 6 SERVINGS

Cajun Chili with Scallion Corn Cakes

SCALLION CORN CAKES
1 package Jiffy corn bread mix
2 scallions, chopped
Butter, for griddle

CAJUN CHILI
1 & 1/2 pounds lean ground pork
1 tablespoon Mexican chili powder
1 tablespoon ground cumin (1/2 palmful)
4 shakes cayenne pepper sauce, such as Frank's Red Hot or Tabasco
1/2 medium yellow onion, chopped
2 cloves garlic, minced
1 rib celery, chopped
1/2 red bell pepper, chopped
1/2 green bell pepper, chopped
1/2 bottle of beer
1 can (14 ounces) crushed tomatoes
A handful chopped fresh cilantro (optional)
Kosher salt, to taste

Follow directions on box for corn cakes, not corn bread. When batter is prepared, stir in chopped scallions.

Meanwhile, heat a pot over high heat and a skillet or griddle with a nonstick surface over medium-high heat.

Dump ground pork into the pot. Season with chili powder, cumin, and cayenne sauce, brown for 5 minutes. Add the onion, garlic, celery, and bell peppers and cook, shaking pan now and then, for another 3 or 4 minutes.

Rub the hot griddle with a little butter and wipe off excess with a paper towel. Pour corn cake batter onto griddle to form up to 4-inch corn cakes; cook until cakes begin to bubble and edges become dry, 3 minutes. Keep finished cakes on a plate in a warm oven until chili is done.

Back to the chili. Add beer and stir up the bits from the bottom of the pot. Stir in the tomatoes and cilantro. Bring to a boil and season with salt. Top bowls of chili with scallion corn cakes. Serve with extra cakes and a chunked vegetable salad on the side. ★

TEX-MEX
ONE POT

1
entree
CAJUN CHILI

2
side dish
SCALLION CORN
CAKES

3
suggested side
CHUNKED
VEGETABLE
SALAD

30-MINUTE MEALS

MENU

ITALIAN
STYLE
CHICKEN

1

entree
ZESTY CHICKEN
CUTLETS
PARMIGIANA

2

suggested side
GREEN SALAD

MAKES 4 TO 6 SERVINGS

Zesty Chicken Cutlets Parmigiana

Salt, to taste

1 pound spaghetti

QUICK MARINARA SAUCE

3 cloves garlic, minced

2 pinches crushed red pepper flakes

2 tablespoons extra-virgin olive oil (evoo)

2 cans (28 ounces each) crushed tomatoes

15 to 20 leaves fresh basil, roughly cut or torn

2 sprigs fresh oregano, leaves stripped from stem and chopped

A handful of chopped fresh flat-leaf parsley

CHICKEN

The juice of 3 lemons, or several tablespoons bottled lemon juice

1/3 cup freshly grated Parmigiano Reggiano or Romano cheese (a good handful)

1 cup Italian bread crumbs (a couple handfuls)

Freshly ground black pepper, to taste

A pinch crushed red pepper flakes

A handful chopped fresh flat-leaf parsley

1 & 1/2 pounds boneless, skinless chicken breast cutlets

2 cloves garlic, popped from skin and left whole

3 tablespoons extra-virgin olive oil (evoo) (three times around the pan)

1 pound fresh mozzarella or fresh smoked mozzarella, thinly sliced

Start a big pot of salted water to boil for pasta. Cook according to package directions, until al dente, or still slightly firm to the bite. Drain.

Meanwhile, throw your sauce together by heating garlic and crushed red pepper in evoo in a pot over medium heat. When the garlic speaks by sizzling in the oil, add tomatoes and fresh herbs. Bring to a bubble, reduce heat, and let the sauce hang out over low heat while you prepare the cutlets.

Squeeze lemon juice into a shallow dish. Mix Parmigiano, bread crumbs, black pepper, red pepper, and parsley on a large plate. Turn each cutlet in lemon juice, then press and coat in breading.

Heat 2 whole cloves garlic in evoo in a large skillet or frying pan over medium heat. When garlic sizzles, remove cloves and sauté chicken cutlets for 4 minutes on each side. When the cutlets are done, arrange on an ovenproof serving dish covered with a layer of sauce. Dot each cutlet with a little more sauce and a slice of fresh mozzarella. Place platter under broiler to just melt cheese.

Take warm platter right to the table. Toss drained spaghetti with remaining sauce. Serve spaghetti and a green salad as side dishes. ★

If you've yet to try fresh mozzarella, please let this be your reason. Look for it in the specialty cheeses case at your local market. Fresh mozzarella is more widely available than ever.

30-MINUTE MEALS

MENU

HUNGARIAN
COMFORT
FOOD

1

entree
GOODNESS
GRACIOUS,
THAT'S GREAT
GOULASH!

2

suggested side
GREEN SALAD

MAKES 6 SERVINGS

Goodness Gracious, That's Great Goulash!

Salt and freshly ground black pepper, to taste

1 pound elbow macaroni

2 pounds lean ground beef

1 medium white onion

2 cloves garlic, minced

1 teaspoon ground cumin (a few healthy pinches)

1 tablespoon paprika (1/2 palmful)

A pinch ground nutmeg

2 sprigs fresh marjoram, chopped, or a healthy sprinkle of dried

1 can (14 ounces) crushed tomatoes

3 rounded tablespoons sour cream

2 pats butter or a drizzle of extra-virgin olive oil (evoo)

Chopped fresh flat-leaf parsley

1 teaspoon caraway seeds (eyeball it)

Put a large pot of water on to boil for the macaroni. When water boils, add salt and pasta. Cook according to package directions.

Meanwhile, heat a deep skillet over medium-high heat. Add ground beef and brown. Grate an onion into the skillet with a hand grater. Add garlic, cumin, paprika, nutmeg, and marjoram. Mix in tomatoes. Heat through, then stir in sour cream. Drain macaroni and toss with butter or evoo, parsley, and caraway seeds.

Serve scoops of goulash over bowls of macaroni, with green salad on the side. ★

Thai Turkey Burgers

WARM PINEAPPLE SALSA

1 fresh, ripe, cored pineapple (available in the produce section)

1 tablespoon sesame oil (once around the pan)

1/4 teaspoon crushed red pepper flakes (a shake or two)

1/2 small red bell pepper, seeded and chopped

1/4 red onion, finely chopped

2 tablespoons dark brown sugar (a palmful)

10 to 15 fresh basil leaves, cut into thin strips

BURGERS

1 & 1/3 pounds ground turkey breast

1 inch fresh gingerroot, peeled and grated, or 2 pinches ground ginger

2 cloves garlic, minced

2 tablespoons dark soy sauce (a couple glugs)

2 teaspoons curry powder (1/3 palmful)

Coarse salt, to taste

2 scallions, finely chopped

4 cornmeal-topped rolls or 4 toasted sandwich-size English muffins, split

Bibb, Boston, or red leaf lettuce for topping

Drain pineapple and cut into pieces that will fit in food processor. Place in processor and process to a coarse, chunky texture. Heat sesame oil and crushed red pepper flakes in a skillet over medium-high heat until oil smokes. Add bell pepper and onions and cook 1 to 2 minutes. Add pineapple and heat through. Sprinkle with brown sugar and cook 1 to 2 minutes. Remove from heat and toss in basil. Let the salsa hang out in the warm pan while you cook burgers.

Heat a nonstick skillet or griddle pan over medium-high heat. Combine turkey, ginger, garlic, soy sauce, curry powder, salt, and scallions. Form into 4 patties and cook on skillet, 4 minutes on each side. Serve on rolls with lots of warm pineapple salsa and lettuce, with a chunked vegetable salad and your favorite chips alongside. ★

EVERYDAY

30-MINUTE MEALS
MENU

THAI-STYLE
COOKOUT

1
entree
THAI TURKEY
BURGERS

2
suggested sides
CHUNKED
VEGETABLE
SALAD AND
CHIPS

30-MINUTE MEALS

MENU

WAY-COOL
DINNER

1

entree
MAMMA'S
BROCCOLINI
AND RICOTTA
PASTA

2

suggested sides
CRUSTY BREAD
AND A TOMATO
& ONION SALAD

Broccolini, a cross between Chinese kale and broccoli, is an item that just appeared in the produce section one day. Science and progress can't be as scary as I thought, since they've come up with bundles of florets with no tough stalks. That means less chopping! A way-cool thing.

✪ ✪ ✪ ✪

MAKES 4 TO 6 SERVINGS

Mamma's Broccolini and Ricotta Pasta

Coarse salt and freshly ground black pepper, to taste

1 pound rigatoni

2 bundles broccolini florets, chopped (3 cups) OR 2 heads broccoli rabe tops, chopped

1 cup water

2 tablespoons extra-virgin olive oil (evoo) (twice around the pan)

1 pound boneless, skinless chicken breasts, diced

4 cloves garlic, minced

2 cups (1 pound) part-skim ricotta cheese

6 to 8 sprigs fresh thyme, leaves stripped from stem and chopped

A couple pinches ground nutmeg

Put a large pot of water over high heat for the pasta. When water boils, add salt and pasta. Cook according to package directions, until al dente. Reserve 1 cup cooking water and drain the rest.

In a small saucepan, simmer broccolini in a cup of water, covered, 5 minutes; drain. If using broccoli rabe, simmer 8 to 10 minutes to extract bitterness. Drain well. Heat evoo in a big, deep skillet over medium heat. Add chicken and garlic. Cook until chicken is cooked through, 5 to 8 minutes. Add broccolini, pasta, ricotta, the reserved pasta cooking water, thyme, nutmeg, salt, and pepper to the pan. Toss until creamy, then transfer to a serving platter. Serve with a tomato and onion salad and crusty bread. ★

Mamma's Broccolini and Ricotta Pasta

30-MINUTE MEALS

MENU

DINNER
WITH THE
BOSS

1

entree
**TONY SOPRANO
STEAK
SANDWICHES
WITH
GIARDINIERA
RELISH**

- - -

2

suggested side
FANCY CHIPS

- - - - -

My salute to the greatest on-screen gangster since Don Corleone. I just love the big-hearted, murderous bastard, and I know he'd love my sandwich. Salute and cent-an', Tony!

✪ ✪ ✪ ✪
MAKES 4 SERVINGS

Tony Soprano Steak Sandwiches with Giardiniera Relish

2 pounds sirloin steak, 1-inch thick, trimmed, and cut into 2 pieces
2 tablespoons balsamic vinegar (2 splashes)
Montreal Steak Seasoning by McCormick or coarse salt and freshly ground black pepper, to taste
1 jar (1 quart) giardiniera salad (pickled vegetables and peppers) (found in Italian aisle)
A handful fresh flat-leaf parsley
The juice of 1/2 lemon
Extra-virgin olive oil (evoo)
1 loaf garlic bread, homemade or prepared, split in half lengthwise
4 leaves romaine from the heart of the lettuce head

Pat trimmed steaks with paper towels and place on a plate. Rub each steak with a splash of balsamic vinegar and a sprinkle of steak seasoning or coarse salt and black pepper. Let meat rest.

Drain giardiniera salad and reserve juice. Place salad in a food processor with parsley, lemon juice, and a drizzle of evoo. Pulse-grind the mixture into a finely chopped relish.

Brown garlic bread loaf under broiler and remove from oven.

Wipe a drop of evoo across a nonstick skillet and heat over medium-high heat until pan smokes. Add steaks and cook 5 minutes on each side. Douse the pan with a few tablespoons of the juice from the pickled relish. Rub the steaks around, picking up the color and juice from the pan. Place steaks on a big cutting board and let rest for 10 minutes, allowing juices to distribute.

Slice steaks very thin, on an angle and against the grain. Pile meat on a plate and scrape juice off board over the top of meat. Wipe off board.

Place garlic bread on board and cover bottom half with relish. Put piles of meat on top of relish. Top with romaine leaves and the other half of garlic bread. Hold bread together with long toothpicks and hack up super sub into 4 big hunks.

Just when you think life couldn't get any better, open up a sack of Terra brand Yukon Gold Garlic and Herb Chips to munch along with your sandwich. Now life is really good. ★

This dish is a fall favorite of my family.

✪ ✪ ✪ ✪
MAKES 4 SERVINGS

Pasta with Pumpkin and Sausage

Coarse salt and freshly ground black pepper, to taste

1 pound penne rigate or rigatoni pasta, cooked until al dente

2 drizzles extra-virgin olive oil

1 pound bulk sweet sausage

1 medium onion, finely chopped

4 cloves garlic, minced

1 bay leaf, fresh or dried

4 to 6 leaves fresh sage, slivered (about 1 & 1/2 tablespoons)

1 cup dry white wine

1 can (14 ounces) chicken broth

1 cup canned pumpkin

1/2 cup heavy cream

2 pinches ground cinnamon

3 pinches ground nutmeg

Romano or Parmigiano cheese, for grating over pasta

Put a large pot of water over high heat for the pasta. When water boils, add salt and pasta. Cook according to package directions until al dente. Drain.

Meanwhile, in a deep pot over medium heat, pour in 1 drizzle of oil and brown sausage in it. Remove to paper towel-lined plate to drain and return pan to heat. Add second drizzle of oil to pan and sauté onion and garlic 5 minutes, till soft and sweet. Add bay leaf, sage, and wine to pot. Reduce wine for 2 minutes. Add broth and pumpkin and combine, stirring sauce until it comes to a bubble. Return sausage to pan, reduce heat, and stir in cream. Season with cinnamon, nutmeg, and salt and pepper and simmer 5 minutes.

To serve, return drained, cooked pasta to the pot you cooked it in. Remove bay leaf from sauce and pour sauce over pasta. Toss pasta and sauce 1 or 2 minutes over low heat so pasta can absorb flavors. Top bowls of pasta with freshly grated Parmigiano or Romano cheese, and serve with green salad on the side. ★

30-MINUTE MEALS
MENU

AUTUMN
COMFORT
FOOD

1
entree
PASTA WITH
PUMPKIN AND
SAUSAGE

2
suggested side
GREEN SALAD

30-MINUTE MEALS
MENU

CREOLE
SURF AND
TURF

1

entree
CREOLE
CHICKEN
BREASTS WITH
CRAB AND
ARTICHOKE
STUFFING

2

suggested sides
GREEN SALAD
AND CRUSTY
BREAD

For my dad, James Claude.

✪ ✪ ✪ ✪
MAKES 4 SERVINGS

Creole Chicken Breasts with Crab and Artichoke Stuffing

1 to 1 & 1/2 pounds chicken breast cutlets, pounded thin
Coarse salt and freshly ground black pepper, to taste
A few pinches poultry seasoning

CRAB AND ARTICHOKE STUFFING
2 shallots, finely chopped
1 rib celery from the heart, finely chopped
2 tablespoons extra-virgin olive oil (evoo) (twice around the pan)
1 can (15 ounces) artichoke hearts in water, drained and chopped
1/2 cup chicken broth (3 or 4 splashes)
8 to 10 ounces canned crabmeat
2 slices white bread, toasted and buttered
1 teaspoon Old Bay seasoning (1/4 palmful)
Coarse salt and freshly ground black pepper, to taste

CREOLE SAUCE
1 tablespoon extra-virgin olive oil (evoo) (once around the pan)
1 pat butter (about 1/2 tablespoon)
1 cup dry sherry
1 cup chicken broth
1 tablespoon cornstarch dissolved in a splash of water or broth

Season chicken cutlets with salt, pepper, and poultry seasoning. Set aside.

For stuffing, in a skillet over medium heat, sauté shallots and celery in evoo, 2 or 3 minutes. Add artichoke hearts and broth; cook 1 minute more. Add crabmeat and heat through, breaking up meat. Cube toast into small dice and add to pan. Season with Old Bay seasoning, salt, and pepper and combine ingredients until bread is moist. Remove from heat.

Place small mounds of stuffing on cutlets and roll up. Secure with toothpicks.

For sauce, heat a nonstick skillet over medium-high heat. Add evoo and butter to pan. Place chicken roll-ups in pan and brown, 2 or 3 minutes on each side. Remove chicken. Add sherry and cook to reduce by half, 1 or 2 minutes. Add broth and bring to a boil. Add cornstarch liquid and stir to thicken sauce. Return chicken to pan. Cover and simmer until chicken is cooked through, about 5 minutes.

Serve chicken with a green salad and crusty French bread. ★

GREEN
CHILI

1

entree
CHILI FOR
"VEG-HEADS"

2

suggested side
TORTILLA CHIPS

Leftovers only get better.

✪ ✪ ✪ ✪
MAKES 4 SERVINGS

Chili for "Veg-Heads"

2 tablespoons olive or vegetable oil
1 medium onion, chopped
1 medium bell pepper, red or green, seeded and chopped
1 jalapeño pepper, seeded and chopped
4 cloves garlic, minced
1 cup beer or vegetable broth
1 can (32 ounces) crushed tomatoes
1 can (14 ounces) black beans, drained and rinsed
1 can (14 ounces) red kidney beans, drained and rinsed
1 to 1 & 1/2 tablespoons ground cumin (1/2 palmful)
1 to 1 & 1/2 tablespoons chili powder (1/2 palmful)
6 dashes cayenne sauce, such as Frank's Red Hot or Tabasco sauce
A few good pinches coarse salt
1 cup spicy vegetarian refried beans
Shredded cheddar cheese, for garnish (optional)
Chopped scallions, for garnish (optional)
Black bean, blue corn, or flavored tortilla chips, for dipping

Heat oil in a deep pot over medium to medium-high heat. Add onion and peppers and sauté, stirring frequently, 3 to 4 minutes. Add garlic and cook 1 minute more. Add beer or broth and scrape up any good stuff from the bottom of the pan. Cook to reduce the liquid by half, 2 or 3 minutes. Add tomatoes and beans and season with cumin, chili powder, cayenne sauce, and salt. Thicken by stirring in refried beans.

Serve in bowls topped with shredded cheese or scallions with plenty of tortilla chips for dipping. ★

✪ ✪ ✪ ✪
MAKES 4 SERVINGS

Lentils and Pasta with Greens

2/3 cup dried lentils, green or other variety

2 bay leaves, fresh or dried

Coarse salt and freshly ground black pepper, to taste

10 to 12 ounces pasta (bow ties or wide egg noodles)

3 tablespoons extra-virgin olive oil (evoo) (3 turns around the pan)

1 small boiling onion, chopped

2 carrots, chopped

1/2 red bell pepper, chopped

3 cloves garlic, minced

1/2 cup red wine (a couple glugs)

2 tablespoons tomato paste

1 can (14 ounces) vegetable broth

1 pound Swiss chard, washed, dried, and chopped

1/4 teaspoon allspice (a couple pinches)

1 teaspoon ground cumin (1/3 palmful)

A handful chopped fresh flat-leaf parsley

Cover lentils with water and bring to a boil. Add a bay leaf and cook until lentils are tender, 20 minutes. Drain and set aside.

Meanwhile, put a large pot of water over high heat for pasta. When water boils, add salt and pasta. Cook according to package directions until al dente. Drain.

Preheat a large skillet and add evoo. Add remaining bay leaf, the onion, carrots, red bell pepper, and garlic. Sauté 10 minutes over medium heat. Add wine and cook to reduce liquid, 1 minute. Stir in tomato paste and cook 1 minute more. Add vegetable broth and Swiss chard; cover. Once greens have wilted, season with allspice, cumin, salt, and pepper. Continue cooking until greens are tender, about 10 minutes.

When greens are tender and no longer bitter, uncover and stir in drained pasta, lentils, and parsley. Adjust seasonings and serve with crusty bread.★

30-MINUTE MEALS
MENU

WINTER PASTA DISH

1

entree
LENTILS AND PASTA WITH GREENS

2

suggested side
CRUSTY BREAD

30-MINUTE MEALS

MENU

MEAT-FREE
COOKOUT

1

entree
PORTOBELLO
BURGERS WITH
GREEN SAUCE
AND SMOKED
MOZZARELLA

2

side dish
SPINACH
ARTICHOKE
PASTA SALAD

Portobellos have a beefy taste once cooked. In this recipe, a balsamic vinegar reduction glazes the mushrooms, adding a sweet, slightly tangy flavor. Popular with meat-eaters and meat-free-ers alike.

✪ ✪ ✪ ✪
MAKES 4 SERVINGS

Portobello Burgers with Green Sauce and Smoked Mozzarella

2 tablespoons extra-virgin olive oil (evoo) (twice around the pan)

4 large portobello mushroom caps

Steak seasoning blend such as Montreal Seasoning by McCormick OR salt and freshly ground black pepper, to taste

1/4 cup balsamic vinegar

1/2 pound fresh smoked mozzarella cheese, sliced

4 crusty rolls, split

1/2 medium red onion, thinly sliced

4 leaves romaine or red leaf lettuce

GREEN SAUCE

1 cup loosely packed basil leaves

1/2 cup fresh flat-leaf parsley

3 tablespoons capers

1/4 cup pignoli nuts (a handful)

1 clove garlic

The juice of 1/2 lemon

1/4 cup extra-virgin olive oil (evoo)

Salt and freshly ground black pepper, to taste

1/2 cup grated Parmigiano Reggiano or Romano cheese

Heat a nonstick skillet over medium-high heat. Add evoo and mushroom caps. Season mushrooms with steak seasoning blend or salt and pepper, and sauté, 5 minutes on each side. Add vinegar and coat the mushrooms in it. When vinegar has evaporated, turn mushrooms cap side up and cover with sliced cheese. Turn off heat and cover pan with foil. Let stand 2 or 3 minutes for cheese to melt.

To make the sauce, combine basil, parsley, capers, pignoli, garlic, and lemon juice in a food processor. Pulse-grind, until finely chopped, and scrape into a bowl. Stir in evoo, salt, pepper, and cheese.

Slather bun tops with green sauce. Place 1 portobello on each bun bottom and top with red onion slices, lettuce, and bun tops. ★

Portobello Burger

✪ ✪ ✪ ✪
MAKES 8 SIDE SERVINGS

Spinach Artichoke Pasta Salad

Coarse salt and freshly ground black pepper, to taste

1 pound penne or other short pasta

1/3 cup extra-virgin olive oil (evoo) (eyeball the amount)

3 tablespoons red wine vinegar (a couple splashes)

The juice of 1 small lemon

Half a sack (6 ounces) baby spinach, chopped

1 can (15 ounces) artichoke hearts in water, drained and coarsely chopped

1/3 pound ricotta salata cheese, crumbled (available in specialty cheese cases)

1/2 cup pitted black olives, such as Kalamata, coarsely chopped

1/2 medium red onion, chopped

1/2 cup fresh flat-leaf Italian parsley (a couple handfuls), chopped

Put a large pot of water over high heat for the pasta. When water boils, add salt and pasta. Cook according to package directions. Drain.

Combine evoo, vinegar, and lemon juice in the bottom of a serving bowl. Add the remaining ingredients plus the pasta to the bowl and toss until well combined. Season with salt and pepper and serve. ★

Pair with a tossed salad and you've got a snack for supper!

✪ ✪ ✪ ✪
MAKES 4 SERVINGS

Stuffed Potatoes with Ham, Thyme, and Gruyère

4 medium to large russet potatoes, washed

A drizzle extra-virgin olive oil (evoo)

FILLING
1 tablespoon extra-virgin olive oil (evoo) (once around the pan)

2 shallots, chopped

1/2 pound baked ham from deli, 1/8-inch-thick slices, cut into 1/4-inch strips

1/2 pound Gruyère cheese, shredded

2 tablespoons butter, in small pieces

1/2 cup milk or half-and-half

6 sprigs fresh thyme, leaves stripped and chopped

Salt and freshly ground black pepper, to taste

Rub potatoes with a drizzle of evoo and pierce with a fork. Microwave on high, 12 minutes or until tender. Cool potatoes 5 minutes, then split down the center and scrape potato flesh into a bowl. Set skins aside on a nonstick baking sheet. Preheat broiler to high with oven rack 6 inches from heat source.

While potatoes are in the microwave, heat a small skillet over medium heat. Add 1 tablespoon evoo and sauté shallots until just tender, 2 to 3 minutes.

To the cooked potato in the mixing bowl, add shallots, ham, cheese, butter, milk or half-and-half, thyme, salt, and pepper. Mash with a potato masher or fork until mixture is combined, but not entirely lump free. Divide mixture evenly among skins and broil to lightly brown on top, 2 or 3 minutes. Serve 2 halves with a green salad, dark bread, and butter. ★

30-MINUTE MEALS
MENU

SNACKS AS SUPPER

1
entree
STUFFED POTATOES WITH HAM, THYME, AND GRUYÈRE

2
suggested sides
GREEN SALAD AND DARK BREAD & BUTTER

30-MINUTE MEALS
MENU

SOUTH OF THE BORDER

1

entree
GRILLED HONEY-
LIME CHICKEN
SANDWICHES
WITH FLAVORED
TORTILLA CHIPS

2

side dish
MEXICAN
CHUNK
VEGETABLE
SALAD

✪ ✪ ✪ ✪

MAKES 4 SERVINGS

Mexican Chunk Vegetable Salad

2 vine-ripe tomatoes, seeded and chopped

1/3 English seedless cucumber, cut into bite-size chunks

1/2 medium red onion, chopped

1 medium red or green bell pepper, cut into bite-size chunks

2 ribs celery, chopped

1 jalapeño pepper, seeded and finely chopped

2 tablespoons chopped cilantro or fresh flat-leaf parsley

2 teaspoons cayenne pepper sauce, such as Frank's Red Hot or Tabasco (several drops)

The juice of 2 limes

2 tablespoons extra-virgin olive oil (evoo) (eyeball it)

Salt and freshly ground black pepper, to taste

Combine vegetables in a bowl. Sprinkle with chopped cilantro or parsley. Dress salad with hot sauce, lime juice, and evoo. Season with salt and pepper. Toss salad and adjust seasonings, to taste. ★

Go south of the
border any night
of the week!

✪ ✪ ✪ ✪
MAKES 4 SERVINGS

Grilled Honey-Lime Chicken Sandwiches with Flavored Tortilla Chips

The juice of 1 lime

2 tablespoons honey (a healthy drizzle)

1 rounded teaspoon cumin (1/3 palmful)

A handful cilantro, finely chopped (about 1 & 1/2 tablespoons)

2 tablespoons extra-virgin olive oil (evoo), canola, or corn oil (a glug)

4 boneless, skinless chicken breasts (6 to 8 ounces each)

1 teaspoon steak seasoning blend such as Montreal Seasoning by McCormick or salt and freshly ground black pepper, to taste

4 crusty rolls, split

TOPPINGS

Lettuce

Sliced tomato

Sliced red onion

Sliced avocado

1 cup prepared salsa verde

Assorted flavored tortilla chips, such as black bean, red corn, blue corn or chili lime chips

Combine lime juice, honey, cumin, cilantro, and evoo in a small bowl to make marinade. Sprinkle chicken with seasoning blend or salt and pepper. Coat chicken in marinade and set aside for 10 minutes.

Grill chicken on an indoor electric grill, 6 to 7 minutes on each side, or pan-fry over medium-high heat in a large nonstick skillet, uncovered, 6 minutes per side.

Slice grilled chicken on an angle and pile on roll bottoms. Top with lettuce, tomato, red onion, and sliced avocado. Spread salsa on roll tops. Serve with Mexican Chunk Vegetable Salad and assorted tortilla chips. ★

✪ ✪ ✪ ✪

MAKES 4 SERVINGS

Spinach Artichoke Calzones

2 cups low-moisture part-skim ricotta cheese

1/4 teaspoon freshly grated nutmeg, or a few pinches ground

Freshly ground black pepper, to taste

1/2 cup grated Parmigiano Reggiano cheese (a couple handfuls)

1 package (10 ounces) frozen chopped spinach, defrosted and squeezed dry

1 can (15 ounces) quartered artichoke hearts in water, drained and coarsely chopped

2 cloves garlic, minced

2 tubes prepared, refrigerated pizza dough (10 ounces each)

2 cups shredded mozzarella cheese (available in pouches on dairy aisle)

2 cups tomato, marinara, or pizza sauce, warmed, for dipping

Preheat oven to 425°F.

Combine ricotta, nutmeg, black pepper, Parmigiano Reggiano, spinach, artichoke hearts, and garlic in a bowl to make the filling.

Roll both tubes of pizza dough out on 2 separate nonstick cookie sheets and cut each dough in half across. Spread 1/2 cup mozzarella and up to 1/4 of the filling over half of each rectangle, then fold dough over top of filling; pinch edges firmly to seal. For a half-moon, pizza parlor look to your calzones, mound filling into a half-moon shape, fold dough over top, and trim edges following the rounded shape, then seal by pinching with fingers. If the dough tears, remove a little of the filling and repair. Repeat process, spacing calzones evenly on a baking sheet, and bake until golden brown, 12 to 15 minutes. Serve with warm tomato, marinara, or pizza sauce for dunking. Add a tossed salad and you've got a complete meal. ★

30-MINUTE MEALS

MENU

SNACKS AS SUPPER 2

1

entree
SPINACH
ARTICHOKE
CALZONES

2

suggested side
GREEN SALAD

MAKES 4 SERVINGS

Turkey Cutlets with Rosemary and Cornmeal-Dusted Ravioli

RAVIOLI
Salt, to taste

1 package (12 to 14 ounces) fresh ravioli, filled either with cheese, spinach and cheese, or mushroom and cheese (found on dairy aisle)

1 cup cornmeal (eyeball it)

1/4 cup grated Parmigiano Reggiano or Romano cheese (a couple handfuls)

1/2 teaspoon freshly grated or ground nutmeg

1/2 teaspoon freshly ground black pepper

2 tablespoons extra-virgin olive oil (evoo) (twice around the pan)

1 tablespoon butter

TURKEY CUTLETS
1 & 1/3 pounds turkey cutlets (available prewrapped in poultry case)

4 to 5 sprigs fresh rosemary, leaves stripped and chopped

Salt and freshly ground black pepper, to taste

A few fresh bay leaves, 1 for each cutlet, (available in produce herb section) or small dried bay leaves

2 to 3 tablespoons extra-virgin olive oil (evoo) (two or three times around the pan)

The grated zest and juice of 2 lemons

1 cup dry white wine or dry vermouth

1 tablespoon butter

Put a large pot of water over high heat for the pasta. When water boils, add salt and ravioli. Cook according to package directions to al dente.

Meanwhile, pour cornmeal onto a plate and combine with grated cheese, then mix in nutmeg and black pepper.

Heat a medium nonstick skillet over medium heat and add evoo and butter. Drain ravioli. Dust hot ravioli in cornmeal on the plate, then add to the skillet and brown on both sides, 3 or 4 minutes total. Set aside.

While ravioli is cooking, preheat a large skillet for turkey cutlets over medium to medium-high heat.

Season cutlets with chopped rosemary, salt, and pepper. Choose small fresh or dried bay leaves or halve large leaves with kitchen scissors. Press a small bay leaf or half leaf into each turkey cutlet. Add evoo to the pan, then the cutlets, bay leaf side down. Sauté in a single layer, working in 2 batches if necessary, 4 or 5 minutes on each side. Transfer to a warm plate.

Add the lemon zest and juice to the pan and deglaze with wine or vermouth, pulling up any pan drippings with a whisk. Add a pat of butter, whisk it in, and pour the sauce down over the cutlets. Serve alongside the fried ravioli. ★

✪ ✪ ✪ ✪
MAKES 4 SERVINGS

Broccoli Rabe with Golden Raisins

2 tablespoons extra-virgin olive oil (evoo) (twice around the pan)
1 small onion, chopped
1/4 cup golden raisins (a couple handfuls)
1 & 1/2 pounds fresh broccoli rabe, trimmed and coarsely chopped
Salt, to taste
1 can (14 ounces) chicken broth or 2 cups water

Heat a deep skillet over medium heat. Add evoo and onion and cook 3 minutes. Add raisins and broccoli rabe, and season with salt. Add broth or water, and bring to a bubble, then reduce heat to simmer. Cover the pan and cook broccoli rabe until tender and no longer bitter, about 12 minutes. Remove lid and allow liquid to reduce by half, 2 or 3 minutes. Transfer cooked broccoli rabe and plumped raisins to a serving dish. ★

✪ ✪ ✪ ✪
MAKES 4 SERVINGS

Warm Cherry, Orange, and Cranberry Compote with Vanilla Ice Cream

1 can (15 ounces) pitted cherries
The grated zest and juice of 1 orange
1/4 cup dried, sweetened cranberries
1 pint vanilla ice cream
Ginger snaps, vanilla wafers, or cinnamon sugar cookies, to garnish

In a microwave-safe bowl, combine cherries and their juice, orange zest and juice, and cranberries. Loosely cover dish with plastic wrap and microwave on high, 1 minute. Stir fruit, and microwave 1 minute longer.

Let fruit stand 5 minutes, then spoon over scoops of vanilla ice cream. Garnish with ginger snaps, vanilla wafers, or cinnamon sugar cookies. ★

The compote may also be prepared on a conventional stove top. Combine ingredients in a small saucepan and simmer over low heat, 7 or 8 minutes or until cranberries plump.

MAKES 4 SERVINGS

Rio Grande Spice Rub Strip Steaks

4 sirloin strip steaks (8 to 10 ounces each), 1 inch thick
1 & 1/2 tablespoons ground ancho chili or dark chili powder (a palmful)
1 & 1/2 tablespoons ground cumin (a palmful)
1 teaspoon ground coriander
1/2 teaspoon cayenne pepper
1 large red onion, cut into 4 thick slices
Extra-virgin olive oil (evoo) or vegetable oil, to coat onion
Salt and freshly ground black pepper, to taste

Remove steaks from refrigerator and let them rest for a few minutes to take the chill off.

Preheat a grill pan or indoor electric grill to high heat.

Combine spice rub ingredients: ground ancho chili, cumin, coriander, and cayenne, and rub well into steaks.

Coat red onion slices in a drizzle of evoo. Season with salt and pepper. Grill steaks and onion slices, 5 minutes on each side. Remove from heat. Let meat stand 5 minutes for juices to redistribute. Season with salt. Top with separated rings of grilled onions. Serve with hot corn and cheese squares and salad. ★

MAKES 6 SERVINGS

Cracked Corn and Cheese Squares

1 package (8 & 1/2 ounces) corn muffin mix
Softened butter, for baking dish
1/3 pound Monterey Jack cheese or pepper Jack cheese, cut into 1/4-inch dice
1/2 cup frozen corn kernels
1 scallion, thinly sliced

Preheat oven to 400°F.

Prepare corn muffin batter according to package directions (don't bake it yet!).

Grease an 8-inch square baking dish with butter. In a mixing bowl, stir cheese, corn, and scallions into corn muffin batter. Pour batter into baking dish and bake until golden, 15 to 18 minutes. ★

✪ ✪ ✪ ✪
MAKES 4 SERVINGS

Mexican Fiesta Salad

2 ripe avocados

3 vine-ripe tomatoes

1/2 sweet onion, sliced

2 tablespoons chopped cilantro

2 limes, halved

Coarse salt, to taste

Extra-virgin olive oil (evoo), for drizzling

Cut avocados in half, working around the pit. Separate the 2 halves. Remove pit and carefully scoop out avocado halves with a spoon. Cut avocados into wedges and pile in the center of a large platter. Seed and wedge tomatoes and arrange around the avocados. Arrange sliced onion over platter and sprinkle all with cilantro. Squeeze the juice of 2 limes evenly over vegetables. Season with coarse salt, drizzle with evoo, and serve. ★

30-MINUTE MEALS
MENU

SATISFACTION
GUARANTEED

1

entree
THE ONLY RECIPE
YOU NEED:
CARBONARA
- - - - -

2

suggested side
GREEN SALAD
- - - - -

3

dessert
SUGARED STONE
FRUITS WITH
COOKIES AND
CREAM
- - - - -

✪ ✪ ✪ ✪
MAKES 4 SERVINGS

The Only Recipe You Need: Carbonara

Salt and freshly ground black pepper, to taste

1 pound rigatoni

1/4 cup extra-virgin olive oil (evoo)

1/4 pound pancetta, chopped

1 teaspoon crushed red pepper flakes (1/3 of a palmful)

5 or 6 cloves garlic, chopped

1/2 cup dry white wine

2 large egg yolks

1/2 cup grated Romano cheese, such as Locatelli

A handful of finely chopped fresh flat-leaf parsley, for garnish (optional)

Put a large pot of water on to boil. Add a liberal amount of salt and rigatoni; cook to al dente, about 8 minutes.

Meanwhile, heat a large skillet over medium heat. Add evoo and pancetta. Brown pancetta 2 minutes. Add red pepper flakes and garlic and cook 2 to 3 minutes more. Add wine and stir up all the pan drippings.

Beat yolks, then add 1 large ladleful (about 1/2 cup) of the pasta cooking water. This tempers the eggs and keeps them from scrambling when added to the pasta.

Drain pasta well and add it directly to the skillet with pancetta and oil. Pour the egg mixture over the pasta. Toss rapidly to coat the pasta without cooking the egg. Remove pan from heat and add a big handful of cheese, lots of pepper, and a little salt. Continue to toss and turn the pasta until it soaks up egg mixture and thickens, 1 to 2 minutes. Garnish with parsley, if desired, and extra cheese. Serve with green salad on the side. ★

Carbonara

★ ★ ★ ★

MAKES 4 SERVINGS

Sugared Stone Fruits with Cookies and Cream

3 **ripe** apricots

2 **ripe** plums

2 **ripe** peaches

2 **tablespoons** sugar

1 **cup** heavy cream

12 sugar cookies, **Nilla Wafers, or ginger snaps, crumbled**

To prepare fruits, section into wedges slicing down to the pits. Pull wedges away from pits. Combine in a bowl and toss with sugar. Set aside or cover and chill until ready to serve.

To serve, spoon fruits into dessert bowls, pour 1/4 cup heavy cream over each serving, and top with crumbled sugar cookies, Nilla Wafers, or ginger snaps. ★

✪ ✪ ✪ ✪

MAKES 4 TO 6 SERVINGS

Anna Maria's Greek Shrimp and Feta Penne

Salt and freshly ground black pepper, to taste

1 pound penne pasta

3 tablespoons extra-virgin olive oil (evoo) (3 turns of the pan)

6 cloves garlic, minced

1 cup dry white wine

1 can (28 ounces) crushed tomatoes

8 ounces feta cheese, crumbled

2 or 3 sprigs fresh oregano, leaves stripped and chopped

2 pounds large shrimp, peeled, deveined, tails removed

A handful chopped fresh flat-leaf parsley

Crusty bread, for the table

Put a large pot of water over high heat for the penne. When water boils, add salt and pasta. Cook according to package directions until al dente. Drain.

Heat evoo in deep skillet over medium heat. Add garlic and sauté 1 or 2 minutes, until garlic sizzles.

Add wine and cook to reduce by half, 2 to 3 minutes. Add tomatoes and bring to a simmer. Add feta and stir constantly, until cheese melts into sauce. Add black pepper and oregano, stir to combine. Add shrimp. Cover and cook 5 minutes, stirring occasionally, until shrimp are pink and firm.

Add parsley and cooked, drained pasta to the shrimp and sauce. Serve immediately with warm, crusty bread and a green salad on the side. ★

30-MINUTE MEALS
MENU

CORNER BISTRO

1
entree
ANNA MARIA'S GREEK SHRIMP AND FETA PENNE

2
suggested sides
GREEN SALAD AND CRUSTY BREAD

MAKES 4 SERVINGS

Super Stuffed Potatoes with the Works

4 slices center-cut bacon, chopped
2 all-purpose potatoes, such as russet
1/2 cup sour cream or reduced-fat sour cream
2 scallions, finely chopped
Salt and freshly ground black pepper, to taste
1 cup shredded cheddar, colby, or smoked cheddar cheese

In a small nonstick skillet over medium-high heat, brown bacon pieces, then drain on a paper towel.

Pierce potatoes a few times each with a fork. Microwave on high for 12 minutes. Let potatoes cool for a few minutes before handling.

Preheat broiler.

Carefully split potatoes and scoop out flesh into a small bowl. Combine with sour cream, scallions, salt, pepper, cheese, and browned bacon. Scoop back into the potato skins, and place under broiler to lightly brown the tops. Serve immediately. ★

MAKES 4 SERVINGS

Hot Buffalo Chicken Sandwiches

4 boneless, skinless chicken breasts (6 ounces each)
Salt and freshly ground black pepper, to taste
1 teaspoon sweet paprika (a few good pinches)
1 teaspoon chili powder (a few good pinches)
A drizzle extra-virgin olive oil (evoo)
2 tablespoons butter
1/2 cup (4 ounces) cayenne pepper sauce, such as Frank's Red Hot or Tabasco
4 crusty rolls, split
Bibb or leaf lettuce leaves
2 cups reduced-fat sour cream
4 scallions, thinly sliced
1/2 pound blue cheese, crumbled
8 ribs celery, cut into sticks
2 large carrots, cut into sticks

I often take restaurant food, even bar food, and try and come up with more healthful and/or quicker versions to make at home. This more adult take on Buffalo hot wings and stuffed potatoes will hit the right flavor bells in your mouth and kids will love it as well! My version calls for boneless, skinless white meat chicken as opposed to deep-fried dark meat with skin, and the blue cheese topping is made with reduced-fat sour cream. The orange freezes, using sherbet, are a not-too-sweet alternative to a milk shake.

Heat a large nonstick skillet over medium-high heat. Season chicken with salt, pepper, paprika, and chili powder, and drizzle with a little evoo to coat. Pan-grill, 5 minutes on each side.

Heat a metal or microwave-safe glass bowl over low heat to melt the butter. Add hot sauce to the butter and combine. When the chicken breasts are done, remove from pan; add chicken to the bowl and coat evenly with the hot sauce mixture.

Place chicken breasts on bun bottoms and top with crisp lettuce. Combine sour cream, scallions, and blue cheese and slather on bun tops. Top sandwiches and serve, using the remaining blue cheese sauce for dipping your veggies. Arrange on dinner plates with Super Stuffed Potatoes and celery and carrot sticks. ★

✪ ✪ ✪ ✪
MAKES 4 SERVINGS

Orange Sherbet Freezes

2 pints or 1/2 gallon orange sherbet
1 pint vanilla ice cream or frozen yogurt
1 liter lemon-lime soda, diet soda, or lemon-lime seltzer
1 lime, for garnish (optional)
Ice cubes

For each freeze, in a blender combine 3 scoops orange sherbet and 1 scoop vanilla ice cream or frozen yogurt. Add 1/4 liter lemon-lime soda. Add ice cubes to the blender to fill. Cover and blend on high until frothy and smooth. Pour into fountain or tall glass and garnish glass rim with a round of lime and a straw. ★

✪ ✪ ✪ ✪

MAKES 4 SERVINGS

Sicilian Eggplant Marinara over Penne

Coarse salt and freshly ground black pepper, to taste

1 pound penne rigate

1 medium eggplant

2 tablespoons extra-virgin olive oil (evoo) (twice around the pan)

4 large cloves garlic, minced

A handful chopped fresh flat-leaf parsley

1 can (28 ounces) crushed tomatoes

20 leaves fresh basil, torn or coarsely chopped

Shaved or grated Parmigiano Reggiano or Asiago cheese, for topping

Preheat oven to 425°F.

Put a large pot of water over high heat for the penne. When water boils, add salt and pasta. Cook according to package directions until al dente. Drain.

Meanwhile, cut several small slits into one side of the eggplant with the tip of a sharp knife. Place eggplant directly on oven rack in the center of the hot oven, slit side up. Roast 20 minutes. Remove from oven and allow to cool. Gently remove skin with a sharp knife; it should pull away easily. Using a food processor, grind the peeled eggplant into a paste.

Heat a skillet over medium to medium-high heat. Add evoo and garlic. When the garlic sizzles, add eggplant paste. Season with salt and pepper. Add parsley, tomatoes, and basil. Heat the sauce through and toss with cooked pasta. Top with grated cheese, and serve immediately with crusty bread and green salad on the side. ★

30-MINUTE MEALS

MENU

SICILIAN
COMFORT
FOOD

1

entree
SICILIAN
EGGPLANT
MARINARA OVER
PENNE
━━ ━━ ━━

2

suggested sides
GREEN SALAD
AND CRUSTY
BREAD
━━ ━━ ━━

When I asked around about chicken fried steaks, EVERY Southerner I know had strong feelings and lots of advice on this roadside diner classic. Many like a traditional white milk gravy, others a deep brown gravy or a red-eye gravy. Still others like their fried steaks plain and crispy. When I came up with my recipe, I decided to fence-sit and make mine with a creamed brown pan gravy, on the side.

✪ ✪ ✪ ✪
MAKES 4 SERVINGS

Chicken Fried Steaks with Creamed Pan Gravy and Biscuits

1 & 1/2 pounds round steak (1/2-inch thick)

1 cup plus 2 tablespoons all-purpose flour

1/3 cup cornmeal

1 teaspoon sweet paprika (a few good pinches)

1 teaspoon salt (a few good pinches)

1/2 teaspoon freshly ground black pepper (eyeball it)

2 eggs, beaten

2 tablespoons water (2 splashes)

4 tablespoons vegetable oil

1 & 1/4 cups beef broth or stock

1/4 cup half-and-half or cream

1 package bake-off biscuits (such as Pillsbury), prepared to directions

Preheat a large, heavy skillet over medium-high heat. Set steaks on a waxed-paper-lined work surface and cover with another piece of waxed paper. Pound steaks to a 1/4-inch thickness. Set steaks aside.

Line work surface with more waxed paper. Make a pile of 1/2 cup flour on both ends of work space. Add cornmeal, paprika, salt, and pepper to one pile of flour. Beat eggs and water in a pie plate or shallow dish.

Cut steaks into 4 portions and coat first in plain flour, then in egg, and then in the seasoned flour and cornmeal mixture.

Add 2 tablespoons oil to hot skillet and brown 2 steaks at a time. As they brown, remove from the pan, and add more oil, as needed. When the last 2 portions are browned, add the first two back to the pan with the others. Cover pan, lower heat to medium-low and cook, covered, 15 minutes. Remove steaks to serving platter and pour off all but 2 to 3 tablespoons drippings. Add 2 tablespoons flour to the drippings, and cook, 2 minutes. Whisk in broth and season with salt and pepper. Add half-and-half or cream and whisk into gravy. When gravy bubbles, remove from heat. Serve steaks and warm biscuits with gravy on top. ★

✪ ✪ ✪ ✪
MAKES 4 SERVINGS

Southern Green Beans

1 & 1/4 pounds green beans, trimmed and cut into 1-inch pieces
2 slices bacon, chopped
1 small onion, finely chopped
2 tablespoons red wine vinegar
2 teaspoons sugar

Cook green beans in a medium skillet in 1 inch simmering water, covered, for 6 minutes. Drain and set aside.

Return skillet to stove and set burner to medium-high. Add bacon, and brown. When fat begins to render, add onions and cook with the bacon until tender. Return cooked green beans to the pan and turn to coat in bacon drippings and onions. When the beans are hot, the bacon crisp at edges, and the onions translucent, add vinegar to the pan and season with sugar. Allow the vinegar to evaporate and the sugar to combine with pan drippings, 1 or 2 minutes, then serve. ★

✪ ✪ ✪ ✪
MAKES 8 SLICES

Quick Chocolate Banana Cream Pie

1 frozen pie shell, pricked several times with a fork
1 package instant chocolate pudding, prepared to package directions
2 ripe bananas, thinly sliced on an angle
Whipped cream (spray-type is fine here)
1 dark chocolate candy bar

Preheat oven to 425°F.

Bake pie shell until golden, 10 to 12 minutes. Remove from oven and let cool.

Line pie shell with half of the prepared chocolate pudding. Add a layer of bananas. Top with remaining pudding and banana slices. Cover with a giant swirl of whipped cream, starting at the center and working out. Shave a chocolate bar with a vegetable peeler and top pie with shavings. Serve immediately. ★

✪ ✪ ✪ ✪

MAKES 4 TO 6 SERVINGS

Country Captain Chicken with White and Wild Rice

RICE
2 & 2/3 cups water
1 tablespoon butter
1 & 1/2 cups white and wild rice or long-grain rice

CHICKEN
2/3 cup all-purpose flour (eyeball it)
1 rounded tablespoon sweet paprika
4 boneless, skinless chicken breasts (6 ounces each)
3 boneless, skinless chicken thighs
Salt and freshly ground black pepper, to taste
2 tablespoons extra-virgin olive oil (evoo) (twice around the pan)
2 tablespoons butter
1 green bell pepper, seeded and chopped
1 red bell pepper, seeded and chopped
1 medium onion, chopped
2 or 3 large cloves garlic, chopped
1 tablespoon curry powder or mild curry paste
1 cup chicken broth
1 can (28 ounces) diced tomatoes or chunky-style crushed tomatoes
1/4 cup golden raisins or currants (a couple handfuls)
2 ounces (1 small pouch) sliced almonds, lightly toasted
3 scallions, chopped, for garnish

Bring water to a boil in a medium saucepan; add butter and rice and return to a boil. Reduce heat to low, cover pot, and cook rice until tender, about 20 minutes. Turn off heat and fluff rice with a fork.

While rice is cooking, combine flour and paprika in a shallow dish. Season chicken with salt and pepper. Cut each chicken breast and thigh in half on an angle. Coat chicken pieces with paprika-seasoned flour.

Heat a large skillet over medium-high heat and add evoo . Brown chicken pieces 3 minutes on each side and remove from the skillet. Add butter to the pan, then stir in peppers, onions, and garlic. Season veggies with salt and pepper and sauté 5 to 7 minutes to soften. Add curry, broth, tomatoes, and raisins. Slide chicken back into the skillet and simmer over medium heat until chicken is cooked through, about 5 minutes. Garnish with sliced almonds. Place skillet on a trivet and serve the chicken from the pan. Transfer rice to a serving dish and garnish with chopped scallions. ★

✪ ✪ ✪ ✪

MAKES 24 TO 30 BALLS

Bourbon Street Candy Balls with Pecans

1 & 1/2 cups crushed vanilla-flavored wafer cookies, such as Nilla wafers

1 cup confectioners' sugar

4 shots bourbon

2 cups chopped pecans

3 tablespoons light Karo syrup

Softened butter

Combine cookies, sugar, bourbon, pecans, and Karo syrup in a bowl. Coat fingertips with a little softened butter to help you roll. Shape mixture into balls 1 & 1/2 inches in diameter. Arrange balls on a dessert platter and serve. Ask for help rolling. Four hands make very quick work of this dessert! ★

This is obviously a grown-ups–only treat!

30-MINUTE MEALS

MENU

GRILL-TOP
DINNER

1

entree
MAPLE-MUSTARD
PORK CHOPS
WITH GRILLED
APPLES

2

side dish
MOM'S OIL AND
VINEGAR
POTATO SALAD
AND 3-BEAN
SALAD

✪ ✪ ✪ ✪
MAKES 4 SERVINGS

Maple-Mustard Pork Chops with Grilled Apples

1/2 cup dark amber maple syrup

1/4 cup spicy brown mustard

1/4 cup apple cider

1/4 medium onion, finely chopped

1/2 teaspoon allspice (eyeball it)

1 teaspoon ground cumin (a few good pinches)

8 center-cut boneless pork loin chops (1/2 to 3/4 inch thick)

Extra-virgin olive oil (evoo), for drizzling

Grill seasoning blend such as Montreal Seasoning by McCormick OR salt and freshly ground black pepper, to taste

3 Golden Delicious apples, sliced across into 1/2-inch rounds, with core and peel intact

The juice of 1/2 lemon

1/2 teaspoon freshly grated or ground nutmeg

Preheat a grill or nonstick griddle pan over medium-high heat, or preheat electric tabletop grill to high. Preheat oven to 350°F.

Combine maple syrup, mustard, cider, onion, allspice, and cumin in a small saucepan and cook over medium heat, 7 to 10 minutes, until sauce begins to thicken.

Coat chops lightly in evoo, season with grill seasoning blend or salt and pepper, and cook on the grill pan of your choice, 3 minutes on each side. Baste chops liberally with sauce and cook, 2 or 3 minutes more, then transfer to a baking sheet. Baste again with sauce and place in hot oven to finish cooking, about 10 to 12 minutes.

While chops are baking, coat apple rounds with lemon juice and a drizzle of evoo. Season with grill seasoning or salt and pepper and a little nutmeg. Cover grill pan surface with as many pieces of apple as possible. As the apples get tender, remove and replace with remaining slices. Apples should cook 3 minutes on each side; you don't want them too soft, just tender.

Serve apples alongside the pork chops. ★

Maple-Mustard Pork Chops

Leftovers of either
salad only get
tastier.

✪ ✪ ✪ ✪
MAKES 6 SERVINGS OF EACH SALAD

Mom's Oil and Vinegar Potato Salad and 3-Bean Salad

POTATO SALAD

16 new red-skinned potatoes
Salt and freshly ground black pepper, to taste
1 red bell pepper, seeded and chopped
1/2 medium red onion, chopped.
1/4 cup chopped fresh mint (a couple handfuls)
1/4 cup chopped fresh flat-leaf parsley (a couple handfuls)
3 tablespoons red wine vinegar (eyeball it)
1/3 cup extra-virgin olive oil (evoo) (eyeball it)

3-BEAN SALAD

1/2 pound fresh green beans, trimmed and cut into thirds
2 rounded teaspoons Dijon mustard
2 tablespoons sugar
1/4 cup red wine vinegar (eyeball it)
1/2 cup extra-virgin olive oil (evoo) (eyeball it)
1 can (15 ounces) red kidney beans, drained
1 can (15 ounces) garbanzo beans, drained
1/4 cup chopped fresh flat-leaf parsley
Salt and freshly ground black pepper, to taste

Put red potatoes in a pot and cover with water. Cover pot and bring to a boil over medium-high heat, then add a liberal amount of coarse salt. Place a colander over boiling pot. Take your first ingredient from the bean salad, the fresh green beans, and place them in the colander. Cover with pot lid and steam beans, 5 minutes, while potatoes boil below. Remove beans and cold-shock them under running water; drain well and set aside.

When the potatoes are just tender, after about 12 minutes, remove from heat, drain, and cold-shock them until just cool enough to handle. Coarsely chop and return them to the warm pot. Add bell pepper, onion, mint, parsley, and vinegar to the pot and toss to allow the potatoes to absorb the vinegar. Add evoo and stir the potatoes until they mash up a bit and salad has a spoonable consistency. Season with salt and pepper, and transfer to a serving bowl.

In another serving bowl, combine mustard, sugar, and vinegar. Whisk in evoo. Add kidney beans, garbanzo beans, steamed green beans, and parsley and toss to coat. Season with salt and pepper and serve. ★

✪ ✪ ✪ ✪
MAKES 4 SERVINGS

Veggie Lo Mein

Coarse salt, to taste

1/2 to 3/4 pound thin spaghetti

2 tablespoons vegetable or wok oil (twice around the pan)

2 cups fresh snow peas (4 handfuls)

1 small red bell pepper, seeded and cut into thin matchsticks

4 scallions, thinly sliced on an angle

1 cup fresh bean sprouts (a couple handfuls) (optional)

1 inch peeled gingerroot, grated or minced

3 or 4 cloves garlic, minced

1/2 cup aged tamari (dark soy sauce)

2 tablespoons toasted sesame oil (several shakes)

Put a large pot of water over high heat for the pasta. When water boils, add salt and pasta. Cook according to package directions. Drain.

Heat a wok, wok-shaped skillet, or large, nonstick skillet over high heat. When pan is hot, add oil—it will smoke a bit—then immediately add snow peas, bell pepper, scallions, and bean sprouts and stir-fry, 2 or 3 minutes. Add ginger and garlic, continue stir-frying 1 minute longer, then add pasta and combine with vegetables until evenly distributed. Add tamari sauce and toss until evenly coated. Transfer to a platter, drizzle with sesame oil, add salt, if desired. Serve with a chunked vegetable salad. ★

30-MINUTE MEALS
MENU

VEGETARIAN STIR-FRY

1
entree
VEGGIE LO MEIN

2
suggested side
CHUNKED VEGETABLE SALAD

30-MINUTE MEALS
MENU

HEALTHY
HUNGER
BUSTER

1

entree
SWORDFISH
STEAKS

2

side dishes
MANGO SALSA

CURRY
COUSCOUS

MAKES 4 SERVINGS

Swordfish Steaks with Mango Salsa and Curry Couscous

SWORDFISH STEAKS

The juice of 1 lime

4 swordfish steaks, 1 & 1/2 inches thick (8 ounces each)

A drizzle extra-virgin olive oil (evoo)

Salt and freshly ground black pepper, to taste

MANGO SALSA

1 ripe mango, peeled and diced

1 small red bell pepper, seeded and diced

1 jalapeño or serrano pepper, seeded and finely chopped

1 inch fresh gingerroot, peeled and grated or minced

1/4 seedless English cucumber, peeled and chopped

20 blades fresh chives, finely chopped

The juice of 1 lime

CURRY COUSCOUS

2 cups chicken broth or water

2 teaspoons curry powder or 1 rounded teaspoon mild curry paste

1/2 teaspoon coarse salt

1 tablespoon extra-virgin olive oil (evoo)

A handful dark or golden raisins

1 cup couscous

2 scallions, sliced on an angle

1 carrot, shredded or grated

1 navel orange, peeled and chopped

1 pouch (2 ounces) sliced almonds (available on baking aisle)

Preheat a grill pan or indoor electric grill to high heat. Squeeze lime juice over fish, and drizzle with a little evoo, rubbing it into the fish to coat well. Season with salt and pepper, and cook steaks 3 to 4 minutes on each side.

Combine all ingredients for the salsa in a small bowl.

For the couscous, bring broth or water to a boil with curry powder, salt, evoo, and raisins. Place couscous in a medium, heatproof bowl. Add boiling liquid, cover, and let couscous stand 10 minutes. Fluff with a fork and combine with scallions, carrot, orange bits, and almonds.

Top swordfish steaks with salsa and serve with generous portions of couscous. ★

✪ ✪ ✪ ✪

MAKES 4 SERVINGS

Noodle Bowls

3 quarts vegetable stock or chicken broth

1 & 1/2 pounds fresh linguini (available on dairy aisle)

1 & 1/2 pounds chicken tenders, cut into bite-size chunks, or chicken breasts cut for stir-fry

8 scallions cut into bite-size pieces on an angle

2 cups shredded carrots (available in pouches in produce section)

1 package fresh shiitake mushrooms (about 24 mushrooms), coarsely chopped

1/2 head bok choy, trimmed and shredded

1/2 pound snow peas, cut in half on an angle

Chopped fresh cilantro and/or chives, for garnish (optional)

Bring vegetable stock or chicken broth to a boil in a soup pot.

Bring a second pot of water to a boil. Add salt and fresh linguini and cook, 3 minutes. Drain pasta just before it's done, as it will finish cooking while it steeps in your soup bowls. Divide pasta equally among 4 deep bowls. Add chicken to boiling broth, and poach chicken, 5 minutes.

Add veggies to bowls of pasta. Ladle broth and chicken equally into the four bowls to cover vegetables and noodles. Cover bowls tightly with small plates and let the soup steep 5 minutes.

Uncover noodle bowls and serve. SLURP away! Where this soup comes from, it is customary to slurp as you eat, using oversized spoons to drag the noodles up to your mouth. You might need a bib, but you will have fun! Garnish with cilantro and/or chives for extra zing, if you prefer. ★

I discovered the wonders of noodle bowls at a Chinese restaurant in Vancouver, Canada, where they hand-pull their own noodles. The owner tried to teach me how to stretch my own homemade noodles. It was a bad scene. My noodles looked like a game of Cat's Cradle gone horribly wrong. In this recipe, storebought fresh pasta comes to the rescue. The noodle bowls can be adapted in tons of ways. Use shrimp, pork, beef, or just veggies—whatever pleases you.

30-MINUTE MEALS
MENU

HEALTHY
HUNGER
BUSTER

1

entree
SWORDFISH
STEAKS
━ ━ ━

2

side dishes
MANGO SALSA
━ ━ ━ ━

CURRY
COUSCOUS
━ ━ ━ ━

MAKES 4 SERVINGS

Swordfish Steaks with Mango Salsa and Curry Couscous

SWORDFISH STEAKS

The juice of 1 lime

4 swordfish steaks, 1 & 1/2 inches thick (8 ounces each)

A drizzle extra-virgin olive oil (evoo)

Salt and freshly ground black pepper, to taste

MANGO SALSA

1 ripe mango, peeled and diced

1 small red bell pepper, seeded and diced

1 jalapeño or serrano pepper, seeded and finely chopped

1 inch fresh gingerroot, peeled and grated or minced

1/4 seedless English cucumber, peeled and chopped

20 blades fresh chives, finely chopped

The juice of 1 lime

CURRY COUSCOUS

2 cups chicken broth or water

2 teaspoons curry powder or 1 rounded teaspoon mild curry paste

1/2 teaspoon coarse salt

1 tablespoon extra-virgin olive oil (evoo)

A handful dark or golden raisins

1 cup couscous

2 scallions, sliced on an angle

1 carrot, shredded or grated

1 navel orange, peeled and chopped

1 pouch (2 ounces) sliced almonds (available on baking aisle)

Preheat a grill pan or indoor electric grill to high heat. Squeeze lime juice over fish, and drizzle with a little evoo, rubbing it into the fish to coat well. Season with salt and pepper, and cook steaks 3 to 4 minutes on each side.

Combine all ingredients for the salsa in a small bowl.

For the couscous, bring broth or water to a boil with curry powder, salt, evoo, and raisins. Place couscous in a medium, heatproof bowl. Add boiling liquid, cover, and let couscous stand 10 minutes. Fluff with a fork and combine with scallions, carrot, orange bits, and almonds.

Top swordfish steaks with salsa and serve with generous portions of couscous. ★

✪ ✪ ✪ ✪
MAKES 4 SERVINGS

Veggie Lo Mein

Coarse salt, to taste

1/2 to 3/4 pound thin spaghetti

2 tablespoons vegetable or wok oil (twice around the pan)

2 cups fresh snow peas (4 handfuls)

1 small red bell pepper, seeded and cut into thin matchsticks

4 scallions, thinly sliced on an angle

1 cup fresh bean sprouts (a couple handfuls) (optional)

1 inch peeled gingerroot, grated or minced

3 or 4 cloves garlic, minced

1/2 cup aged tamari (dark soy sauce)

2 tablespoons toasted sesame oil (several shakes)

Put a large pot of water over high heat for the pasta. When water boils, add salt and pasta. Cook according to package directions. Drain.

Heat a wok, wok-shaped skillet, or large, nonstick skillet over high heat. When pan is hot, add oil—it will smoke a bit—then immediately add snow peas, bell pepper, scallions, and bean sprouts and stir-fry, 2 or 3 minutes. Add ginger and garlic, continue stir-frying 1 minute longer, then add pasta and combine with vegetables until evenly distributed. Add tamari sauce and toss until evenly coated. Transfer to a platter, drizzle with sesame oil, add salt, if desired. Serve with a chunked vegetable salad. ★

VEGETARIAN STIR-FRY

1
entree
VEGGIE LO MEIN

2
suggested side
CHUNKED VEGETABLE SALAD

I like spring rolls, but I don't want to fry them. The method used here is the same I use to make a spanakopita-like Greek spinach and feta roll that is one of my all-time favorite recipes. One night I was making the spinach and feta rolls and I thought, "Hmmm...this could be a cool, quick twist on an Asian spring roll, too!" The pastry roll-ups make a great party offering, and the method can be adapted to incorporate cooked shredded pork or shrimp.

✪ ✪ ✪ ✪
MAKES 4 SERVINGS

Baked Crab Spring Rolls

1 tablespoon vegetable oil or olive oil

1/2 red bell pepper, finely chopped

2 ribs celery from the heart, finely chopped

6 water chestnuts, finely chopped

1/2 small onion, finely chopped

1/4 cup fresh bean sprouts (a handful), chopped

2 cans (6 ounces each) lump crabmeat, drained and flaked

2 tablespoons tamari (dark soy sauce)

1/2 teaspoon dried thyme leaves (eyeball it)

4 sheets defrosted phyllo dough (13x17 inches each)

3 tablespoons melted butter

Preheat oven to 400°F.

Preheat a skillet over medium to medium-high heat and add oil. Sauté bell pepper, celery, water chestnuts, and onion, 2 to 3 minutes. While veggies are still a little crunchy, transfer to a bowl. Add bean spouts, crabmeat, tamari, and thyme. Combine well with a spoon.

Paint half of a sheet of phyllo dough with melted butter and fold sheet in half, making almost a square. Pile a few spoonfuls of filling 2 inches from the bottom of sheet and leaving 2 inches at either side of sheet. Fold bottom flap up and side edges in, then roll up and over until you reach the top of the sheet. Your crab pastry will look like a spring roll. Dab the edges and sides of your roll with melted butter and place seam-side down on a pastry sheet. Assemble all and bake on center rack until lightly golden all over, about 15 minutes. ★

Chicken Not-Pot-Pie

2 sprigs fresh rosemary, leaves stripped from stem and chopped

4 boneless, skinless chicken breasts

Salt and freshly ground black pepper, to taste, or crushed red pepper, to taste

2 teaspoons balsamic vinegar (a splash)

1 large, round loaf crusty peasant bread, top cut off and inside scooped out

1 can (15 ounces) artichoke hearts in water, drained

2 whole (4 halves) roasted red bell peppers from a jar, drained

1/4 medium Spanish onion, thinly sliced

2 plum tomatoes, sliced

1/4 pound sliced provolone, smoked provolone, or rustico with red pepper cheese

A handful pepper salad, pepperoncini, or pepper rings

Baby greens or baby spinach

Extra-virgin olive oil (evoo), for drizzling

Rub the rosemary leaves on the chicken and coat chicken with salt, pepper, and vinegar. Heat a griddle pan over high heat. Cook the chicken 5 minutes on each side. Remove from heat.

Place the chicken in the bottom of the hollowed-out loaf of bread. Pile artichokes, peppers, onions, tomatoes, cheese, pepper salad, and greens on top (you can use any antipasto combination you like). Drizzle evoo over the pie. Sprinkle with salt and pepper or crushed red pepper, to taste. Place the lid on the bread. Cut into wedges and serve with a green salad. ★

EVERYDAY

30-MINUTE MEALS

MENU

PEASANT
BREAD
SURPRISE

1

entree
CHICKEN NOT-
POT-PIE

2

suggested side
GREEN SALAD

Fluffernutter Brownies

Butter Bean Salad

Honey Mustard BBQ Chicken

Corn on the Cob with Chili and Lime

30-MINUTE MEALS
MENU

BACKYARD
PICNIC

1
entree
HONEY
MUSTARD BBQ
CHICKEN

2
side dish
BUTTER BEAN
SALAD

CORN ON THE
COB WITH CHILI
AND LIME

3
dessert
FLUFFERNUTTER
BROWNIES

✪ ✪ ✪ ✪
MAKES 4 SERVINGS

Honey Mustard BBQ Chicken

SAUCE

2 tablespoons vegetable oil (eyeball it)

1/2 red onion, chopped

1/4 cup apple cider vinegar

1/4 cup packed brown sugar (a couple handfuls)

1 cup chicken broth

1/2 cup prepared honey mustard, such as Honey Cup brand

1/2 teaspoon allspice (eyeball it)

1/2 teaspoon curry powder (eyeball it)

CHICKEN

4 pieces boneless, skinless chicken breast (6 to 8 ounces each)

4 boneless, skinless chicken thighs

Vegetable oil, for drizzling

Salt and freshly ground black pepper, to taste

Preheat grill pan or griddle over medium-high heat.

To make the sauce, place a small saucepan over medium heat and add vegetable oil. Add red onions and sauté, 3 to 5 minutes. Add vinegar and cook to reduce by half, 1 to 2 minutes. Add brown sugar and cook 1 minute to incorporate. Whisk in broth, honey mustard, allspice, and curry powder. Bring sauce to a bubble and reduce heat to lowest setting.

Coat chicken with a drizzle of oil and some salt and pepper. Place chicken on hot grill and cook 4 to 5 minutes, then turn. Baste chicken liberally with sauce and grill another 5 minutes. Turn once again and baste. Cook 2 or 3 minutes more, then transfer chicken to a platter and serve. ★

✪ ✪ ✪ ✪
MAKES 4 SERVINGS

Butter Bean Salad

2 cans (15 ounces each) butter beans, rinsed and drained

1/2 red bell pepper, diced

1/2 green bell pepper, diced

1/4 red onion, chopped

2 cloves garlic, minced

1 teaspoon ground cumin (a few good pinches)

2 tablespoons extra-virgin olive oil (evoo) (a glug)

The juice of 1 large lemon

Coarse salt and freshly ground black pepper, to taste

69

I am often asked where my recipes come from. Many come from my family. Others are versions of wonderful foods I've had during my travels.

Combine all ingredients in a medium bowl. Toss to coat beans and vegetables evenly in dressing. ★

✪ ✪ ✪ ✪
MAKES 4 SERVINGS

Corn on the Cob with Chili and Lime

4 ears sweet corn, shucked and cleaned of silk
1 lime, cut into wedges
1/3 stick butter, cut into pats
Chili powder, for sprinkling
Salt, to taste

In a medium pot, bring water to a boil, and simmer corn until just tender, 3 to 5 minutes.

Drain and arrange the ears on a shallow plate in a single row. Squeeze lime juice liberally over all the ears. Nest pats of butter into paper towels and rub lime-doused hot corn with butter. Season with a sprinkle of chili powder and salt, and serve immediately. ★

✪ ✪ ✪ ✪
MAKES 12 BROWNIES

Fluffernutter Brownies

1 package chocolate brownie mix
1 cup peanut butter chips
Softened butter, for baking dish
1 package (2 ounces) chopped nuts (available on baking aisle)
1 cup mini marshmallows

Preheat oven to 425°F.

Mix brownie mix according to package directions (don't bake it yet!).

Stir peanut butter chips into brownie batter. Grease an 8x8-inch baking dish with softened butter and spread the brownie batter into an even layer. Sprinkle with chopped nuts and bake, 20 to 22 minutes total, scattering marshmallows on top for the last 3 to 5 minutes of baking time. Remove from oven and cut into 12 brownies. ★

✪ ✪ ✪ ✪

MAKES 4 TO 6 SERVINGS

Twilight Time Turkey Patties and Cranberry Sauce

1 handful pecan pieces (found in bulk in candy and nuts section)

1 cup instant mashed potato flakes

1 & 1/3 pounds ground turkey breast

1 small white onion

1 handful chopped fresh flat-leaf parsley

2 sprigs fresh thyme, leaves stripped from stems and chopped

1 teaspoon poultry seasoning

Salt and freshly ground black pepper, to taste

2 tablespoons extra-virgin olive oil (evoo) (twice around the pan)

1 can (16 ounces) whole berry cranberry sauce

Grind pecans in a food processor or place in plastic bag and whack with a blunt instrument. Mix pecans with mashed potato flakes in a shallow dish. Place turkey in a bowl and grate the onion over and into same bowl with a handheld grater. Combine with parsley, thyme, poultry seasoning, salt, and pepper. Form into 6 patties.

Heat evoo in a nonstick skillet over medium-high heat. Coat patties in potato-and-nut mixture. Cook patties 5 minutes on each side.

Serve with plenty of cranberry sauce, a green salad, and bread and butter. ★

30-MINUTE MEALS

MENU

TASTY TURKEY BURGERS

1

entree
TWILIGHT TIME TURKEY PATTIES AND CRANBERRY SAUCE

2

suggested sides
GREEN SALAD AND BREAD & BUTTER

✪ ✪ ✪ ✪
MAKES 4 SERVINGS

Too-Easy Chicken with Leeks

2 leeks

4 pieces boneless, skinless chicken breasts (6 to 8 ounces each)

Salt and freshly ground black pepper, to taste

2 tablespoons extra-virgin olive oil (evoo) (twice around the pan)

1 cup dry white wine

Trim leeks of tough green ends and roots. Split them lengthwise, then cut across into 1/2-inch slices. Place sandy slices of leeks into a colander. Run under cold water, separating the layers of each slice to free the grains of sand. Drain leeks very well and place within arm's reach of the stovetop.

Heat a large nonstick skillet over medium-high heat. Season chicken breasts with salt and pepper. Add evoo to coat skillet, then add chicken breasts and brown, 3 to 4 minutes on each side; transfer to a plate. Add a little more oil to the pan, then add leeks, and sauté, 5 minutes, until they become soft. Add wine to the pan and nest chicken breasts down into leeks. Reduce heat to simmer for another 5 to 7 minutes. To serve, remove chicken from pan and slice on an angle. Fan and arrange sliced chicken breasts over a bed of sautéed leeks on each dinner plate or warm serving platter. ★

✪ ✪ ✪ ✪
MAKES 4 SERVINGS

Lemon Rice Pilaf

1 tablespoon extra-virgin olive oil (evoo) (once around the pan)

1 tablespoon butter

1 large shallot, finely chopped

1 & 1/2 cups long-grain rice

1/2 cup dry white wine

A few sprigs fresh thyme, leaves stripped and chopped

1 can (14 ounces) or 2 cups chicken broth

1 cup water

The grated zest of 1 lemon

A handful chopped fresh flat-leaf parsley

Slivered almonds, toasted, for garnish

Heat a medium saucepan over medium heat. Add evoo and butter and shallots to pan. Sauté, 2 minutes, then add rice, and lightly brown, 3 to 5 minutes. Add wine and allow it to evaporate entirely, 1 to 2 minutes. Add thyme and chicken broth. Add a cup of water to pot and bring to a boil. Cover rice, reduce heat, and cook until tender, about 20 minutes. Stir in lemon zest and parsley. Transfer to dinner plates or warm serving dish and garnish with toasted slivered almonds. ★

✪ ✪ ✪ ✪
MAKES 4 SERVINGS

Whatever-Your-Garden-Grows Salad

1/4 pound fresh wax beans, trimmed

1/4 pound fresh green beans, trimmed

1 small yellow squash, cut into strips

1 red bell pepper, cut into thin strips

2 scallions, thinly sliced on an angle

2 cups baby spinach or arugula leaves, shredded

DRESSING

1 teaspoon Dijon mustard

2 tablespoons white wine vinegar or tarragon vinegar (a couple splashes)

The juice of 1/2 lemon

1/4 cup extra-virgin olive oil (evoo)

2 tablespoons chopped fresh tarragon and/or fresh flat-leaf parsley

Salt and freshly ground black pepper, to taste

In a deep skillet bring 3 inches of water to a boil. Add wax and green beans and julienne-sliced yellow squash to the pot, and simmer, 2 minutes. Add red peppers and simmer, 1 minute longer. You want the vegetables to remain full of color and bite. Drain vegetables in a colander and cold-shock under running water. Place drained vegetables in a serving dish and combine with sliced scallions and shredded spinach or arugula.

Whisk together mustard, vinegar, and lemon juice. Add evoo in a slow stream, whisking to get a nice emulsion. Add herbs, adjust salt and pepper to taste, and pour dressing over salad, tossing to combine flavors and coat evenly. ★

As the title implies, try any and every mix of veggies. Substitutions are encouraged!

73

30-MINUTE MEALS
MENU

FRENCH
CUISINE IN
30

1

entree
CHICKEN
CHASSEUR WITH
HERBED EGG
FETTUCCINE

2

suggested side
GREEN SALAD

Everyone who tastes this, flips. It is a thirty-minute version of the classic French hunter's chicken.

MAKES 4 TO 6 SERVINGS

Chicken Chasseur with Herbed Egg Fettuccine

PASTA

Salt, to taste

1 pound fresh egg fettuccine

3 tablespoons butter

1 large shallot, finely chopped

12 blades fresh chives, chopped

A handful fresh flat-leaf parsley, chopped

CHICKEN

1/4 teaspoon ground thyme

Coarse salt and freshly ground black pepper, to taste

1/2 cup all-purpose flour (a couple handfuls)

1 & 1/2 pounds boneless, skinless chicken breast cutlets, cut into large pieces (3 per breast)

2 tablespoons extra-virgin olive oil (evoo) (twice around the pan)

2 tablespoons butter

8 to 10 baby carrots, thinly sliced

1 rounded teaspoon sugar

2 large shallots, minced

12 crimini mushroom caps, chopped

1 cup dry red wine (3 or 4 times around the pan in a slow stream)

1 can (28 ounces) crushed tomatoes

4 sprigs fresh tarragon, leaves stripped and chopped

Put a large pot of water over high heat for the pasta. When water boils, add salt and pasta. Cook according to package directions until al dente. Drain.

Start the chicken: Mix thyme, salt, pepper, and flour in a dish. Coat chicken in flour, set aside. Discard flour. Heat evoo and butter in large, deep skillet over medium heat. Brown chicken pieces 4 minutes on each side and remove. Put carrots in pan, sprinkle with sugar, and cook 1 minute. Add shallots and mushrooms and cook 3 to 5 minutes to soften. Add wine and cook to reduce by half. Add tomatoes and tarragon and return chicken to pan. Give the pan a shake. Simmer until chicken is cooked through, another 3 to 5 minutes.

Back to the pasta: Melt butter in a large skillet over medium heat. Add shallots and cook 5 minutes. Add herbs and toss in egg fettuccine. Serve alongside chicken. Add a green salad for a complete meal. ★

✪ ✪ ✪ ✪

MAKES 4 SERVINGS

Herb and Cheese Oven Fries

3 all-purpose potatoes, such as russet, cut into thin wedges

2 or 3 tablespoons extra-virgin olive oil (evoo), just enough to coat potatoes

1 teaspoon dried Italian seasoning, or 1/2 teaspoon each dried oregano, thyme, and parsley

Salt and freshly ground black pepper, to taste

1/2 cup grated Parmigiano Reggiano cheese

Preheat oven to 500°F.

Place potato wedges on a cookie sheet. Drizzle with just enough evoo to coat. Season with Italian seasoning, salt, and pepper. Roast potatoes and turn after 15 to 20 minutes. Sprinkle cheese liberally on potatoes and roast, another 10 minutes. Serve. ★

✪ ✪ ✪ ✪

MAKES 4 SERVINGS

Sausage, Pepper, and Onion Hoagies

3/4 pound sweet Italian sausage

3/4 pound hot Italian sausage

3 tablespoons extra-virgin olive oil (evoo)

2 large cloves garlic, crushed

1 large onion, thinly sliced

2 cubanelle peppers (light-green mild Italian peppers), seeded and thinly sliced

1 red bell pepper, seeded and thinly sliced

Salt and freshly ground black pepper, to taste

2 or 3 hot cherry peppers, banana peppers, or pepperoncini, finely chopped

3 tablespoons hot pepper juice from the jar

BREAD

4 crusty, semolina submarine sandwich rolls (8 inches each), sesame seed or plain

1 tablespoon extra-virgin olive oil (evoo)

3 tablespoons butter

1 large clove garlic

1 & 1/2 teaspoons dried Italian seasoning (half palmful), OR 1/2 teaspoon each, oregano, thyme, and parsley

Place the sausages in a large nonstick skillet. Pierce the casings with a fork. Add 1 inch water to the pan. Bring liquid to a boil. Cover sausages; reduce heat and simmer, 10 minutes.

Heat a second skillet over medium-high heat. Add 2 tablespoons evoo (twice around the pan). Add garlic, onion, cubanelle, and red bell peppers. Season with salt and pepper.

Drain sausages and return pan to stove, raising heat back to medium-high. Add the remaining tablespoon evoo (a drizzle) to the skillet; brown and crisp the casings. Remove sausages, slice into 2-inch pieces on an angle and set pieces back in the pan to sear.

Prepare the bread: Preheat the broiler to high. Split the bread and toast it under the broiler.

Melt evoo and butter together in a small pan over medium heat. Add garlic and let it sizzle 1 to 2 minutes. Brush rolls with garlic butter and sprinkle with a little Italian seasoning.

Combine the cooked peppers and onions with the sausages in a skillet. Add hot peppers and hot pepper juice. Toss and turn the sausage, peppers, and onions, picking up all the drippings from the pan. Pile the meat and peppers into the garlic rolls and serve. ★

✪ ✪ ✪ ✪
MAKES 4 SERVINGS

Date Shakes

1 cup pitted dates, coarsely chopped
1 quart skim milk
2 pints French vanilla ice cream
1 teaspoon grated fresh nutmeg

For each date shake, place 1/4 cup dates (a handful), in a blender. Add 1 cup cold skim milk and 2 big scoops of French vanilla ice cream. Grate 1/4 teaspoon fresh nutmeg into blender and blend until smooth. ★

✪ ✪ ✪ ✪

MAKES 4 SERVINGS

Herb Smashed Potatoes with Goat Cheese

3 large all-purpose potatoes, peeled and cut into chunks

Salt and freshly ground black pepper, to taste

1 tablespoon extra-virgin olive oil (evoo) (once around the pan)

2 tablespoons butter, cut into pieces

1 shallot, chopped

10 blades chives, chopped or snipped (3 tablespoons)

3 or 4 sprigs fresh thyme, leaves stripped and chopped

1 cup chicken broth

1 small log (4 ounces) herb, peppercorn, or plain goat cheese

Bring a medium pot of water to a boil. Add potatoes and salt. Boil potatoes until fork-tender, about 15 minutes.

Drain cooked potatoes and return empty pot to stove. Adjust heat to medium. Add evoo, then butter. When butter has melted, add shallots and sauté, 2 to 3 minutes. Add chives and thyme, then potatoes to the pot. Mash potatoes, adding broth as you work to achieve desired consistency. Season with salt and pepper.

Remove goat cheese from packaging and cut into 4 disks. Serve potatoes on dinner plates and top each mound with a disk of goat cheese. ★

30-MINUTE MEALS

MENU

THANKSGIVING FOR EVERYDAY

1

entree
TURKEY AND WILD MUSHROOM MEAT LOAF PATTIES WITH PAN GRAVY

2

side dishes
HERB SMASHED POTATOES WITH GOAT CHEESE

GREEN BEANS WITH LEMON AND TOASTED ALMONDS

Complete this menu with pecan pie and whipped cream (store-bought).

✪ ✪ ✪ ✪

MAKES 4 SERVINGS

Turkey and Wild Mushroom Meat Loaf Patties with Pan Gravy

3 tablespoons extra-virgin olive oil (evoo)

8 crimini (baby portobello) mushrooms, chopped

8 shiitake mushrooms, chopped

1 shallot, chopped

Salt and freshly ground black pepper, to taste

1 & 1/3 pounds (1 package) ground turkey

3 or 4 sprigs fresh sage, leaves stripped and chopped

1 tablespoon Worcestershire sauce (eyeball it)

1/2 cup Italian bread crumbs

1 egg, beaten

2 tablespoons butter

2 tablespoons all-purpose flour

2 cups chicken or turkey broth

1 teaspoon poultry seasoning

Heat a nonstick skillet over medium-high heat. Add 2 tablespoons evoo (twice around the pan). Add chopped mushrooms and shallots and season with salt and pepper. Sauté mushrooms until dark and tender, 5 or 6 minutes. Remove from heat. Transfer mushrooms to a bowl and return pan to stovetop to preheat to cook patties.

Place turkey in a mixing bowl. Make a well in the center of the meat. Add sage, Worcestershire, bread crumbs, and beaten egg. Scrape sautéed mushrooms and shallots into the bowl. Add salt and pepper. Mix together and make a small, 1-inch patty. Place patty in the hot pan and cook 1 minute on each side. Taste for seasonings and adjust seasonings in raw meat loaf mixture accordingly. Divide meat loaf mixture into 4 equal parts by scoring the meat before you form patties. Form into oval patties, 1 inch thick. Add 1 tablespoon evoo to the pan, and arrange patties in the pan. Cook 6 minutes on each side and transfer to a serving plate or individual dinner plates.

Return pan to heat and add butter. When butter has melted, whisk in flour and cook 1 to 2 minutes. Whisk in broth and season gravy with poultry seasoning, salt, and pepper. Thicken gravy to your liking and pour over patties, reserving a little to pass at the table. ★

✪ ✪ ✪ ✪
MAKES 4 SERVINGS

Green Beans with Lemon and Toasted Almonds

1 package (2 ounces) sliced almonds (available on baking aisle)
1 pound green beans, trimmed
1 tablespoon butter
The juice of 1/2 lemon
Salt and freshly ground black pepper, to taste

In a medium pan, toast almonds over medium heat. Remove from pan and set aside.

Add 1/2 inch water to pan. Bring water to a boil, add beans, and cover pan. Reduce heat. Cook beans until just tender yet still green, 4 or 5 minutes. Drain beans and set aside.

Return pan to stovetop and melt butter over medium heat. Add lemon juice to butter (juice lemon half right-side up to keep seeds in lemon rather than in your beans). Add beans to lemon butter and coat evenly. Season with salt and pepper, to taste. Transfer green beans to dinner plates or serving plate and top with almonds. ★

✪ ✪ ✪ ✪
MAKES 4 SERVINGS

Asparagus and Green Beans with Tarragon Lemon Dip

1 pound fresh asparagus, trimmed
1 pound fresh green beans, trimmed

TARRAGON LEMON DIP
1 cup mayonnaise
The zest and juice of 1 lemon
1 small shallot, finely chopped
2 tablespoons chopped fresh tarragon (4 springs)
2 tablespoons chopped fresh flat-leaf parsley
A few grinds fresh black pepper
Sprigs of tarragon and parsley, for garnish

In a large skillet, cook asparagus spears and green beans in 1 inch of salted boiling water, covered, 3 or 4 minutes. Drain and cool the vegetables and arrange them on a serving plate. Combine dip ingredients in a small bowl and garnish with sprigs of parsley and tarragon and set alongside vegetables on a serving dish. ★

✪ ✪ ✪ ✪
MAKES 4 SERVINGS

French Dip Roast Beef Sandwiches

2 tablespoons butter
1 shallot, chopped
1 & 1/2 tablespoons flour
1 shot dry sherry (optional)
2 cans (14 ounces each) beef consommé
1 & 1/2 pounds deli-sliced roast beef
Steak seasoning blend such as Montreal Seasoning by McCormick OR coarse salt and freshly ground black pepper to taste
4 torpedo sandwich rolls, split

In a large, shallow skillet over medium heat, melt the butter. Sauté shallots in the butter 2 minutes. Add flour and cook 1 minute longer. Whisk in sherry and cook liquid out. Whisk in consommé in a slow stream. Bring sauce to a bubble and allow to simmer over low heat until sandwiches are ready to serve.

Pile roast beef loosely across a large work surface, and season with grill seasoning or salt and black pepper. Gather 4 ramekins or small soup cups for dipping sauce, and 4 split torpedo rolls. Using tongs to help you

assemble, dip meat into sauce and pile into rolls. Set ramekins with extra sauce next to the sandwiches. ★

✪ ✪ ✪ ✪
MAKES 4 SERVINGS

Chocolate Fondue

FONDUE

3/4 cup heavy whipping cream (reserve 1/4 cup to thin fondue, if necessary)

4 bittersweet chocolate bars (3 & 1/2 ounces each), chopped

2 tablespoons Frangelico or Amaretto liqueur (optional)

1/4 cup finely chopped hazelnuts or almonds (optional)

SUGGESTED "DIP-ABLES," CHOOSE 3 OR 4 OF THE FOLLOWING:

Hazelnut or almond biscotti

Salted pretzel sticks

Cubed pound cake

Sliced bananas

Stem strawberries

Sectioned navel oranges

Ripe fresh pineapple, diced

Heat cream in a heavy nonreactive saucepan over medium heat until cream comes to a low boil. Remove pan from heat and add chocolate, allowing it to stand in hot cream, 3 to 5 minutes to soften, then whisk together with the cream. Stir in liqueur and/or chopped nuts and transfer to a fondue pot or set the mixing bowl on a rack above a small lit candle. If fondue becomes too thick, stir in reserved cream, 1 tablespoon at a time, to desired consistency. Arrange your favorite "dip-ables" in piles on a platter alongside chocolate fondue with fondue forks, bamboo skewers or seafood forks as dipping utensils. ★

✪ ✪ ✪ ✪

MAKES 4 SERVINGS

Oven Fries with Herbes de Provence

3 all-purpose potatoes, scrubbed and dried

Extra-virgin olive oil (evoo), for drizzling (about 2 tablespoons)

4 teaspoons dried herbes de Provence (a palmful), or 1 teaspoon each: dried parsley, sage, rosemary, and thyme

Salt, to taste

Preheat oven to 500°F.

Cut potatoes into thin wedges and place on a cookie sheet. Coat potatoes in a thin layer of evoo, then sprinkle very liberally with herbes de Provence. Toss potatoes to coat evenly. Roast potatoes until crisp and golden at edges, about 25 minutes. Season hot wedges with salt. ★

✪ ✪ ✪ ✪

MAKES 4 SERVINGS

Tomato and Spinach Soup

2 tablespoons extra-virgin olive oil (evoo) (twice around the pan)

1 large shallot, finely chopped

2 cloves garlic, chopped

1 can (14 ounces) diced tomatoes in juice, drained

1 can (28 ounces) crushed tomatoes

2 cups good-quality vegetable stock (available on soup aisle)

1/2 ten-ounce sack triple-washed spinach, stems removed and spinach shredded with knife

Salt and freshly ground black pepper, to taste

Heat a medium soup pot over medium heat. Add evoo, shallots, and garlic. Sauté 5 minutes. Add diced and crushed tomatoes; stir. Add stock and stir to combine. Stir in spinach in handfuls to wilt it and combine with soup. Season with salt and pepper to taste. Bring soup to a bubble, reduce heat, and simmer 10 to 15 minutes to reduce. ★

✪ ✪ ✪ ✪

MAKES 4 SERVINGS

Rachael's Tuna Pan Bagnat

2 baguettes

1/2 to 2/3 cup (18 to 24 olives) Kalamata olives

2 cans (6.5 ounces each) Italian or French imported tuna in oil, drained (available in canned fish or international foods aisles)

1 tin (6 fillets) flat anchovies, drained and chopped

3 tablespoons capers, drained

1/2 red onion, chopped

1 can (15 ounces) artichoke hearts in water, drained and coarsely chopped

1/2 cup drained sun-dried tomatoes in oil, chopped

1/4 to 1/3 cup (a couple handfuls) fresh flat-leaf parsley, chopped

4 or 5 sprigs fresh rosemary, leaves stripped and chopped

1 lemon, halved

1 tablespoon red wine vinegar

Freshly ground black pepper, to taste

3 tablespoons extra-virgin olive oil (evoo) (eyeball it)

Preheat oven to 400°F.

Crisp baguettes in hot oven, about 1 to 2 minutes, then cool to handle. Cut baguettes in half across, on an angle, then split each half horizontally. Hollow out some of the soft middle to make room for the filling.

If the olives are pitted, coarsely chop them. If the olives have pits, place an olive or two on a cutting board. Place the flat of a knife blade on top of the olives and—just like peeling garlic—whack the heel of your hand on the knife and the pits of the olives will be exposed. Remove pits and discard; chop olives.

Place tuna in a bowl and separate with a fork. Add anchovies, capers, red onion, artichokes, sun-dried tomatoes, olives, parsley, and rosemary.

Squeeze lemon juice into the bowl by holding the lemon halves cut side up, allowing juice to spill over sides (seeds will stay with the lemon half). Add vinegar and pepper and drizzle salad liberally with evoo. Toss to combine, and adjust pepper to taste. Pack the tuna salad into hollowed baguette halves and set tops in place. Press down to set the bread and salad together. The bread will absorb the evoo and salad juices. Cut each half baguette in half again, making 8 pieces total. ★

This tasty lunch also makes a picture-perfect picnic. To take this menu on the road, pour the soup into a large thermos and rather than making the oven fries, buy a sack of specialty potato chips instead. Garlic-and-onion flavored Terra brand chips, available on the snack aisle of your market, are a good example.

✪ ✪ ✪ ✪
MAKES 4 SERVINGS

Pasta al Forno

Salt and freshly ground black pepper, to taste

1 pound ziti rigate or penne rigate (with lines)

Softened butter, for baking dish

2 tablespoons extra-virgin olive oil (evoo) (twice around the pan)

1 small onion, finely chopped

3 cloves garlic, chopped

1 can (15 ounces) crushed tomatoes

1/2 cup heavy cream

2 pinches cinnamon

3 ounces prosciutto (one thick slice from deli counter), chopped

1/4 to 1/3 cup grated Parmigiano Reggiano cheese

Put a pot of water over high heat to boil. When it comes to a boil, add salt and pasta. Cook pasta until al dente on the chewy side, about 7 minutes. Once pasta water comes to a boil, preheat oven to 500°F.

Butter a medium-size baking dish or casserole. Add evoo to a medium skillet over medium heat. Cook onions and garlic in evoo, 3 to 5 minutes. Stir in tomatoes and bring to a bubble. Add cream and season sauce with cinnamon, salt, and pepper. Add chopped prosciutto to sauce and stir with cooked pasta to combine. Adjust seasonings and transfer pasta to buttered baking dish. Cover pasta with cheese and place in oven; bake until top is lightly brown and pasta is bubbling, about 10 minutes. Serve hot from the oven. ★

✪ ✪ ✪ ✪
MAKES 4 SERVINGS

Veal Involtini with Pancetta on Bed of Spinach

1 pound veal scaloppini (from the butcher counter)

1/4 cup chopped fresh flat-leaf parsley (a couple handfuls)

Salt and freshly ground black pepper, to taste

1 pound smoked fresh mozzarella cheese, thinly sliced

1 jar (16 to 18 ounces) roasted red peppers, drained and sliced

1/3 pound pancetta, sliced, or thin-cut bacon (from the deli counter)

2 tablespoons extra-virgin olive oil (evoo) (twice around the pan), plus more for drizzling

1 clove garlic, cracked with the flat of a knife

1 sack (10 ounces) baby spinach or triple-washed spinach leaves

1/4 to 1/3 cup white wine or dry vermouth

Veal Involtini

Arrange scaloppini on waxed paper or plastic wrap. Sprinkle with parsley, salt, and pepper. Place a thin layer of cheese and a few slices of roasted pepper on each scaloppini. Roll veal and wrap each roll with a slice of pancetta. Secure with toothpicks.

Fry veal rolls in 2 tablespoons (a thin layer) of evoo until golden all over and pancetta is crisp, 5 or 6 minutes. Remove from pan to a warm platter. Return skillet to heat. Add a drizzle evoo and the garlic to pan. Wilt spinach in pan, add a touch of wine or vermouth to lift drippings and combine them with greens. Using tongs, place a bed of spinach on each dinner plate and top with veal rolls. Serve immediately. ★

✪ ✪ ✪ ✪
MAKES 4 SERVINGS

Pears with Vanilla Ice Cream and Chocolate Sauce

2 cans (15 ounces each) pears in heavy syrup
1/4 cup amaretto or dark rum
4 ounces bittersweet chocolate chips or chopped chocolate bar
1 pint French vanilla ice cream

Drain pears over a small saucepan. Reduce syrup over medium-high heat, 12 to 15 minutes. Stir in liquor and cook 2 minutes longer. Add chocolate and stir to melt. Remove from heat.

Slice pears and place in cocktail glasses. Pour hot chocolate sauce over pears and top glasses with small scoops of vanilla ice cream. ★

✪ ✪ ✪ ✪
MAKES 6 SERVINGS

Blackberry Napoleons

2 half-pint containers blackberries

2 tablespoons granulated sugar

18 wonton wrappers

3 tablespoons butter, melted

1/4 cup packed brown sugar

1 canister real whipped cream (from dairy aisle)

Preheat oven to 400°F.

Combine berries with granulated sugar and let stand 20 minutes.

Meanwhile, arrange wonton wrappers on a nonstick cookie sheet. Brush with melted butter and sprinkle with brown sugar. Bake 5 to 7 minutes, until deep golden. Remove from oven and cool until ready to serve.

To assemble, layer whipped cream and berries in between 3 pieces of toasted wonton. Repeat to assemble 6 individual napoleons. ★

30-MINUTE MEALS
MENU

MIDDLE
EASTERN
MEAT-FREE
DINNER

1
entree
GARLIC AND
RED PEPPER
PITA CHIPS WITH
GREEN OLIVE
HUMMUS

2
side dish
VEGETABLE AND
COUSCOUS
STACKS

3
dessert
BLACKBERRY
NAPOLEANS

✪ ✪ ✪ ✪

MAKES 6 SERVINGS

Vegetable and Couscous Stacks

2 cloves garlic, cracked away from skin with the flat of a knife

1 cup extra-virgin olive oil (evoo)

1 medium eggplant, sliced 1/2 inch thick

1 medium zucchini, thinly sliced on an angle

4 or 5 sprigs rosemary, leaves stripped and finely chopped (3 tablespoons)

7 or 8 sprigs fresh thyme leaves, leaves stripped and chopped (3 tablespoons)

Coarse salt and freshly ground black pepper, to taste

2 roasted red peppers (available in bulk near deli or in jars), drained and quartered

6 slices red onion, 1/2 inch thick

1 can (14 ounces) chicken broth (about 2 cups), empty can reserved

2 cups couscous

1/2 cup grated Parmesan cheese

1 pound fresh smoked mozzarella, sliced into 12 thin slices

12 leaves fresh basil

2 vine-ripe tomatoes, thinly sliced

Preheat oven to 400°F and preheat a grill pan to high.

Warm garlic and evoo in a small skillet over low heat. Brush eggplant and zucchini slices lightly with garlic oil and arrange in single layers on 2 cookie sheets. Season with about 2 tablespoons each of rosemary and thyme. Add salt and pepper and place in oven to roast until tender, 15 minutes.

Brush peppers and onions with garlic oil and grill until charred and just tender. Season with salt and pepper.

Pour broth into a saucepan and bring to a boil with 2 tablespoons of the warmed garlic oil. Take the top and bottom off the broth can with a can opener. Rinse can and reserve. When stock boils, remove from heat. Add remaining 1 tablespoon each rosemary and thyme, and the couscous. Cover and let stand 5 minutes. Fluff with a fork and toss with grated cheese.

To assemble, place the can upright on a large serving platter. Set 2 slices of eggplant down into can, then 2 slices zucchini. Press the vegetables down as you work, using a rubber spatula. Pack a rounded 1/2 cup couscous into the can, then a piece of grilled roasted red pepper and a thin slice of onion. Next, 2 thin slices smoked mozzarella, 2 leaves basil, and finally, 2 thin slices tomato. Season top of the stack with salt and pepper. Remove can and repeat 5 more times with remaining ingredients. Garnish with any remaining basil or mixed sprigs of herbs. ★

✪ ✪ ✪ ✪
MAKES 6 SERVINGS

Garlic and Red Pepper Pita Chips with Green Olive Hummus

3 pita breads, 6 to 8 inches in diameter

2 cloves garlic, minced

1/4 cup extra-virgin olive oil (evoo)

2 teaspoons crushed red pepper flakes

Salt, to taste

1 & 1/2 cups store-bought roasted garlic hummus, any brand

10 to 12 large green pitted olives, chopped (1/2 cup), plain, herb, or hot pepper flavored (available near deli in bulk bins)

2 scallions, thinly sliced

Preheat oven to 400°F.

Separate each pita, making 6 pieces out of 3 pitas. Stack breads and cut into 6 wedges, making 36 pieces total. Combine garlic, evoo, and 1 teaspoon red pepper flakes in the bottom of a bowl. (If you have garlic oil remaining from the previous recipe for vegetable stacks, that may be used up in this recipe, just add crushed red pepper flakes and no garlic.) Add pita bread wedges and toss with your fingertips to combine and coat evenly. Scatter the wedges in a single layer on a cookie sheet and bake 5 minutes until browned and crisp. Season hot pita chips with a sprinkle of coarse salt.

Combine hummus with the remaining 1 teaspoon crushed red pepper flakes and chopped green olives. Transfer to a bowl and garnish with scallions. Surround with pita chips and serve. ★

✪ ✪ ✪ ✪
MAKES 4 SERVINGS

My Sister Ria's Favorite Fajitas

MARINADE

3 tablespoons cayenne pepper sauce, such as Frank's Red Hot or Tabasco

2 tablespoons ground cumin (a palmful)

1 teaspoon allspice

2 tablespoons chili powder (a palmful)

A handful fresh oregano and thyme leaves combined (3 or 4 stems each)

1/2 bottle of beer

A drizzle extra-virgin olive oil (evoo)

THE GUTS

1 & 1/2 pounds flank steak, or 4 boneless, skinless chicken breasts
   (8 pieces)

Extra-virgin olive oil (evoo)

1 large Spanish onion, cut in half and then into 1/2-inch strips

1 red bell pepper, seeded and cut into 1/2-inch strips

1 green bell pepper, seeded and cut into 1/2-inch strips

2 poblano chiles, cut into strips (if none are available in your market,
   use cubanelle long Italian peppers)

Salt and freshly ground black pepper, to taste

THE TOPPING

Prepared pico di gallo (fresh salsa made of only finely chopped tomato,
   serrano or jalapeño chiles, minced onion, cilantro, mint, and salt) or
   any store-bought salsa.

THE WRAPS

Small flour tortillas (6 inches) or 4 large tortillas (9 to 12 inches)

Mix all marinade ingredients together.

Coat the meat or poultry in the marinade and let it hang out. Heat two
pans, a nonstick griddle to high, a nonstick frying pan to medium-high.
Drizzle the frying pan with evoo. Cook the onions, peppers, and chiles, with
an occasional shake, until they darken around the edges, about 5 minutes.
Sprinkle with salt and pepper and turn off heat.

Drop meat or chicken onto the very hot griddle pan. Sear for 2 minutes on
each side. Remove from heat. Slice very thin, on the bias, and return strips
to griddle to brown and cook through. Drop cutting board and knife into
sink to sanitize.

Heat tortillas according to package directions. Fill with sizzling meat or
chicken, veggies, and a scoop or two of pico di gallo. Wrap and chow down.
Serve with a side of refried beans and your beverage of choice (margaritas
or mockaritas are not a bad choice). ★

TEX-MEX IN NO TIME

1
entree
MY SISTER RIA'S
FAVORITE
FAJITAS

2
suggested side
REFRIED BEANS

93

✪ ✪ ✪ ✪

MAKES 6 SERVINGS

Mexican Ice Cream Pie

1 jar (8 ounces) chocolate fudge topping

1 graham cracker piecrust (available on baking aisle)

3 pints coffee or vanilla ice cream, softened in microwave on defrost 30 seconds

2 cups small breakfast cereal flakes, such as Grape Nuts Flakes or Special K

1 teaspoon cinnamon

1 tablespoon cocoa powder or instant hot cocoa mix

1/4 cup (2 ounces) Spanish peanuts

Honey, for drizzling

1 canister real whipped cream (from dairy aisle) (optional)

Take the lid off fudge sauce and heat 10 seconds in a microwave on high to make it spreadable. Cover bottom of graham cracker crust with a thin layer of fudge sauce. Fill and mound the crust with coffee or vanilla ice cream using a rubber spatula. Smooth the top of the pie with a spatula, making the surface of the pie smooth and free of lumps. Mix cereal, cinnamon, cocoa, and nuts. Using handfuls of the mix, coat the pie liberally with topping, pressing it into the ice cream as you apply it. Cover pie with plastic storage wrap and set in freezer to set.

When ready to serve, cut pie into 6 wedges. Drizzle each slice with honey and garnish with a rosette of whipped cream. ★

✪ ✪ ✪ ✪

MAKES 6 SERVINGS

Calabacitas Casserole with Polenta and Cheese

2 tubes (16 ounces each) prepared polenta

3 tablespoons extra-virgin olive oil (evoo)

2 cups frozen corn kernels, defrosted

4 cloves garlic, chopped

1 green chile pepper, seeded and chopped, or 2 jalapeños, seeded and chopped

2 small to medium zucchini, diced

1 small to medium yellow squash, diced

1 large yellow onion, chopped

Salt and freshly ground black pepper, to taste

2 teaspoons dark chili powder

1 can (14 ounces) stewed tomatoes

2 cups (10 ounces) shredded Monterey Jack cheese (available preshredded on the dairy aisle)

3 scallions, chopped

2 tablespoons chopped cilantro or fresh flat-leaf parsley

Preheat oven to 500°F.

Cut one tube of polenta into 1/2-inch slices lengthwise. Drizzle 1 tablespoon evoo (just eyeball it) into a shallow baking dish or casserole. Spread the oil around with a pastry brush to evenly coat the bottom and sides of the dish. Line the bottom of the dish with the long slices of polenta. Slice the remaining tube of polenta in 1/2-inch slices across, making several disks of polenta. Reserve.

Heat a large skillet over medium-high heat. Add remaining 2 tablespoons evoo, the corn, garlic, and chiles. Sauté 3 minutes, add zucchini, yellow squash, and onions; season with salt, pepper, and chili powder; cook 7 to 8 minutes. Add stewed tomatoes and heat through. Transfer vegetables to baking dish. Top with reserved polenta disks and the cheese. Place in hot oven to melt cheese and warm polenta, 8 to 10 minutes. Garnish with chopped scallions and cilantro or parsley. ★

This is another great menu to entertain with designed to please both meat eaters and meat-free-ers alike. I am not a veg-head, but I eat meat-free meals often, and some of my friends and coworkers are vegetarians or they are partnered with vegetarians. More and more, I find a need to cook recipes that can please both groups of eaters at the same time.

These quesadillas are all-veggie favorites, inspired by a trip to Santa Fe.

Grilled Green Chile Quesadillas

3 fresh chile peppers, such as poblanos (any variety may be used, according to your tolerance for heat)

4 large (12-inch) flour tortillas

1 & 3/4—pound brick smoked cheddar cheese, shredded (3 cups)

1 cup salsa verde (available on chip and snack aisle or in Mexican foods section)

1 cup sour cream

2 tablespoons chopped fresh cilantro, for garnish

Heat a grill pan over high heat. Place whole chiles on grill and char all over, 10 minutes. Remove from heat and split chiles. Scrape away seeds with a spoon and discard; slice chiles.

Heat a large nonstick skillet or griddle over medium-high heat. Char a tortilla and blister it on one side, 20 seconds, then flip tortilla. Cover half of the tortilla with cheese and chiles, then fold over. Press down gently with spatula. Cook quesadilla 15 seconds more on each side then transfer to a cutting board. Repeat with remaining tortillas. Pile up 2 completed quesadillas at a time and cut into 3 generous wedges. The yield will be 12 pieces from 4 quesadillas.

Serve slices on a large platter with small dishes of salsa verde and sour cream for topping. Garnish the platter and toppings with chopped cilantro.★

Grilled Green Chile Quesadillas

30-MINUTE MEALS

MENU

RAINY
NIGHT
RELIEF

1

entree
SAUSAGE,
BEANS, AND
BROCCOLI RABE
"STOUP"

2

side dish
ITALIAN GRILLED
CHEESE AND
TOMATO
SANDWICHES

✪ ✪ ✪ ✪

MAKES 2 SERVINGS

Sausage, Beans, and Broccoli Rabe "Stoup"

2 tablespoons extra-virgin olive oil (evoo) (twice around the pan)

1 pound bulk Italian sweet sausage

1 medium onion, chopped

1 carrot, chopped

1 starchy Idaho potato, peeled and chopped into small dice

2 cloves garlic, chopped

1 bay leaf

1 can (15 ounces) white beans, drained

Salt and freshly ground black pepper, to taste

1 bunch broccoli rabe, chopped (3 cups)

1 quart chicken broth

Grated Parmigiano Reggiano or Romano cheese, for serving

Heat a medium pot or a deep skillet over medium-high heat. Add evoo and sausage and brown, crumbling with a spatula. Add onions, carrots, potatoes, garlic, bay leaf, and beans. Season with salt and pepper. Cook to begin to soften the vegetables, 5 minutes. Add broccoli rabe and cook just until wilted. Add chicken broth and cover pot. Raise heat and bring stoup to a boil. Reduce heat to simmer and cook 15 minutes. Remove bay leaf, adjust seasonings, and serve stoup with grated cheese for topping. ★

✪ ✪ ✪ ✪

MAKES 2 SERVINGS

Italian Grilled Cheese and Tomato Sandwiches

2 tablespoons extra-virgin olive oil (evoo) (twice around the pan)

1 large clove garlic

4 slices crusty Italian bread

6 deli slices provolone cheese

1 vine-ripe tomato, cut into 6 slices

Salt and freshly ground black pepper, to taste

8 fresh basil leaves, torn into pieces

Heat a large griddle or large nonstick skillet over medium heat. Add evoo and garlic and cook 1 minute. Add bread to the pan to soak up garlic oil. Top each slice of bread with 1 & 1/2 slices provolone each. Add 3 tomato slices each to 2 slices bread and season with salt and pepper. Top tomatoes with lots of basil. Set the other two slices of bread on top of the basil to form sandwiches. Cook grilled cheeses until golden brown and cheese has melted, flipping and pressing with a spatula. Cut from corner to corner and serve. ★

✪ ✪ ✪ ✪

MAKES 2 SERVINGS

Marinated Grilled Flank Steak with BLT—Smashed Potatoes

2 cloves garlic, minced

1 tablespoon grill seasoning blend, such as Montreal Seasoning by McCormick

1 teaspoon smoked paprika, ground chipotles, chili powder, or ground cumin

2 teaspoons cayenne pepper sauce, such as Frank's Red Hot or Tabasco (eyeball it)

1 tablespoon Worcestershire sauce

2 tablespoons red wine vinegar (2 splashes)

1/3 cup extra-virgin olive oil (evoo), plus a drizzle

1 & 1/2 pounds flank steak

1 & 1/2 pounds small new red-skinned potatoes

1 leek, trimmed of tough tops

4 slices thick-cut smoky bacon, such as applewood-smoked bacon, chopped

1 small can (15 ounces) diced tomatoes, well-drained

1/2 cup sour cream, half-and-half, or chicken broth

Salt and freshly ground black pepper, to taste

Mix garlic, grill seasoning, paprika, hot sauce, Worcestershire sauce, vinegar, and 1/3 cup evoo in a shallow dish. Place meat in dish and coat it evenly in marinade. Let stand 15 minutes.

Meanwhile, cut larger potatoes in half; leave very small potatoes whole. Place potatoes in a small pot and cover with water. Cover pot. Bring water to a boil, remove lid, then cook potatoes until tender, 12 to 15 minutes.

Heat a grill pan or cast-iron pan over high heat.

Cut leek in half lengthwise. Chop into 1/2-inch pieces. Place leeks in a bowl of water and swish, separating the layers, to release the dirt. Drain leeks in a colander or strainer.

Grill flank steak on hot pan; 4 minutes on each side for medium-rare to medium, and 6 or 7 minutes on each side for medium-well.

Heat a small skillet over medium-high heat. Add a drizzle of evoo and the bacon. Cook bacon until it begins to crisp and has rendered most of its fat, 3 to 5 minutes. Add leeks and cook until tender, 2 to 3 minutes. Add tomatoes and heat them through, 1 minute.

Drain potatoes and return them to the hot pot. Smash potatoes with sour

Marinated Grilled Flank Steak

cream, half-and-half, or chicken broth and the BLT (bacon, leeks, and tomatoes). Season with salt and pepper.

Remove flank steak from grill and let it sit a few minutes before slicing. Thinly slice meat on an angle, cutting against the grain. Serve sliced flank steak next to BLT potatoes. ★

✪ ✪ ✪ ✪
MAKES 2 SERVINGS

Lemon-Butter Broccolini

1 pound broccolini
1/2 lemon
1 cup water
2 tablespoons butter
Salt, **to taste**

Trim ends from broccolini so stalks are 4 to 5 inches long. Trim a few pieces of peel off the lemon. Place broccolini in a bowl and add 1 cup water and the lemon peel. Cover the bowl with plastic wrap and microwave on high 6 minutes. Test the broccolini: It should be just tender but still bright green. Cook 2 minutes more if stems are still tough. Drain off water. Squeeze the juice from the lemon half over the broccolini and toss with butter and salt. ★

✪ ✪ ✪ ✪

MAKES 6 SERVINGS

Rigatoni, Rapini, and Ricotta Salata Pasta

Salt and freshly ground black pepper, to taste

1 pound rigatoni

4 cloves garlic, minced

2 tablespoons extra-virgin olive oil (evoo) (twice around the pan)

2 bunches rapini (broccoli rabe) roughly cut into 2-inch pieces (bottom 2 inches discarded)

1 can (14 ounces) fat-free chicken broth

1/4 teaspoon nutmeg (a couple shakes)

1 bunch fresh thyme, leaves stripped from stems and chopped

1/2 pound ricotta salata, crumbled

Start a large pot of salted water to boil. Cook rigatoni according to package directions until al dente and drain.

In a large skillet over medium heat, sauté garlic in evoo until garlic sizzles. Add rapini and cook 3 or 4 minutes. Add broth and nutmeg. Cover pan loosely with foil and cook until rapini is tender, another 10 minutes or so. Add pasta to rapini and broth. Toss with thyme, crumbled ricotta salata, and salt and pepper. Dump out onto a serving platter. Serve with bread and a salad of chunked tomatoes and sliced onions drizzled with extra-virgin olive oil. ★

30-MINUTE MEALS

MENU

THE THREE R'S

1

entree
RIGATONI, RAPINI, AND RICOTTA SALATA PASTA

2

suggested sides
BREAD AND A TOMATO & ONION SALAD

✪ ✪ ✪ ✪

MAKES 4 SERVINGS

Open-Face Hot Turkey Sammies with Sausage Stuffing and Gravy, Smashed Potatoes with Bacon, Warm Apple-Cranberry Sauce

POTATOES

2 pounds new potatoes or baby Yukon gold potatoes

Salt and freshly ground black pepper, to taste

1/2 cup sour cream

2 tablespoons butter

3 strips Ready Crisp bacon, crisped in microwave according to package directions and chopped

Milk or chicken broth, for thinning potatoes (optional)

WARM APPLE-CRANBERRY SAUCE

1 cup store-bought applesauce

1 can (14 ounces) whole berry cranberry sauce

STUFFING

2 slices whole-grain bread

1 tablespoon butter, softened

1 tablespoon extra-virgin olive oil (evoo) (once around the pan)

1 pound maple sausage, bulk or large links removed from casing

1 medium onion, chopped

2 ribs celery, chopped

2 teaspoons poultry seasoning

Salt and freshly ground black pepper, to taste

1 cup chicken broth or turkey broth

GRAVY AND TURKEY

2 tablespoons butter

2 tablespoons all-purpose flour

2 cups chicken or turkey broth

Salt and freshly ground black pepper, to taste

1 & 1/2 to 2 pounds turkey breast meat (rotisserie turkey breast or thick-cut deli turkey), at room temperature

4 slices whole-grain bread

2 tablespoons chopped fresh flat-leaf parsley or chives, for garnish

Preheat a medium skillet over medium-high heat.

Start the potatoes: Cut larger potatoes in half; leave smaller ones whole. Place potatoes in a medium pot. Cover with water and place over high heat

with lid on. When water boils, add salt. Cook potatoes with lid off until tender, 10 or 11 minutes.

Make apple-cranberry sauce: Place a second medium pot over low heat. Add applesauce and canned cranberry sauce. Stir to combine the two and gently heat through, 10 minutes.

Make the stuffing: Toast bread, and butter heavily, 1/2 tablespoon per slice. Chop into small cubes and reserve.

Put a medium skillet over medium-high heat and when hot, add evoo and sausage. Brown and crumble sausage with a wooden spoon or heat-safe spatula. Add onions and celery then season with poultry seasoning, salt, and pepper; cook 5 minutes. Add bread and stir to combine. Dampen the stuffing with chicken broth and turn to combine. Turn off heat and cover pan loosely with aluminum foil.

Back to the potatoes: Drain cooked potatoes and return to hot pot. Smash with sour cream, butter, and bacon. Season with salt and pepper. If they're too thick, thin them out with a splash of milk or broth.

Make the gravy: Preheat a medium skillet over medium heat. Add 2 tablespoons butter and let it melt. Whisk in flour and cook 1 minute. Whisk in 2 cups broth. Add a pinch of salt and a few grinds of pepper. Allow gravy to thicken slightly.

Cut rotisserie meat away from the bones of turkey breast. If you are using deli turkey, remove from packaging and separate slices. Set turkey in gravy and turn to coat.

Assemble the sammies: Place a bread slice on each dinner plate. Top with a slice of turkey. Use a large ice cream scoop to place a mound of stuffing on the turkey. Place another turkey slice on top of stuffing. Serve the smashed potatoes and cranberry sauce on the side. Spoon hot extra gravy over potatoes and turkey sandwiches. Sprinkle the plates with chopped parsley or chives and serve. ★

✪ ✪ ✪ ✪
MAKES 6 TO 8 SERVINGS

Oil-and-Vinegar Slaw

2 tablespoons red wine vinegar

2 tablespoons water

1 tablespoon sugar

2 tablespoons peanut or vegetable oil (eyeball it)

1 sack (16 ounces) shredded cabbage mix for slaw salads (available on the produce aisle)

Salt and freshly ground black pepper, to taste

In a large bowl, mix vinegar, water, and sugar. Whisk in oil. Add cabbage to dressing and season with salt and pepper. Toss with fingers to combine. Adjust seasoning. Let stand 20 minutes. Retoss and serve. ★

✪ ✪ ✪ ✪
MAKES 4 SERVINGS

Devilish Chili-Cheese Dogs

1 tablespoon extra-virgin olive oil (evoo) (once around the pan)

1 pound ground sirloin

Salt and freshly ground black pepper, to taste

2 teaspoons Worcestershire sauce (eyeball it)

1 small onion, chopped

2 cloves garlic, chopped

1 tablespoon chili powder (1/2 palmful)

1 can (8 ounces) tomato sauce

8 fat or foot-long beef franks

1 tablespoon butter

1 tablespoon cayenne pepper sauce, such as Frank's Red Hot or Tabasco

8 hot dog buns, toasted

2 cups (1 sack, 10 ounces) shredded cheddar cheese (preshredded is available on dairy aisle)

Heat a medium skillet over medium-high heat. Add evoo and meat and season with salt and pepper. Brown and crumble beef. Add Worcestershire, onion, garlic, and chili powder; cook together 5 minutes. Add tomato sauce and reduce heat to low.

Boil franks in a shallow skillet of water to warm through, 5 minutes. Drain and return pan to medium heat. Score casings on dogs. Melt butter in skillet and add hot sauce. Add dogs to skillet, browning and crisping the casings in hot sauce and butter.

Devilish Chili-Cheese Dogs

Preheat the broiler.

Place devilish dogs in buns and top with chili and lots of cheese. Place devilish dogs under broiler and melt cheese. Serve immediately.

✪ ✪ ✪ ✪
MAKES 4 SERVINGS

Summer-ish Succotash Salad

2 cups frozen corn kernels, thawed
1 can (15 ounces) butter beans, drained
1 small red bell pepper, chopped
1/2 small red onion, chopped
1 tablespoon red wine vinegar
2 tablespoons chopped fresh flat-leaf parsley (a palmful)
2 tablespoons peanut oil or vegetable oil
Salt and freshly ground black pepper, to taste

Combine corn, beans, bell pepper, and onions and toss with vinegar, parsley, oil, salt, and pepper. ★

✪ ✪ ✪ ✪

MAKES 2 SERVINGS

Pizza Salad

All-purpose flour, for dusting

1 store-bought pizza dough

1/2 cup pizza sauce

2 cups shredded mozzarella or Italian 4-cheese blend (preshredded is available in sacks on dairy aisle)

2 cloves garlic, chopped

1 teaspoon crushed red pepper flakes

1/3 pound sliced prosciutto di Parma

3 cups arugula leaves

The juice of 1/2 lemon

Extra-virgin olive oil (evoo), for drizzling

Salt and freshly ground black pepper, to taste

Preheat oven to 425°F.

Sprinkle a little flour on a clean work surface. Roll or press out dough to form a 12-inch pie and place dough on a pizza pan or cookie sheet. Spread pizza sauce on dough and top with lots of cheese. Scatter garlic and red pepper flakes over the cheese. Bake pizza until cheese is bubbly and crust is crisp, about 12 minutes. Top the hot pizza with sliced prosciutto, working all the way to the crust's edge and covering the whole pie. Toss arugula with lemon juice and a little evoo. Season arugula with salt and pepper. Pile arugula up on the center of the pizza. Cut into quarters and serve with a chunked vegetable salad on the side. ★

30-MINUTE MEALS

MENU

YOUR NEW FAVORITE MEAL

1

entree
PIZZA SALAD

2

suggested side
CHUNKED VEGETABLE SALAD

✪ ✪ ✪ ✪

MAKES 4 SERVINGS

Italian Mini Meat Loaves with Mac 'n Three Cheeses

MEAT LOAVES

1 & 1/3 pounds ground sirloin

1 large egg, beaten

2/3 cup Italian bread crumbs (a couple of handfuls)

1/4 cup grated Parmigiano Reggiano cheese (a handful)

1/2 small green bell pepper, chopped

1/2 small onion, finely chopped

4 cloves garlic, chopped

3 tablespoons tomato paste

Salt and freshly ground black pepper, to taste

2 tablespoons extra-virgin olive oil (evoo)

MAC 'N CHEESE

Salt, to taste

1 pound cavatappi (hollow, corkscrew-shaped pasta) or small shell pasta

2 tablespoons butter

2 tablespoons all-purpose flour

2 cups milk

2 cups shredded sharp cheddar cheese

1/2 cup shredded Asiago cheese

1/2 cup grated Parmigiano Reggiano cheese

1 teaspoon freshly ground black pepper

1/2 cup Italian bread crumbs

2 tablespoons extra-virgin olive oil (evoo)

2 tablespoons chopped fresh thyme leaves

3 to 4 sprigs fresh rosemary, leaves stripped and chopped

1/4 cup chopped fresh flat-leaf parsley

Put a large pot of water on to boil for the pasta.

Preheat oven to 425°F.

Place meat in a bowl. Make a well in meat. Fill well with egg, bread crumbs, Parmigiano Reggiano cheese, bell pepper, onion, garlic, tomato paste, salt, and pepper. Mix meat and breading and form 4 individual oval meat loaves, about 1 inch thick. Coat loaves with 2 tablespoons evoo and arrange on a baking sheet. Roast until done, 18 to 20 minutes. Remove meat and switch oven heat to broiler.

When the pasta water boils, add salt then pasta. Cook until slightly undercooked—pasta will continue to cook when combined with cheese sauce. Drain.

For the mac 'n cheese, melt butter in a saucepan and stir in flour. Whisk in milk. Bring to a bubble. Cook to thicken milk, 2 to 3 minutes. Add cheddar, Asiago, Parmigiano Reggiano, and black pepper. Stir to melt cheeses. Add pasta and combine with cheese sauce; transfer to a baking dish or casserole. Place bread crumbs in a bowl, add evoo, thyme, rosemary, and parsley. Stir to combine and top the pasta and cheese. Place under broiler to brown bread crumbs. Serve mac and cheese alongside meat loaves. ★

✪ ✪ ✪ ✪
MAKES 4 SERVINGS

Seared Greens with Red Onion and Vinegar

2 tablespoons vegetable oil or other light oil

1/2 red onion, sliced

1 teaspoon mustard seed

1 & 1/2 to 2 pounds red or yellow Swiss chard, stems removed and tops coarsely chopped

1/4 cup red wine vinegar

Salt and freshly ground black pepper, to taste

Heat a large skillet over high heat. Add oil then onion and mustard seeds. Sear onion and mustard seeds, 2 minutes. Add greens and toss with tongs in oil. Sear greens 2 to 3 minutes. Add vinegar and toss with greens. Remove pan from heat and season greens with salt and pepper. ★

✪ ✪ ✪ ✪

MAKES 4 SERVINGS

Beef and Watercress Dumpling "Stoup"

2 pounds beef sirloin (1 inch thick), trimmed

2 tablespoons vegetable oil

4 slices hickory- or applewood-smoked bacon, chopped

2 medium onions, chopped

4 ribs celery, chopped

2 fresh or dried bay leaves

4 sprigs fresh thyme, leaves stripped and chopped, or 1 teaspoon dried thyme

2 tablespoons all-purpose flour

1 cup dry red wine (eyeball it)

1 rounded tablespoon spicy brown mustard or grainy Dijon mustard

1 quart beef broth or stock

1 box biscuit mix (5 to 6 ounces), such as Jiffy brand

1 cup chopped watercress

1/4 to 1/2 teaspoon Liquid Smoke (optional)

Salt and freshly ground black pepper, to taste

Heat a large, wide heavy-bottom pot or pan over high heat. Cut sirloin into large cubes. Add oil to the pan, then add meat. Sear meat until caramelized, 2 minutes on each side. Remove to a shallow dish and tent with aluminum foil. Reduce heat to medium-high. Add bacon to the pan and cook until brown at edges, rendering fat. Add onions, celery, bay leaves, and thyme. Stir and cook 5 minutes. Sprinkle in flour, stir, and cook 1 minute. Whisk in wine and mustard and scrape up pan drippings. Add broth. Cover and bring liquid to a boil, 1 to 2 minutes.

Mix biscuit mix according to package directions, adding watercress at the beginning. Add meat back to the pan and settle it in so that it is covered with sauce. Add Liquid Smoke (if using), and season with salt and pepper. Drop large spoonfuls of watercress dumpling mix onto the surface of the stew and cover the pan. Cook until dumplings are plump and cooked through, about 8 minutes. Serve hot. ★

✪ ✪ ✪ ✪
MAKES 4 SERVINGS

Hot Spiked Cider

2 quarts apple cider

2 cloves

2 cinnamon sticks

8 shots apple brandy

In a large pot over medium-high heat, heat cider with cloves and cinnamon. Pour 2 shots of apple brandy into each of 4 mugs and fill with cider. ★

✪ ✪ ✪ ✪
MAKES 4 SERVINGS

Maple-Walnut Ice Cream Cups

1 cup pure maple syrup

1 cup granola

2 pints maple-walnut ice cream

1 canister real whipped cream (available on dairy aisle)

Cinnamon, **for sprinkling**

1/2 cup chopped walnuts

Place syrup in a small pitcher or cup and microwave on high to warm, 15 seconds.

Place 1/4 cup granola in each of 4 small dessert cups or bowls. Drizzle with syrup. Add 2 scoops ice cream each. Top with whipped cream, another drizzle of syrup, a sprinkle of cinnamon, and chopped nuts. Serve. ★

30-MINUTE MEALS
MENU

I CAN'T
BELIEVE I
MADE THIS

1
appetizer
SPINACH-
ARTICHOKE
CASSEROLE

2
entree
SHRIMP
NEWBURG

3
side dish
RICE WITH
SWEET RED
PEPPERS

✪ ✪ ✪ ✪

MAKES 6 SERVINGS

Spinach-Artichoke Casserole

1 small round loaf (1 pound) crusty bread
2 boxes (10 ounces each) frozen chopped spinach
2 tablespoons extra-virgin olive oil (evoo) (eyeball it)
2 cloves garlic, cracked away from skin with the flat of a knife
1 can (15 ounces) quartered artichoke hearts, drained
1 teaspoon coarse salt
2 extra-large eggs, beaten
1/2 cup heavy cream
2 cups shredded Swiss or Gruyère cheese
1/2 cup grated Manchego or Parmigiano Reggiano cheese
Freshly ground black pepper, to taste

Preheat oven to 425°F.

Trim two sides of the loaf and thickly slice the bread. Place slices and ends on a baking sheet in the oven to toast.

Defrost spinach in the microwave, then squeeze dry in a clean kitchen towel.

Pour evoo into a 13-inch oval casserole dish or a 9x13-inch rectangular dish, liberally coating the sides and bottom with the oil. Rub toasted bread with cracked garlic and cut into large chunks. Reserve toasted bread ends for Shrimp Newburg (recipe follows), or for salad croutons on another night. Arrange the toasted, garlic-rubbed pieces of bread in a single layer in dish. Do not pack tightly. Add the quartered artichoke hearts to the dish, nesting them in and around the bread. Sprinkle the spinach around the casserole and season with salt. Beat eggs with cream and pour evenly over the dish. Top casserole with cheeses and pepper and bake until golden on top, 17 minutes. ★

✪ ✪ ✪ ✪

MAKES 6 SERVINGS

Rice with Sweet Red Peppers

3 cups chicken broth
2 tablespoons butter
1 & 1/2 cups white rice
1/2 small red bell pepper, finely chopped
3 tablespoons chopped fresh parsley, flat-leaf or curly

These way-cool
retro dishes still
work!

Bring broth to a boil with butter in a medium pot with a tight-fitting lid. Add rice and reduce heat to simmer. Cover and cook 15 minutes. Add red pepper bits, cover, and cook 2 to 3 minutes longer. Fluff rice with fork and combine rice mixture with parsley. ★

✪ ✪ ✪ ✪
MAKES 6 SERVINGS

Shrimp Newburg

The juice of 1 lemon

2 bay leaves

2 & 1/2 pounds large raw shrimp, peeled, deveined, and tails removed

1 tablespoon extra-virgin olive oil (evoo) (once around the pan)

4 tablespoons (1/2 stick) butter

1 large shallot, finely chopped

2 tablespoons all-purpose flour

1/2 cup chicken broth

1 cup heavy cream

3 tablespoons dry sherry

1/4 teaspoon ground nutmeg

Salt and freshly ground black pepper, to taste

Toasted bread crusts or day-old baguette

1 teaspoon sweet paprika

2 tablespoons chopped fresh flat-leaf parsley

1/2 cup grated Parmigiano Reggiano, parmesan, or Manchego cheese (optional)

Preheat broiler to high or oven to 425°F.

Bring 3 to 4 inches of water to a boil in a large pot. Add lemon juice, bay leaves, and shrimp. Reduce heat to simmer, cover, and cook shrimp 5 minutes.

To a large skillet over medium heat add evoo, 2 tablespoons butter, and shallots. Sauté shallots 2 minutes, then add flour and cook 1 minute. Whisk in broth and thicken 1 minute. Add cream and bring to a bubble. Stir in sherry then season sauce with nutmeg, salt, and pepper. Allow sauce to reduce until thick enough to coat a spoon, 2 to 3 minutes more. Drain shrimp and place in a shallow serving dish. Season cooked shrimp with salt.

Melt remaining 2 tablespoons butter in microwave, 15 seconds. Grate toasted or stale bread with a large box grater. Toss bread with melted butter, paprika, and parsley. Cheese may be added for a more deeply brown, saltier topping. Set aside.

Pour hot sherry sauce over shrimp. Add bread topping and toast under broiler until golden, 2 minutes, or bake in hot oven, 5 minutes. ★

30-MINUTE MEALS

MENU

**TURBO
CLASSICS
MEAL**

1

entree
GARLIC ROAST
CHICKEN WITH
ROSEMARY AND
LEMON

2

side dishes
PESTO-SMASHED
POTATOES

MIXED GREENS
SALAD WITH
GORGONZOLA
DRESSING

✪ ✪ ✪ ✪

MAKES 2 SERVINGS

Garlic Roast Chicken with Rosemary and Lemon

1 & 1/2 to 2 pounds boneless, skinless chicken breasts, cut into large chunks

4 cloves garlic, crushed

4 sprigs fresh rosemary, leaves stripped and chopped

3 tablespoons extra-virgin olive oil (evoo) (eyeball it)

The grated zest and juice of 1 lemon

1 tablespoon grill seasoning blend, such as Montreal Seasoning by McCormick or salt and freshly ground black pepper

1/2 cup dry white wine or chicken broth

Preheat oven to 450°F.

Arrange chicken in a baking dish. Add garlic, rosemary, evoo, lemon zest, and grill seasoning. Toss chicken to coat, then place in oven. Roast 20 minutes. Add wine and lemon juice to the dish and combine with pan juices, then spoon over chicken. Return to oven and turn oven off. Let stand 5 minutes longer, then remove chicken from the oven. Place baking dish on trivet and serve, spooning pan juices over the chicken pieces. ★

✪ ✪ ✪ ✪

MAKES 2 SERVINGS

Pesto-Smashed Potatoes

1 & 1/2 pounds small red-skinned potatoes

Salt, to taste

1/2 cup chicken broth

1/2 cup store-bought pesto

Cut larger potatoes in half and leave small potatoes whole. Place potatoes in a pot and cover with water; bring water to a boil. Add salt and cook until potatoes are tender, 10 to 12 minutes. Drain potatoes and return them to hot pot. Add chicken broth and smash the potatoes up. Add pesto and smash to desired consistency. Serve hot. ★

✪ ✪ ✪ ✪
MAKES 2 SERVINGS

Mixed Greens Salad with Gorgonzola Dressing

1 heart romaine lettuce, chopped

1 bulb endive, chopped

1/4 cup walnut pieces (a handful)

2 tablespoons red wine vinegar

1/4 cup extra-virgin olive oil (evoo) (eyeball it)

3 ounces (1/4 cup) gorgonzola cheese, crumbled

Salt and freshly ground black pepper, to taste

Combine lettuce, endive, and walnuts in a large salad bowl. Pour vinegar into a small bowl and whisk in evoo. Stir in gorgonzola. Toss salad with dressing and season with salt and pepper. ★

30-MINUTE MEALS
MENU

GO FISH!

1

entree
SWORDFISH
KEBABS

▪▪ ▪▪ ▪▪ ▪▪

2

side dish
TOMATO,
ONION, AND
ARUGULA SALAD

▪▪ ▪▪ ▪▪ ▪▪

✪ ✪ ✪ ✪

MAKES 2 SERVINGS

Swordfish Kebabs with Tomato, Onion, and Arugula Salad

1 & 1/2 pounds swordfish steak

The grated zest of 1 lemon

A handful fresh flat-leaf parsley leaves

1 large clove garlic

1 teaspoon salt

Extra-virgin olive oil (evoo), for drizzling

3 small vine-ripe tomatoes, seeded and chopped

1/2 cup chopped white onion

2 cups arugula, chopped

Freshly ground black pepper, to taste

Lemon wedges, for serving

Preheat the broiler.

Cube swordfish into 1-inch pieces and thread onto 2 metal skewers. Pile lemon zest with parsley and garlic and chop together. Add salt and rub it into the mixture with the flat of the knife, forming a paste. Drizzle fish with evoo and rub the paste evenly over kebabs. Place kebabs on broiler pan and broil on top rack until fish is firm and opaque, about 3 minutes on each side.

Make the salad: Mix tomatoes, onions, and arugula together. Drizzle with evoo and season with salt and pepper. Divide the salad between 2 plates. Top with a skewer of fish and serve with wedges of lemon. ★

Swordfish Kebabs

30-MINUTE MEALS
MENU

TV DINNER

1

entree
CHICKEN
CACCIATORE
SUBS

2

side dish
AL FREDO'S
POPCORN

✪ ✪ ✪ ✪
MAKES 4 SERVINGS

Chicken Cacciatore Subs

2 tablespoons extra-virgin olive oil (evoo) (twice around the pan), plus more for drizzling

4 boneless, skinless chicken breasts (6 to 8 ounces each)

Grill seasoning blend, such as Montreal Seasoning by McCormick or salt and freshly ground black pepper, to taste

4 sub rolls, split

2 cloves garlic, cracked away from skins with the flat of a knife

1 teaspoon crushed red pepper flakes

2 large portobello mushroom caps, sliced

1 green bell pepper, seeded and sliced

1 large onion, sliced

1 teaspoon dried oregano (1/3 palmful)

Salt and freshly ground black pepper, to taste

1/2 cup dry red wine or chicken or beef broth

1 can (14 ounces) crushed tomatoes

2 to 3 tablespoons chopped fresh flat-leaf parsley (a handful)

1/3 pound deli-sliced provolone cheese

Heat a grill pan or large skillet over medium to medium-high heat. Drizzle evoo on chicken, making sure it's coated, and season with grill seasoning blend or salt and pepper. Grill or pan-fry 6 minutes on each side. Set aside.

Preheat the broiler. Place rolls on a cookie sheet and lightly toast them; remove, but leave the broiler on.

Heat a large skillet over medium-high heat. Add 2 tablespoons evoo, the garlic, red pepper flakes, mushrooms, bell peppers, onions, and oregano. Sauté veggies and season with salt and pepper. Cook 5 minutes, then add wine or broth. Scrape up tasty browned bits off the bottom of the pan with a wooden spoon or heat-safe spatula. Add tomatoes and parsley. Slice chicken breasts on an angle and set into sauce. Pile chicken and veggies into sub rolls and cover with sliced provolone. Place sandwiches on cookie sheet and melt cheese under hot broiler. Serve. ★

Park yourself on the couch and enjoy this dinner late night!

✪ ✪ ✪ ✪

MAKES 4 SERVINGS

Al Fredo's Popcorn

3 tablespoons vegetable oil

1 cup popping corn

4 tablespoons (1/2 stick) butter

1 clove garlic, cracked away from skin with the flat of a knife

1 cup grated parmesan cheese

Salt and freshly ground black pepper, to taste

Place oil in a heavy pot with a lid and heat over medium-high heat. Add corn and pop, shaking the pan until popping slows to 2 or 3 seconds between pops, then remove from heat. Place butter and garlic in a microwave-safe dish and melt in the microwave, 15 seconds on high. Discard garlic clove. Pour butter over corn and sprinkle cheese over corn. Turn to coat. Season the popcorn with salt and pepper. ★

30-MINUTE MEALS

MENU

DESTINATION:
COUCH

1

appetizer
SUN-DRIED
TOMATO DIP WITH
CHIPS AND
VEGGIES

2

entree
SUPER-STUFFED
FRENCH BREAD
PIZZA RUSTICA

✪ ✪ ✪ ✪

MAKES 4 SERVINGS

Super-Stuffed French Bread Pizza Rustica

1 package (10 ounces) frozen chopped spinach

1 loaf (2 feet long) French bread

1 tablespoon extra-virgin olive oil (evoo) (once around the pan)

1 pound bulk sweet Italian sausage

1 small red bell pepper, seeded and chopped

1 small onion, chopped

2 large cloves garlic, chopped

Salt and freshly ground black pepper, to taste

1 & 1/2 cups part-skim ricotta cheese

1/2 cup grated parmesan cheese

1/2 pound sweet sopressata, sliced thick from the deli, chopped

1/2 stick pepperoni, chopped

1 sack (10 ounces) preshredded mozzarella cheese

1 sack (10 ounces) preshredded provolone cheese

1 teaspoon dried oregano

1 teaspoon crushed red pepper flakes

Preheat oven to 425°F.

Defrost spinach in the microwave, 6 minutes on high. Wring spinach dry in a clean kitchen towel.

Split bread lengthwise and hollow it out. Cut in half across, making 4 shells for pizzas.

Heat a medium skillet over medium-high heat, add evoo, then sausage. Brown and crumble sausage using a wooden spoon. Add bell pepper, onions, and garlic. Cook 3 to 5 minutes, then add spinach. Remove mixture from heat and season with salt and pepper. Transfer to a bowl.

Combine sausage mixture with ricotta, parmesan, sopressata, and pepperoni. Fill pizzas with the mixture and top with mounded mozzarella and provolone cheeses. Place on a cookie sheet and bake until cheese melts and bubbles and bread is super crisp, 10 to 12 minutes. Top pizzas with oregano and hot pepper flakes. Serve immediately, but snack all night! ★

✪ ✪ ✪ ✪
MAKES 4 SERVINGS

Sun-Dried Tomato Dip with Chips and Veggies

3/4 pound feta cheese, crumbled

1/2 cup drained sun-dried tomatoes in oil, coarsely chopped

1 clove garlic or 1/2 teaspoon granulated garlic

1 teaspoon dried thyme

1/2 teaspoon dried oregano

1 cup milk

1 teaspoon freshly ground black pepper

1 sack Mediterranean-flavored gourmet potato chips, such as Terra brand Onion and Garlic Yukon Gold Chips

1 pound baby-cut carrots

1 green bell pepper, cut into strips

4 ribs celery, cut into sticks

Combine cheese, sun-dried tomatoes, garlic, thyme, oregano, milk, and black pepper in a food processor and process until smooth. Transfer to a small bowl. Serve with chips and veggies. ★

Minestrone is literally a BIG soup. This one tastes as if it simmered all day. For a strictly vegetarian minestrone, omit the pancetta or prosciutto, and use a vegetable broth or stock instead of the chicken.

✪ ✪ ✪ ✪
MAKES 4 SERVINGS

Green Minestrone

2 tablespoons extra-virgin olive oil (evoo) (twice around the pan)

4 slices pancetta or 1/4 pound thick-cut prosciutto, chopped

1 medium onion, chopped

2 ribs celery, chopped

2 large cloves garlic, crushed

1 bay leaf, fresh or dried

1 medium zucchini, diced

Salt and freshly ground black pepper, to taste

1 can (15 ounces) white cannellini beans

1 can (15 ounces) garbanzo beans

8 cups chicken broth (two 1-quart paper containers)

1 cup ditalini pasta or mini penne pasta

1/2 pound green beans, trimmed and cut into 1-inch pieces

1 sack (10 ounces) triple-washed spinach, stems removed, leaves coarsely chopped

1/2 cup grated Parmigiano Reggiano or Romano cheese, plus extra to pass at the table

12 to 16 leaves fresh basil, torn or shredded OR 1/4 cup chopped fresh flat-leaf parsley

Heat a soup pot over medium-high heat. Add evoo and pancetta or prosciutto. Sauté 2 minutes, then add onions, celery, garlic, bay leaf, and zucchini to the pot, and season with salt and pepper. Sauté 5 minutes, stirring frequently. Add white beans, garbanzo beans, and chicken broth to the pot; cover, and bring to a boil. Add pasta and green beans and cook 8 minutes, or until pasta is just tender. Stir in spinach to wilt, 1 minute. Stir in grated cheese and ladle soup into bowls. Top with basil or chopped parsley. ★

Green Minestrone

Panzanella is a great use for leftover, good quality, chewy bread. The combination of vegetables can be as simple as tomato and basil or as varied as everything your garden grows.

✪ ✪ ✪ ✪
MAKES 4 SERVINGS

Tomato Basil Panzanella

1/2 pound day-old chewy farm-style bread, cubed
Bottled spring water, to cover bread
4 vine-ripe tomatoes, seeded and chopped
1/2 medium red onion, chopped
1 cup loosely packed basil leaves, torn or shredded
2 tablespoons red wine vinegar
1/4 cup extra-virgin olive oil (evoo)
Salt and freshly ground black pepper, to taste

Place bread in a medium mixing bowl, cover with water, and allow it to soak, 3 to 5 minutes. In small handfuls, remove bread from the water and wring it out without mashing or tearing bread. You do not want wet bread, so wring it carefully.

Combine tomatoes with onions and basil in a second bowl and dress with vinegar, evoo, salt, and pepper. Add bread to tomato salad and combine. Adjust seasonings and serve. ★

✪ ✪ ✪ ✪
MAKES 6 SLICES

Lemon Coconut Angel Food Cake

1 store-bought prepared angel food cake
1 jar (9 to 11 ounces) lemon curd (found on the jam and jelly aisle)
The grated zest of 1 lemon
1 cup sweetened shredded coconut

Place the cake on a serving plate. Warm lemon curd over low heat and stir in the lemon zest. Pour the warm sauce down over the cake in a slow stream to glaze it. Sprinkle shredded coconut liberally over the lemon-glazed cake and serve. ★

✪ ✪ ✪ ✪

MAKES 2 SERVINGS (WITH LEFTOVERS OR BIG SECONDS)

Chili Verde

2 tablespoons vegetable, sunflower, or corn oil

1 & 1/3 pounds ground turkey breast or chicken breast

2 & 1/2 tablespoons ground cumin (a generous palmful)

2 tablespoons cayenne pepper sauce, such as Frank's Red Hot or Tabasco

1 & 1/2 tablespoons grill seasoning blend, such as Montreal Seasoning by McCormick

1 jalapeño, seeded and chopped

3 cloves garlic, chopped

1 small white onion, chopped

1 small zucchini

1 small yellow or green bell pepper, seeded

12 tomatillos, husks removed

2 to 3 tablespoons chopped cilantro leaves (a generous palmful)

1 & 1/2 tablespoons fresh thyme leaves or 1 teaspoon dried thyme

1 can (15 ounces) pinto beans, drained well

Shredded cheddar, Monterey Jack, pepper Jack, or smoked cheddar cheese, for topping chili (optional)

2 scallions, chopped

Corn chips, polenta chips, or soy chips, for dipping and scooping (optional)

Heat a deep skillet over medium-high heat. Add oil and turkey. Season turkey with cumin, hot sauce, and grill seasoning. Start to brown and crumble the turkey and add jalapeño, garlic, and onion to the pan. Chop and add zucchini and bell peppers as you work—chop and drop into the pan. Let the vegetables and turkey cook while you chop tomatillos. Stir in tomatillos; add cilantro, thyme, and beans, then cover the pot. Reduce heat to medium. Cook 5 minutes, covered; remove the lid and cook another 3 to 5 minutes. Adjust seasonings.

Ladle chili verde into bowls. Top with cheese, if using, and chopped scallions. Serve with tortilla chips for dipping, if desired. ★

30-MINUTE MEALS

MENU

ONE-HOT-POT

1
entree
CHILI VERDE

2
suggested side
TORTILLA CHIPS

RACHAEL RAY
CLASSIC
30-MINUTE MEALS

PARTIES

30-MINUTE MEALS

MENU

AT HOME
SUNDAY

1

entree
ALDO'S COLD
HERB-ROASTED
CHICKEN

2

side dish
BLANCHED
GREEN BEANS
WITH PARSLEY

Heads up: Try this recipe on a night when you have more than 30 minutes to spare.

✪ ✪ ✪ ✪

MAKES 4 TO 6 SERVINGS

Aldo's Cold Herb-Roasted Chicken and Blanched Green Beans with Parsley

2 small young chickens, cut up by butcher—breasts, thighs, legs, 12 pieces total (use backs and wings for soup or stock)

Extra-virgin olive oil (evoo)

1 teaspoon coarse salt

1/4 teaspoon black pepper

1 teaspoon dried herbes de Provence seasoning blend (parsley, sage, rosemary, thyme)

1 & 1/2 pounds green beans, trimmed

A pinch coarse salt

A few sprigs fresh flat-leaf parsley, chopped

Preheat oven to 400°F.

Wash and pat chickens dry. Coat chickens lightly with evoo. Combine salt, pepper, and herbs in a small dish. Rub seasoning into the skin of chicken pieces. Arrange chicken on a rack in roasting pan in a single layer. Place in the center of oven and reduce heat to 375°F. Roast chicken 30 to 40 minutes, depending on size of pieces, basting every 15 minutes with pan juices. Place aluminum foil tent over top of pan once skin begins to brown to keep it from becoming too dark. Remove chicken from oven when meat thermometer reads 165°F, or when juices run clear when skin is pricked at deepest part of thigh.

Bring chicken to room temperature before lifting to a plate or storage container.

To prepare beans, add just enough water to cover the bottom of a skillet. Set beans in pan and bring to a boil. Reduce heat to lowest setting, cover, and cook 3 minutes. Drain beans in colander and run under cool water. Pat beans dry and transfer to a shallow bowl. Drizzle beans with a little evoo and sprinkle with just a touch of coarse salt and a little parsley. Beans can be stored in fridge in airtight container; bring back to room temperature before serving.

To serve, arrange chicken down the center of a long oval platter and surround with blanched beans. ★

30-MINUTE MEALS
MENU

ITALY
MEETS
GREECE

1

entree
SICILIAN
SAUSAGE AND
FENNEL PASTA

2

side dish
GREEK DINER
SALAD

MAKES 4 TO 6 SERVINGS

Sicilian Sausage and Fennel Pasta

Salt and freshly ground black pepper, to taste

1 pound penne

3/4 pound bulk sweet sausage

1 bulb fresh fennel, tops and outer layer trimmed away

1/2 medium white onion

3 cloves garlic

A pinch allspice

1 cup chicken broth

1/3 cup Pernod or anisette liqueur

3 tablespoons heavy cream or half-and-half (three times around the pan)

Grated Parmigiano Reggiano cheese, for the table

Put a large pot of water over high heat. When water boils, add salt and pasta and cook according to package directions until al dente. Drain.

Meanwhile, break up sausage in a deep skillet and brown over medium heat. Cut fennel and onion into chunks and process with garlic in a food processor or mince by hand.

Add fennel, onion, and garlic to skillet. Sprinkle with allspice and pepper. Give the pan a good shake. Add broth. Cover and reduce heat to low. Simmer 10 minutes, until fennel bits are tender.

Uncover and bring heat up to medium again. Let the broth reduce by half, about 5 minutes. Douse with Pernod. Bring mixture back to a boil. Add cream to sauce and give the pan a shake. Toss immediately with the pasta. Serve with plenty of grated cheese and extra black pepper. ★

✪ ✪ ✪ ✪

MAKES 4 TO 6 SERVINGS

Greek Diner Salad

2 cloves garlic, minced

1/3 cup extra-virgin olive oil (evoo)

The juice of 1 large lemon

A pinch allspice

Kosher salt and freshly ground black pepper, to taste

2 hearts romaine lettuce, chopped

2 plum tomatoes, diced

1/2 medium red onion, very thinly sliced

1/2 seedless cucumber, thinly sliced

A handful pepperoncini hot peppers, chopped

1/4 pound feta or flavored feta cheese, crumbled

A handful pitted oil-cured or Kalamata black olives

2 tablespoons chopped fresh oregano (a palmful)

In an ovensafe bowl, cover the garlic with evoo. Heat in warm oven or in microwave on high for 30 seconds until garlic sizzles. You are infusing the garlic flavor into the oil by adding heat. Whisk in lemon juice, allspice, salt, and pepper. Set aside.

Combine lettuce, tomatoes, red onion, cucumber, hot peppers, feta cheese, olives, and oregano in a bowl. Toss with dressing. ★

MMMMM PASTA!

1

entrees
BUCATINI ALL
'AMATRICIANA

2

suggested side
GREEN SALAD
AND CRUSTY
BREAD

Pancetta is Italian rolled, cured pork, similar to bacon, but not smoked. Look for it at your deli counter. Bacon may be substituted; it will result in a smoky-tasting tomato sauce.

✪ ✪ ✪ ✪
MAKES 6 SERVINGS

Bucatini all'Amatriciana

2 tablespoons extra-virgin olive oil (evoo)

1/4 pound (4 or 5 slices) pancetta, chopped

1 medium onion, chopped

4 to 6 cloves garlic, chopped

1 teaspoon crushed red pepper flakes

1 can (28 ounces) crushed tomatoes

2 tablespoons chopped fresh flat-leaf parsley (a handful)

Salt and freshly ground black pepper, to taste

1 pound bucatini (hollow spaghetti)

Grated Parmigiano Reggiano, grana padano, or Romano cheese, to pass at table

Bring a large pot of water to a boil.

Meanwhile, heat a large, deep skillet over medium-high heat. Add evoo and pancetta. Cook pancetta 2 or 3 minutes, then add onions, garlic, and red pepper flakes. Cook until onions are translucent, 7 or 8 minutes. Add tomatoes and parsley. Season with salt and pepper. Simmer over low heat until ready to serve.

Add salt and pasta to boiling water. Cook pasta to al dente (with a bite to it), about 10 minutes. Drain pasta well (do not rinse; starchy pasta holds more sauce) and toss with sauce. Pass grated cheese at the table and serve with green salad on the side. ★

Bucatini all'Amatriciana

30-MINUTE MEALS
MENU

FOOD FOR SPORTS FANS

1

entree
SUPER SUB BALLS

- - - -

2

side dish
PIGSKIN POTATOES

- - - - -

✪ ✪ ✪ ✪
MAKES 4 SERVINGS

Pigskin Potatoes

4 white-skinned or scrubbed Idaho potatoes

Extra-virgin olive oil (evoo)

Montreal Steak Seasoning or salt, freshly ground black pepper, paprika, and garlic powder

Preheat oven to 425°F.

Cut potatoes lengthwise into thin wedges. Toss potato wedges into a big bowl and coat with a little evoo. Sprinkle with seasonings. Pour wedges out onto a cookie sheet.

Roast until brown and crisp, about 20 minutes. ★

✪ ✪ ✪ ✪
MAKES 4 SERVINGS

Super Sub Balls

1 & 1/2 pounds lean ground beef

1 egg

1/2 teaspoon crushed red pepper flakes (a shake or two)

3 cloves garlic, minced

1/4 medium Spanish onion, minced

A handful chopped fresh flat-leaf parsley

1 cup Italian bread crumbs (a couple of good handfuls)

4 shakes Worcestershire sauce

2/3 pound provolone cheese, cut into 16 small cubes

Olive oil, for baking sheet

QUICK MARINARA
2 tablespoons extra-virgin olive oil (evoo)

3 cloves garlic, minced

2 pinches crushed red pepper flakes

2 cans (28 ounces each) crushed tomatoes

15 to 20 leaves fresh basil, roughly cut or torn

2 sprigs fresh oregano, leaves stripped from stem and chopped

A handful chopped fresh flat-leaf parsley

4 sesame-seed sub rolls

Preheat oven to 425°F.

Combine meat, egg, red pepper flakes, garlic, onions, parsley, bread crumbs, and Worcestershire in a bowl. Pull a palmful of meat mixture into your hand. Nest a piece of provolone in the middle of the meat and form a ball. Place on a nonstick cookie sheet brushed with a little olive oil. Repeat until mixture is gone, about 16 balls later. Place cookie sheet in oven and bake until cooked through, 12 to 15 minutes.

For marinara sauce, warm evoo in a deep frying pan or pot over medium heat; add garlic and red pepper flakes and cook until garlic sizzles. Add tomatoes and herbs. Bring to a boil, reduce heat, and simmer over low heat until ready to serve.

Drop the stuffed sub balls into sauce. Scoop up sauced sub balls and place in rolls. Serve with Pigskin Potatoes and a simple salad. ★

Timing Tip: Throw the potatoes in the oven first, then put the meatballs in the oven and cook together for the last 12 to 15 minutes. You will be wowed by this fresh take on the traditional sub, which is usually made with fried meatballs and covered with melted, salty, sorta-mozzarella cheese product. My version is not only better tasting, it's better for you.

✪ ✪ ✪ ✪
MAKES 12 SERVINGS

Sweet Sausage-Stuffed Portobellos

PORTOBELLOS

1/4 cup extra-virgin olive oil (evoo)

4 cloves garlic, popped from skin

6 portobello mushroom caps, stems removed (save 2 or 3 stems to chop for stuffing)

1/2 cup sherry, port, or Marsala wine

STUFFING

1 pound bulk sweet Italian sausage, or 4 links, casings removed

1 package defrosted chopped frozen spinach, squeezed dry

4 tablespoons (1/2 stick) butter, salted or unsalted

2 tablespoons extra-virgin olive oil (evoo) (twice around the pan)

1/2 red bell pepper, seeded and finely diced

1/2 to 2/3 cup finely chopped mushroom stems (2 to 3 portobello stems)

1 medium onion, chopped

2 cloves garlic, minced

A handful chopped fresh flat-leaf parsley

2 to 3 good pinches ground nutmeg

Freshly ground black pepper, to taste

6 slices white bread, toasted and lightly buttered

1 egg

1/4 cup grated Parmigiano Reggiano cheese

1 package (10 ounces) shredded provolone or mozzarella cheese

Preheat oven to 350°F.

Get started on the portobello caps: Heat evoo and garlic in a big skillet over medium heat. Add mushroom tops and cook until tender, 10 to 12 minutes, preparing stuffing while you wait. Douse pan with sherry, port, or Marsala, coating caps. Remove caps from pan and place on a cookie sheet. (Reserve juices in a small bowl and serve alongside stuffed mushrooms for dipping.)

Meanwhile, prepare the stuffing: Brown sausage in a medium skillet over medium-high heat. Drain away fat. Transfer sausage to a bowl and combine with spinach. Wipe out pan and return to heat. Melt butter and evoo. Add peppers, mushrooms, onions, garlic, and parsley and cook until soft, 3 to 5 minutes, stirring frequently. Add sausage and spinach mixture to pan and combine. Sprinkle with nutmeg and pepper. Dice up toasted, buttered bread and add to pan. Beat egg, combine it with cheese, and pour over pan. Mush it all together to cook the egg.

30-MINUTE MEALS
MENU

A GREAT GATHERING

1
entree
SWEET SAUSAGE-STUFFED PORTOBELLOS

2
side dishes
ANTIPASTICKS

GIARDINIERA

FRESH FIGS AND MELON WITH PROSCIUTTO

Place a mound of stuffing on half of each cap and top with a generous sprinkle of provolone or mozzarella cheese. Fold the cap over, like an omelet. Place caps in oven for 5 minutes to melt cheese. Cut caps into pizza-like wedges, transfer to a serving platter, and serve immediately. ★

✪ ✪ ✪ ✪
MAKES ONE QUART OF SALAD

Giardiniera

1 head cauliflower, stem removed, broken into florets
2 large carrots, thinly sliced
1/2 cup pepper rings from a jar, drained (found in Italian food aisle)
1/2 red bell pepper, seeded and chopped
1/4 cup sugar
1 cup white vinegar
1 teaspoon mustard seeds
1/2 teaspoon black peppercorns

Combine cauliflower, carrots, pepper rings, and bell pepper in a bowl.

Heat sugar, vinegar, mustard seeds, and peppercorns in a small saucepan over low heat until sugar dissolves. Pour marinade over veggies and refrigerate, stirring occasionally, for at least 24 hours. Drain and serve. ★

✪ ✪ ✪ ✪
MAKES 12 SERVINGS

Antipasticks

24 bamboo skewers (8-inch size)
2 dried Italian sausages, about 1 pound each (sopressata is the most common), each cubed into 24 pieces (choose sweet or hot dried sausage, or mix Genoa or hard salamis as a substitute)
1 pound provolone, cubed into 24 pieces (ask for two 1-inch-thick hunks at deli)
Hot or sweet Italian cherry peppers

Skewer ingredients, alternating 2 cubes of sausage or salami with 1 cube of cheese and one hot pepper to make each antipastick. Pile up on a platter and serve. ★

The marinated vegetables will take minutes to make, but should be made at least one day before your party to allow flavors to develop fully.

✪ ✪ ✪ ✪
MAKES 12 SERVINGS

Fresh Figs and Melon with Prosciutto

8 fresh figs, sliced

1 ripe cantaloupe, sliced

1/2 pound thinly sliced prosciutto di Parma (available at deli counter)

Arrange figs and cantaloupe on a serving platter with thinly sliced prosciutto, for an elegant Italian offering. ★

30-MINUTE MEALS

MENU

LEMON
HEAVEN

1

entree
BROILED COD

2

side dish
AMALFI-COAST
LEMON LINGUINI

3

suggested side
GREEN SALAD

Italy's Amalfi coast is lemon flavored. Lemon trees grow on terraced soil, from the sea up to the sun, and the lemons are as big as grapefruit. The smell of citrus is always in the air. Mamma and I, we tried lemon everything—lemon liqueurs and lemon candy, lemon sodas and lemon ices—they even put lemons on pasta! We have tried to re-create this very rich creamy sauce. We paired it with a broiled piece of cod and the results are yummy and a real stunner for your guests or your family.

MAKES 4 TO 6 SERVINGS

Broiled Cod and Amalfi-Coast Lemon Linguini

Coarse salt, to taste

1 pound linguini or tagliatelle

2 & 1/2 pounds fresh cod (see Note), 1 inch thick (don't let them give you tails)

2 tablespoons butter, softened

2 tablespoons good, sugar-free mayonnaise, such as Hellmann's

Chopped fresh parsley or fresh chives, for garnish

Lemon slices, for garnish (optional)

AMALFI LEMON SAUCE

8 tablespoons (1 stick) butter

8 tablespoons lemon juice (the juice of 4 lemons)

The grated zest of 3 lemons (2 tablespoons packed, grated rind)

1 cup heavy (whipping) cream

1 cup grated Parmigiano Reggiano cheese

Salt and freshly ground black pepper, to taste

1/2 cup chopped fresh flat-leaf parsley (half a bunch)

Put a large pot of water over high heat for the pasta. When water boils, add salt and linguine. Cook according to package directions, until al dente. Drain.

Meanwhile, preheat broiler.

Wash and dry fish. Sprinkle lightly with salt. Mix butter and mayonnaise and spread mixture over fish. Place a splash of water on a shallow pan and set fish on it. Set aside and start sauce.

For the sauce, in a large skillet, melt butter over medium-low heat. Add lemon juice and zest and simmer 3 or 4 minutes. Whisk in cream and half the Parmigiano Reggiano. Bring just to a simmer and remove from heat.

Place fish under broiler, 5 inches from heat, and cook 6 to 8 minutes, removing when golden and firm. Transfer fish carefully to a serving plate and garnish with chives and lemon slices.

Toss drained pasta with lemon sauce and salt and pepper. Transfer to a serving platter. Top pasta with remaining cheese and parsley. Serve with green salad on the side. ★

Note: Fresh fish is firm and shows no signs of breaking.

30-MINUTE MEALS
MENU

A WALK ON
THE WILD
SIDE

1

entree
WILDLY
DELICIOUS WILD
MUSHROOM
FETTUCCINE

2

suggested side
SALAD AND
CRUSTY BREAD

✪ ✪ ✪ ✪

MAKES 4 TO 6 SERVINGS

Wildly Delicious Wild Mushroom Fettuccine

Coarse salt and freshly ground black pepper, to taste
1 pound egg fettuccine
1/4 cup extra-virgin olive oil (evoo)
2 shallots, minced
2 portobello mushroom caps, halved and thinly sliced
6 crimini mushroom caps, halved and thinly sliced
6 shiitake mushroom caps, slivered
1/4 teaspoon ground thyme (a pinch)
2 pinches ground nutmeg
1/2 cup good sherry
1 cup chicken broth
2/3 cup heavy cream (4 trips around pan in slow and steady stream)
6 blades fresh chives, for garnish
1/2 cup toasted chopped hazelnuts, for garnish (optional)
Grated Romano or pepato cheese, for passing

Put a large pot of water over high heat for the pasta. When water boils, add salt and fettucine. Cook according to package directions, until al dente. Drain.

Meanwhile, heat evoo in a large skillet over medium heat. Add shallots, sauté 2 minutes, then add mushrooms. Sauté mushrooms 2 minutes, then cover pan, reduce heat to medium-low, and cook until juices are extracted and mushrooms are dark and tender, another 3 to 5 minutes. Uncover and raise heat back to medium. Add thyme, nutmeg, salt, and pepper. Toss mushrooms with a good shake of the pan. Add sherry and cook to reduce liquid by half, 2 or 3 minutes. Add broth, then cream. Simmer until sauce thickens so that it coats the back of a spoon, about 5 minutes. Toss with hot pasta and top with chives and toasted hazelnuts. Serve with grated cheese, crusty bread, and a green salad. ★

Wildly Delicious Wild Mushroom Fettuccine

MAKES 6 SERVINGS

Roasted Salsa with Mint and Cilantro

4 plum tomatoes

1 jalapeño pepper, halved and seeded

1 small onion, peeled and cut across into 3 thick slices

3 or 4 sprigs fresh mint, leaves stripped

A handful cilantro leaves

Coarse salt, to taste

Place whole tomatoes and the seeded jalapeño, skin side down, plus onion slices in a dry pan over high heat. Allow them to char on all sides, then place in a food processor. Pulse-grind with mint and cilantro leaves. Season with coarse salt. Pour salsa into a strainer, drain off liquid, and transfer to a serving dish. ★

MAKES 12 BURRITOS, 6 OF EACH FILLING

Spicy Black Bean Filling and Chicken, Red Peppers, and Chorizo Filling

BLACK BEAN FILLING

1 tablespoon vegetable or olive oil (once around the pan)

1 jalapeño pepper, seeded and chopped

2 cloves garlic, chopped

1 medium onion, chopped

2 cans (15 ounces each) black beans, drained

2 tablespoons chopped cilantro (a palmful)

1 teaspoon ground cumin (eyeball it in your palm)

Coarse salt, to taste

1 teaspoon cayenne pepper sauce, such as Frank's Red Hot or Tabasco

CHICKEN, RED PEPPERS AND CHORIZO FILLING

1 tablespoon vegetable or olive oil (once around the pan)

3/4 pound boneless chicken tenders, diced

1 teaspoon dark chili powder

Coarse salt, to taste

2 cloves garlic, chopped

1 red bell pepper, seeded and chopped

1/2 pound chorizo, casing removed, diced

12 burrito-size flour tortillas

Heat 2 nonstick skillets over medium-high heat. In the first, start the black beans: Add 1 tablespoon oil, jalapeño, garlic, and onions. Sauté 2 or 3 minutes, then add black beans, cilantro, cumin, salt, and cayenne pepper sauce. Reduce heat to low and simmer.

In the second skillet make the chicken: Add oil and, when hot, chicken. Season with chili powder and salt, and lightly brown the meat, 2 to 3 minutes. Add garlic, red peppers, and chorizo, and sauté, 5 to 6 minutes, then reduce heat to low.

Char and soften tortillas by heating them over hot burner flame, 15 seconds on each side. If you do not have gas burners, heat the dry skillet you used for salsa and cook tortillas one at a time, 15 seconds on each side.

Pile tortillas near stove and line up your toppings and sides. Serve fillings directly out of the pans. ★

First, set salsa ingredients in a pan to char. Next, make warm fillings and refried beans. Finally, arrange cold toppings and sides.

✪ ✪ ✪ ✪

MAKES 6 SERVINGS

Refried Beans

2 cans (15 ounces each) spicy vegetarian refried beans

1 can (4 ounces) sliced jalapeño pepper, drained

1 teaspoon garlic powder

Combine refried beans with jalapeños and garlic powder and heat in a bowl in the microwave. Loosely cover bowl with plastic wrap. Stop the timer and stir beans occasionally as you heat them. This should take 2 to 3 minutes. Serve alongside burritos. ★

✪ ✪ ✪ ✪

Toppings and Sides

Sour cream

2 cups roasted salsa

1 & 1/2 cups grated pepper Jack cheese

1 & 1/2 cups white smoked cheddar cheese (preshredded is available)

4 to 6 scallions, chopped

1 heart romaine lettuce, chopped

Lime wedges

MENU

TAPAS PARTY

1

tapas
POTATO
TORTILLA

— — — —

CHORIZO AND
VEGETABLE
CONFETTI
TORTILLA

— — — —

HERBED
CHICKEN TAPAS

— — — —

MUSHROOM
CAPS IN GARLIC
SAUCE

— — — —

Tapas are the "little dishes" of Spain. These pretty and very easy-to-make foods are wonderful party offerings. Since they are quite substantial, you don't need to make many varieties. Tapas should be served warm. Center this party around the kitchen and chat through the last-minute preparations. Pace the offerings. Cook a few tapas and let everyone enjoy them, yourself included. Then prepare a few more. This is the way they are eaten in Spain—over the course of a few hours with lots of conversation and a little wine.

One day before party

Do your shopping. Trim meats and place on paper-towel-lined dishes. Cover and refrigerate. Set out glasses and disposables.

Day of party

Assemble all of your serving dishes near the stove so you can keep filling them. Place shot glasses filled with long bamboo picks or skewers around counters or serving table with small piles of party napkins alongside.

One to two hours before guests arrive

Make tortillas and cover loosely with plastic wrap. Cut meat into pieces. Have all ingredients near the stove to assemble first tapas offerings.

More Party Tips

• If you are throwing a party for a family member, decorate with the things he or she loves—books or sheet music, art supplies, or sports equipment. Anything can be turned into a decoration if you set your mind to it.

• Greenery is as close as your own backyard. Trim a few branches, collect a few pinecones—no one sets a more elegant table than Mother Nature.

• The only things you should have left to purchase when you have gone through your house are candles and napkins. Try the dollar store for these—really. There are candles in every shape and size and wonderful prints or solid-colored disposables in every so-called dollar or "junk" store. Go and see for yourself—it's usually a fun, inexpensive shopping spree.

✪ ✪ ✪ ✪
THE RECIPES FOR THIS PARTY WILL FEED 20 PEOPLE

Potato Tortilla

2 medium white-skinned potatoes, peeled and very thinly sliced
Coarse salt, to taste
1/4 cup extra-virgin olive oil (evoo) (4 times around the pan)
Half a large sweet onion, thinly sliced
4 large eggs

Season potato slices with a little salt. Heat evoo in a 7- or 8-inch nonstick skillet over medium heat. Place potato and onion slices in pan in alternating single layers and gently cook, turning occasionally, not allowing potatoes to brown, for 10 minutes, or until potatoes are tender.

Beat eggs until frothy with a pinch of salt and a splash of cold water. Pour over potatoes. Use a spatula to lift potatoes and onions so liquids can settle under them. Shake pan to keep omelet from sticking as the eggs begin to set. Continue to shake pan and cook until tortilla is set. Place a flat dinner plate over top of pan, flip, and transfer inverted tortilla to plate. Return eggs to pan on flip side. Shake pan to keep tortilla from sticking. Let the bottom set, then flip another time or two, mostly because it makes you feel incredibly talented. Place tortilla on a serving plate and let cool before covering loosely with plastic wrap until ready to serve, at room temperature. Wipe pan and return to stove for next tortilla. To serve, cut into 10 small wedges. ★

✪ ✪ ✪ ✪
FEEDS 20 PEOPLE

Herbed Chicken Tapas

2 pounds chicken tenders
1/2 cup extra-virgin olive oil (evoo) (3 glugs)
The juice of 1 lemon
2 sprigs fresh rosemary, leaves striped from stem and minced
4 sprigs fresh thyme, leaves stripped and chopped
Coarse salt and freshly ground black pepper, to taste

Toss chicken in evoo, lemon juice, rosemary, thyme, salt, and pepper. Get a nonstick skillet smoking hot over medium-high heat. Add half the chicken tenders, lifting them out of the marinade and shaking off excess first. Cook 6 to 7 minutes, shaking pan frequently. Transfer to plate and repeat with next batch. After last batch, add any leftover marinade to pan and scrape up the good stuff stuck to the pan. Pour these juices over chicken. Serve with long picks and eat hot. ★

Chicken "tenders" are chicken breast tenderloins, packaged and sold as such in supermarkets.

149

✪ ✪ ✪ ✪
FEEDS 20 PEOPLE

Chorizo and Vegetable Confetti Tortilla

3 tablespoons (3 times around the pan) plus 1 teaspoon (a drizzle) extra-virgin olive oil (evoo)

1/4 to 1/3 pound chorizo, chourico, or linguiça, skinned and diced

1 small onion, diced

1/4 green bell pepper, diced

1/4 red bell pepper, diced

6 eggs

A handful frozen green peas, defrosted and drained

Pinch salt

Place a drizzle evoo in a 7- or 8-inch nonstick skillet over medium heat and cook chorizo and onion 5 minutes. Add peppers and cook another 1 to 2 minutes. Transfer mixture to a plate. Rinse out pan and dry and return to medium heat.

Add 3 tablespoons evoo and heat while beating eggs. Fold peas and salt into eggs. Add eggs to pan and spread chorizo mixture on them. As eggs set, lift with spatula and allow liquids to continue to settle. When tortilla is set firmly, turn tortilla onto a flat dinner plate and invert. Slide tortilla back into pan and cook until opposite side is set. Turn a few more times, then transfer to a serving plate. Let cool until room temperature. Cover loosely with plastic wrap until ready to serve. Cut into 10 wedges. ★

✪ ✪ ✪ ✪
FEEDS 20 PEOPLE

Mushroom Caps in Garlic Sauce

2 tablespoons butter

2 tablespoons extra-virgin olive oil (evoo) (twice around the pan)

40 small whole mushroom caps

12 cloves garlic, minced

1/2 cup Spanish sherry (a couple good splashes)

Coarse salt and freshly ground black pepper, to taste

A handful fresh flat-leaf parsley, chopped

Melt butter in a skillet over medium-high heat and add evoo. Sauté mushrooms until brown. Add garlic and shake pan, cooking 1 minute. Douse pan with sherry. Cook 1 to 2 minutes more to reduce sherry by half, shaking pan frequently. Sprinkle with salt, pepper, and a handful of parsley. Turn off heat and let stand until ready to serve. ★

Mushroom Caps in Garlic Sauce

Chorizo and Vegetable Confetti Tortilla

Herbed Chicken Tapas

✪ ✪ ✪ ✪
MAKES 8 SERVINGS

Grilled Polenta Crackers with Roasted Red Pepper Salsa

1 tube (18 ounces) store-bought polenta, plain or sun-dried tomato flavor, cut into 1/2-inch slices
1/4 cup extra-virgin olive oil (evoo) (eyeball it)
3 roasted red peppers (16-ounce jar), drained well
1/2 cup Kalamata olives, pitted
2 tablespoons capers
1/2 cup fresh flat-leaf parsley leaves (a couple handfuls)
1/4 red onion
1 to 2 cloves garlic
1/2 teaspoon crushed red pepper flakes

Preheat a grill pan to high. Brush polenta slices lightly with evoo. Grill 2 or 3 minutes on each side to score the "crackers" and warm them.

Place peppers, olives, capers, parsley, onion, garlic, and red pepper flakes in a food processor and pulse to chop salsa. Top polenta with spoonfuls of salsa and serve. ★

✪ ✪ ✪ ✪
MAKES 8 SERVINGS

Lavash Pizzas with Smoked Cheese and Ham

1 package lavash flat bread, plain or flavored
Extra-virgin olive oil (evoo), for drizzling
1 pound smoked mozzarella, diced into small cubes (28 to 32 pieces)
1/4 pound prosciutto, cut into 1/2-inch strips
1 cup arugula leaves (a couple handfuls), chopped
Freshly ground black pepper, to taste

Preheat oven to 375°F.

Cover 2 cookie sheets with lavash. Drizzle lavash with little evoo and turn over. Dot lavash with cubes of smoked mozzarella, spacing 1 inch apart. Make rows of cheese dots down and across the flat bread.

Place bread in oven to melt cheese, 5 minutes. Remove from oven and top with ham strips, draping them over the cheese. Scatter chopped arugula over the pizza. Cut into squares and drizzle with evoo and season with pepper. Transfer to plate and serve. ★

✪ ✪ ✪ ✪
MAKES 12 APPETIZER SERVINGS

Tomato and Garlic Bread Rounds

1 loaf crusty French or Italian bread, about 24 inches long
3 cloves garlic, popped from skin and left whole
3/4 cup extra-virgin olive oil (evoo)
2 large, vine-ripe tomatoes

Preheat oven to 325°F.

Cut bread into 24 slices. Place bread rounds on a cookie sheet and toast in oven until lightly browned, 7 or 8 minutes.

Warm garlic and evoo in microwave on high for 45 seconds or in a small saucepan over medium-low heat, until the garlic sizzles. Brush rounds with garlic oil.

Cut tomatoes in half and rub the oil-brushed sides of the bread against the flesh of the ripe tomatoes, rubbing six rounds with each half-tomato. Serve immediately. ★

✪ ✪ ✪ ✪
MAKES 12 SERVINGS

Assorted Olives

Olives are always a welcome party food, too. Whether green, black, or violet (indicating degree of ripeness) they are a healthy, delicious snack. Try tasting different kinds. Some are slightly bitter, others more aromatic. They shouldn't be too salty, as a rule, and good olives are firm, not soft. You can save money by buying them in bulk in your market. ★

✪ ✪ ✪ ✪
MAKES 12 SERVINGS

Sangria Slushes

2 pints lemon ice or sorbet
3 bottles Spanish Rioja red wine

Drop a scoop or two of lemon ice into wine glasses and fill up with red wine. ★

Heads up: Try this on a night when you have more than 30 minutes to spare. For the meat tapas, long bamboo skewers make great mini-spears. Put them in a small glass alongside the meats.

✪ ✪ ✪ ✪
MAKES 8 SERVINGS

Grilled Polenta Crackers with Roasted Red Pepper Salsa

1 tube (18 ounces) store-bought polenta, plain or sun-dried tomato flavor, cut into 1/2-inch slices

1/4 cup extra-virgin olive oil (evoo) (eyeball it)

3 roasted red peppers (16-ounce jar), drained well

1/2 cup Kalamata olives, pitted

2 tablespoons capers

1/2 cup fresh flat-leaf parsley leaves (a couple handfuls)

1/4 red onion

1 to 2 cloves garlic

1/2 teaspoon crushed red pepper flakes

Preheat a grill pan to high. Brush polenta slices lightly with evoo. Grill 2 or 3 minutes on each side to score the "crackers" and warm them.

Place peppers, olives, capers, parsley, onion, garlic, and red pepper flakes in a food processor and pulse to chop salsa. Top polenta with spoonfuls of salsa and serve. ★

✪ ✪ ✪ ✪
MAKES 8 SERVINGS

Lavash Pizzas with Smoked Cheese and Ham

1 package lavash flat bread, plain or flavored

Extra-virgin olive oil (evoo), for drizzling

1 pound smoked mozzarella, diced into small cubes (28 to 32 pieces)

1/4 pound prosciutto, cut into 1/2-inch strips

1 cup arugula leaves (a couple handfuls), chopped

Freshly ground black pepper, to taste

Preheat oven to 375°F.

Cover 2 cookie sheets with lavash. Drizzle lavash with little evoo and turn over. Dot lavash with cubes of smoked mozzarella, spacing 1 inch apart. Make rows of cheese dots down and across the flat bread.

Place bread in oven to melt cheese, 5 minutes. Remove from oven and top with ham strips, draping them over the cheese. Scatter chopped arugula over the pizza. Cut into squares and drizzle with evoo and season with pepper. Transfer to plate and serve. ★

Mushroom Caps in Garlic Sauce

Chorizo and Vegetable Confetti Tortilla

Herbed Chicken Tapas

✪ ✪ ✪ ✪

FEEDS 20 PEOPLE

Meat Tapas with Garlic & Sherry

3 tablespoons extra-virgin olive oil (evoo) (three times around the pan)

3 cloves garlic, peeled, coarsely sliced

3 pounds meat tenderloin, cubed into 1/2- to 1-inch pieces (use beef tenderloin filet, pork tenderloin, or chicken tenders, or a combination totaling 3 pounds)

Coarse salt and freshly ground black pepper, to taste

1 cup Madeira wine or good Spanish sherry

A handful chopped fresh flat-leaf parsley

Bamboo or wooden skewers (8 inch), for serving

Heat evoo and garlic in a heavy skillet over medium-high heat. Pat meat with paper towels to dry just before dropping into heated skillet. Cook meat until browned, 7 or 8 minutes. Sprinkle with coarse salt and pepper. Douse pan with Madeira or sherry, scraping off all the juicy bits from the bottom of pan. Reduce the liquid for 1 minute and transfer meat to a serving bowl. Sprinkle with parsley for color. ★

✪ ✪ ✪ ✪

FEEDS 20 PEOPLE

Warm Chili and Cheese Dip with Tri-Color Peppers and Tortilla Chips

1 can (15 ounces) chili with meat, no beans

1 brick (8 ounces) cream cheese or reduced-fat cream cheese

1 small can (4 ounces) sliced jalapeño peppers, drained and chopped

1 sack (10 ounces) shredded cheddar or reduced-fat cheddar

A handful fresh cilantro, chopped

1 yellow bell pepper, seeded and cut lengthwise into thin strips

1 green bell pepper, seeded and cut lengthwise into thin strips

1 red bell pepper, seeded and cut lengthwise into thin strips

3 bags assorted tortilla chips (10 to 12 ounces each), blue corn, red corn, black bean, white corn, etc.

Combine chili, cream cheese, jalapeños, and cheddar in a saucepan and cook over medium-low heat until smooth. Stir in cilantro and transfer to a fondue pot or oven-safe bowl, warmed in a 350°F oven for 10 minutes.

Place a platter of tricolored pepper strips and a basket of assorted tortilla chips next to your chili-cheese concoction for dipping. ★

Grilled Polenta Crackers

Lavash Pizzas

This recipe is my take on chimichurri: oil, vinegar, onions, garlic, herbs, and spices—to serve as both marinade and dipping sauce.

✪ ✪ ✪ ✪
MAKES 8 SERVINGS

Rachael's Chimichurri Chicken Bites

2 serrano or jalapeño peppers

1 rounded tablespoon sweet paprika

1/2 cup fresh flat-leaf parsley leaves (a couple handfuls)

4 sprigs oregano, leaves stripped

5 or 6 sprigs fresh thyme, leaves stripped and chopped

2 bay leaves, crumbled

1/2 small white onion, coarsely chopped

3 cloves garlic

1 cup extra-virgin olive oil (evoo) (eyeball it)

3 tablespoons red wine vinegar (3 splashes)

1 teaspoon coarse salt

1 & 1/2 to 1 & 3/4 pounds chicken tenders

Preheat a grill pan over high heat.

Char peppers by holding over a gas flame or placing under the broiler for 1 to 2 minutes to blister them all over. Seed and coarsely chop the peppers and place in a food processor. Add paprika, herbs, onion, and garlic. Pulse until finely chopped. Transfer to a bowl and stir in evoo, vinegar, and salt. Taste to adjust seasonings.

Cut chicken tenders into thirds and place in a shallow dish. Wash your hands. Spoon half of the chimichurri over the chicken and coat completely and evenly. Using tongs, transfer the chicken bites to the hot grill and cook, 2 or 3 minutes on each side. Transfer bites to a serving plate. Serve with party picks and reserved chimichurri sauce for dipping. ★

★ ★ ★ ★
MAKES 8 SERVINGS

Lemon Pepper Chicken Tenders

The grated zest and juice of 2 lemons

1/3 cup extra-virgin olive oil (evoo) (eyeball it)

2 pounds chicken breast tenders (20 pieces)

Salt and freshly ground black pepper, to taste

20 bamboo skewers (6 inches long)

Heat a large nonstick skillet, grill pan, or indoor grill to medium-high heat. In a shallow dish, combine lemon zest and juice with evoo. Season chicken with salt and pepper. Pour half of the marinade over chicken and reserve half. Turn chicken in marinade to coat lightly. Cook tenders in 2 batches, in a single layer in a very hot skillet or grill, 3 minutes on each side, while basting occasionally with reserved marinade. Transfer chicken to a serving platter and place skewers alongside. ★

★ ★ ★ ★
MAKES 8 SERVINGS

Chickpea and Rosemary Dip with Zucchini "Chips"

Makes 8 servings

2 cans (15 ounces each) chickpeas (garbanzo beans), drained

1 small jar (6 ounces) roasted red peppers, drained and coarsely chopped

The juice of 1/2 lemon

2 cloves garlic, cracked away from skin with the flat of a knife

4 sprigs fresh rosemary, leaves stripped from stems (about 3 tablespoons)

Coarse salt and freshly ground black pepper, to taste

2 tablespoons extra-virgin olive oil (evoo) (eyeball it)

1 package "everything-flavored" flat breads

1 pint grape tomatoes

1 zucchini, sliced into 1/8-inch disks

Combine chickpeas, roasted red pepper, lemon juice, garlic, rosemary, salt, and pepper in a food processor. Turn the processor on and stream in evoo. Remove spread to a serving bowl and surround with flat breads, grape tomatoes, and zucchini. ★

LITTLE
BITES
PARTY

1

appetizers
LEMON PEPPER
CHICKEN
TENDERS

CHICKPEA AND
ROSEMARY DIP
WITH ZUCCHINI
"CHIPS"

SPINACH AND
ARTICHOKE-
STUFFED
PORTOBELLOS

Chickpea and Rosemary Dip

Lemon Pepper Chicken Tenders

Spinach- and Artichoke-Stuffed Portobellos

✪ ✪ ✪ ✪

MAKES 8 SERVINGS

Spinach- and Artichoke-Stuffed Portobellos

PORTOBELLOS

2 teaspoons extra-virgin olive oil (evoo) (a drizzle)

5 medium portobello mushroom caps

Salt and freshly ground black pepper, to taste

2 tablespoons balsamic vinegar

STUFFING

1 tablespoon extra-virgin olive oil (evoo) (once around the pan)

3 cloves garlic, chopped

1 small yellow onion, chopped

1 pound fresh spinach, coarsely chopped

1 can (15 ounces) artichoke hearts in water (6 to 8 count), drained well
  on paper towels

Salt and freshly ground black pepper, to taste

4 to 6 sprigs fresh thyme, leaves stripped and chopped

3 slices Italian bread, toasted and chopped into small cubes

1 cup chicken or vegetable stock

1/4 cup grated Parmesan cheese (a handful)

6 ounces fontina cheese, shredded

Preheat oven to 400°F.

Prepare the mushroom caps: Heat a large nonstick skillet over medium-high heat. Add a drizzle of evoo and the mushroom caps. Season caps with salt and pepper, and cook 3 minutes on each side. Add vinegar to the pan and allow it to cook away as it coats the caps. Transfer balsamic-glazed caps to a cookie sheet.

Make the stuffing: Return pan to the stove and add evoo, garlic, and onion. Sauté, 3 minutes; add spinach to the pan and let it wilt. Coarsely chop artichoke hearts and add to the spinach. Season veggies with salt, pepper, and thyme. Add chopped toast and dampen stuffing with chicken or vegetable stock. Combine stuffing and sprinkle in Parmesan. Top each mushroom with 1/5 of the stuffing and sprinkle lightly with a few strands fontina. Set mushrooms in oven for 5 minutes to set the mushrooms and melt the cheese strands. Cut each mushroom into 4 pieces and transfer to a serving dish. ★

Your friends will love you for this healthy, great-tasting party menu. The lemon pepper chicken is cooked with olive oil, and the dip replaces fattening cream cheese and sour cream spreads normally passed at parties. The mushrooms have a little cheese, but no sausage or rich crabmeat, and the stuffing is held together with broth, not butter. It's all figure-friendly, easy to make, and oh, so good.

✪ ✪ ✪ ✪
MAKES 4 SERVINGS

Olive Rosemary Crostini

2 cloves garlic, cracked away from skin with the flat of a knife

1/4 cup extra-virgin olive oil (evoo) (eyeball it)

1 small loaf crusty bread, sliced

1/2 pound oil-cured black and Sicilian green olives, pitted and chopped

3 tablespoons capers, drained

1/2 teaspoon crushed red pepper flakes

2 sprigs fresh rosemary, leaves stripped from stems

Preheat the broiler.

Heat evoo over low heat in a small skillet and sauté 2 cloves garlic until soft and golden, about 5 to 6 minutes.

Toast bread slices under hot broiler on both sides. Using a pastry brush, dab charred bread with garlic oil. Place the rest of the oil in a small bowl with chopped olives.

Pile garlic cloves on a cutting board together with capers, red pepper flakes, and rosemary. Finely chop mixture, and combine with the olives and oil. To assemble crostini, spread this olive tapenade on toasts. Enjoy! ★

✪ ✪ ✪ ✪
MAKES 4 SERVINGS

Pesce Spada Rollotini (Rolled Swordfish)

1 & 1/2 pounds thin-cut swordfish steaks (ask at fish counter for 3 steaks cut as thinly as possible, no more than 1/2 inch thick)

1 & 1/2 cups plain bread crumbs

A handful fresh flat-leaf parsley

1 large clove garlic, peeled

The grated zest of 1 lemon

Coarse salt

2 tablespoons extra-virgin olive oil (evoo) (twice around the pan)

Pat swordfish steaks dry. Trim away skin and dark connective tissue, and place between 2 sheets of waxed paper. Pound with a rubber mallet as you would chicken or veal cutlets. Cut the thin slices into several rectangular pieces, about 2x4 inches. ★

Place bread crumbs in a shallow dish. Pile parsley, garlic, lemon zest, and a little coarse salt on a cutting board. Finely chop the lemon-garlic mixture, then combine with plain bread crumbs. Gently press the fish slices into the crumb mixture, coating both sides. Roll up the coated fish strips tightly into small bundles.

Preheat a medium nonstick skillet over medium heat, coat with a thin layer of evoo, and cook several swordfish rolls until just golden and firm, 3 to 4 minutes on each side. Remove from pan and serve swordfish with lemon wedges, slaw salad, and crostini. ★

✪ ✪ ✪ ✪
MAKES 4 SERVINGS

Fennel Slaw Salad

A palmful golden raisins (2 tablespoons)
The juice of 1 navel orange
2 to 3 tablespoons hot water
2 bulbs fresh fennel, trimmed of tops and fronds, cored and thinly sliced lengthwise
1 medium head radicchio lettuce, shredded
4 scallions, thinly sliced on an angle
A handful fresh flat-leaf parsley, chopped
3 tablespoons pignoli nuts, toasted (a handful)
2 tablespoons balsamic vinegar (eyeball it)
3 tablespoons extra-virgin olive oil (evoo) (3 times around the bowl)
Coarse salt and freshly ground black pepper, to taste

Place raisins in a small dish, cover with the orange juice and 2 to 3 tablespoons hot water. Let raisins plump and soften, 5 minutes. Combine fennel, radicchio, scallions, and parsley in a bowl. Add plumped raisins in juice and the pignoli nuts to the slaw and toss with balsamic vinegar and evoo to lightly coat. Season with coarse salt and pepper. ★

When in Sicily, I have these swordfish rolls as a favorite lunch or late-night snack. Here, I use my grandfather's lemon, parsley, and garlic coating to bread my own fish rolls, and the results would make him proud!

✪ ✪ ✪ ✪
MAKES 4 SERVINGS

John's Fish: Tilapia with Tomatillo Sauce and Avocados with Creamy Maque Choux (Corn and Peppers)

TILAPIA

4 fillets tilapia (1 & 1/4 to 1 & 1/2 pounds total)

Coarse salt and freshly ground black pepper, to taste

1 teaspoon ground cumin (eyeball it)

1/2 teaspoon sweet paprika (eyeball it)

2 tablespoons extra-virgin olive oil (evoo)

The juice of 1 lime

1/2 medium red onion chopped

1 jalapeño or serrano pepper, seeded and finely chopped

2 or 3 large cloves garlic, minced

8 to 10 tomatillos, peeled and diced with juice

1/2 bottle pale beer

2 tablespoons chopped cilantro (a palmful), plus a few sprigs for garnish

AVOCADOES AND MAQUE CHOUX

1 tablespoon extra-virgin olive oil (evoo) (once around the pan)

1/2 red onion, chopped

1 jalapeño pepper, seeded and finely chopped

1 small red bell pepper, seeded and chopped

4 ears fresh corn on the cob, husked

A sprinkle of sugar

Dash cayenne pepper

Dash salt

2 tablespoons butter

2 ripe avocados

The juice of 1 lime

Coarse salt

Season tilapia on both sides with salt, pepper, cumin, and paprika. Preheat a nonstick skillet over medium-high heat. Add 1 tablespoon evoo (once around the pan) to the hot skillet and sauté tilapia 3 minutes on each side, turning carefully with a thin spatula. Squeeze the juice of 1/2 lime over the fish, and transfer fillets to a warm serving platter.

Return skillet to the stove over medium-high heat. Add 1 tablespoon evoo, red onion, jalapeño, and garlic, and sauté, 1 or 2 minutes, then add

Tilapia with Tomatillo Sauce

tomatillos. Season with salt and pepper, and sauté, another 1 or 2 minutes. Add beer and the remaining lime juice, and bring sauce to a boil. Reduce heat to low and simmer, 5 minutes.

While sauce is simmering, make the maque choux: Get a second skillet hot over medium heat. Add evoo, onion, jalapeño, and bell pepper and sauté, 2 or 3 minutes. Working on a plate to catch the milky juices, scrape corn off the cob. Break up kernels and pour corn and its juices into the skillet. Combine with peppers and onions. Season with sugar, cayenne, and salt. When mixture bubbles, reduce heat to a simmer. Cut butter into pieces, stir into corn mixture, and simmer until creamy, 5 to 7 minutes.

Cut avocados in half lengthwise and remove pits. Squeeze lime juice over the avocados to keep them from browning and season with a little coarse salt.

Back to the sauce for fish: Add cilantro, and adjust salt and pepper. Spoon hot tomatillo sauce over the fish and garnish with sprigs of cilantro.
To serve, set 1/2 an avocado per person alongside a serving of fish topped with tomatillo sauce. Fill the avocado with maque choux, allowing the corn to spill down and over the sides. The ripe avocado is spooned away from its skin with bites of creamy, warm corn and peppers. ★

These icy, frozen treats, a combination after-dinner drink and dessert, are refreshing following a spicy meal.

✪ ✪ ✪ ✪
MAKES 4 SERVINGS

Margarita Granita

The juice of 2 limes
1 tray ice cubes
1 pint lime sherbet (4 large scoops)
4 shots good-quality tequila
2 shots orange liqueur, such as Cointreau

Combine all ingredients in a blender and blend on high, 1 or 2 minutes or until smooth and frothy. Spoon into glasses and serve. ★

✪ ✪ ✪ ✪
MAKES 4 SERVINGS

Grilled Halibut Sandwiches

1 & 1/4 to 1 & 1/2 pounds fresh halibut, cut into 4 servings (4 to 6 ounces each, 1 inch thick)

Vegetable or olive oil, for drizzling

2 teaspoons Old Bay Seasoning (found near seafood counter in most markets)

Salt and freshly ground black pepper, to taste

2 tablespoons butter, melted

The juice of 1/2 lemon

ZESTY TARTAR SAUCE

1 cup mayonnaise or reduced-fat mayonnaise

2 tablespoons sweet pickle relish

1 dill or half-sour pickle, finely chopped

2 tablespoons finely chopped onion

2 tablespoons chopped fresh dill

10 blades fresh chives, chopped, or 2 thin scallions thinly sliced

The juice of 1/2 lemon

A few drops cayenne pepper sauce, such as Frank's Red Hot or Tabasco

4 crusty rolls, split

1 large ripe tomato, sliced

4 leaves green leaf or Boston lettuce

1 bag gourmet chips, such as Terra Chips in Yukon Gold Onion and Garlic flavor

Preheat a nonstick skillet or well-seasoned cast-iron grill pan over medium-high heat. Drizzle halibut with oil, season with Old Bay, salt, and pepper, and grill on hot pan, 4 or 5 minutes on each side. Place melted butter in a small dish and add lemon juice. Set aside.

Combine all ingredients for the tartar sauce in a small bowl: mayonnaise, sweet relish, chopped pickle, onion, dill, chives, lemon juice, and hot sauce. Stir to combine.

Lightly toast buns on grill pan when you remove fish from heat.

To assemble, brush bun bottoms and fish with reserved lemon butter. Place a portion of fish on each bun bottom and top with tomato and lettuce; slather the bun tops with tartar sauce, then serve with Asparagus Pasta Salad and chips. ★

30-MINUTE MEALS

MENU

MAKE YOUR OWN TAKE-OUT

1
entree
GRILLED HALIBUT SANDWICHES

2
side dish
ASPARAGUS PASTA SALAD

3
dessert
FRUIT SALAD WITH ORANGE LIQUEUR AND SORBET

To trim asparagus, hold a spear at each end and snap it. The spear will break where the tender top meets the tough bottom. Line the broken spear up with the bundle of cleaned asparagus. Cut using the guidline of the snapped spear.

✪ ✪ ✪ ✪
MAKES 4 SERVINGS

Asparagus Pasta Salad

Salt and freshly ground black pepper, to taste

1/2 pound farfalle (bow-tie pasta)

1 small shallot or 1/2 large shallot, finely chopped

1/3 cup extra-virgin olive oil (evoo) (eyeball it)

1 pound thin asparagus spears, trimmed

2 endives, cored and thinly sliced

1/2 small red bell pepper, chopped

1/2 cup frozen green peas

1/4 cup chopped fresh flat-leaf parsley (a couple handfuls)

3 tablespoons white wine vinegar

Put a pot of water over high heat to boil. When it comes to a boil, add salt and pasta. Cook pasta according to package directions, until al dente. Drain.

Meanwhile, heat the shallots and evoo in the microwave in a covered dish for 30 seconds or in a small pan on the stovetop over medium-low heat for 5 minutes. Let cool.

Pour 1 inch water into a pot with a tight-fitting lid; bring to a simmer. Parboil the asparagus in simmering water, covered, 3 to 5 minutes, until just tender but still bright green. Cool under cold running water and drain. Cut into 1-inch pieces on an angle and place in a bowl. Combine with endive, red bell pepper, cooked pasta, peas, and chopped parsley. (The peas will defrost as you toss the salad.)

Pour vinegar into a small bowl and whisk in cooled shallot oil. Pour dressing over salad and toss. Season with salt and pepper and toss again. ★

✪ ✪ ✪ ✪
MAKES 4 SERVINGS

Fruit Salad with Orange Liqueur and Sorbet

2 fresh ripe peaches, pitted and diced OR 1 can (15 ounces) whole peaches, drained and diced

1 ripe Bartlett or Anjou pear, diced

1 pint ripe strawberries, halved

2 kiwis, peeled and sliced

2 ounces orange liqueur, such as Grand Marnier

1 pint orange or strawberry sorbet

Combine fruit in a bowl and douse with liqueur. Let stand a few minutes for flavors to combine. To serve, spoon fruit into dessert cups and top with scoops of sorbet. ★

30-MINUTE MEALS
MENU

FIRESIDE FEAST

1

entrees
VEAL
DUMPLINGS AND
EGG
FETTUCCINE

2

suggested sides
GREEN SALAD
AND CRUSTY
BREAD

✪ ✪ ✪ ✪
MAKES 4 TO 6 SERVINGS

Veal Dumplings and Egg Fettuccine

Coarse salt and freshly ground black pepper, to taste
1 box (14 to 16 ounces) egg fettuccine
1 pound ground veal
1 large egg, beaten
1 cup bread crumbs
1/2 small onion, grated
1/2 teaspoon ground nutmeg
1/2 cup grated Romano or Parmigiano Reggiano cheese
2 tablespoons butter, cut into bits
4 sprigs fresh thyme, stripped from stems and chopped
2 cloves garlic, minced
One 28-ounce can plus one 14-ounce can crushed tomatoes

Put a large pot of water over high heat for the pasta. When water boils, add salt and fettucine. Cook according to package directions, until al dente. Drain.

Meanwhile, heat a second, deep pot of water to a boil. Combine veal, egg, bread crumbs, onion, nutmeg, cheese, and black pepper. Roll mixture into 1/2-inch balls. Drop balls into boiling water, reduce heat, and cook 12 minutes, covered. Drain and set dumplings aside.

Return dumpling pot to medium heat and melt butter. Add thyme and garlic. When garlic sizzles, add tomatoes and veal dumplings. Add coarse salt, to taste. Simmer 5 minutes. Toss pasta with veal dumplings and sauce. Serve with green salad and crusty bread. ★

30-MINUTE MEALS
MENU

BIG NIGHT DINNER

1

entree
BRANDY AND
ORANGE
CHICKEN
TOPPED WITH
STUFFED SHRIMP

2

side dish
FRUITED WHITE
AND WILD RICE

3

dessert
MAPLE NUT
COFFEE ICE
CREAM DESSERT

✪ ✪ ✪ ✪

MAKES 4 SERVINGS

Brandy and Orange Chicken Topped with Stuffed Shrimp

STUFFED SHRIMP

1 tablespoon extra-virgin olive oil (evoo) (once around the pan)

2 tablespoons butter

1 rib celery, finely chopped

1 small onion, finely chopped

1/4 red bell pepper, finely chopped

6 ounces, drained weight, fresh lump crabmeat (available at fresh fish counter) or 2 cans (5 & 1/2 ounces each), drained

1/2 teaspoon ground thyme or poultry seasoning (eyeball it)

1 teaspoon sweet paprika

Salt and freshly ground black pepper, to taste

2 thin slices white bread, toasted and buttered, then diced

2 to 3 tablespoons chopped fresh flat-leaf parsley (a handful)

3 tablespoons melted butter

8 jumbo shrimp, peeled and deveined, tails intact (ask for easy peels at the fish counter)

CHICKEN

4 pieces boneless, skinless chicken breast (6 to 8 ounces each)

1 teaspoon ground thyme or poultry seasoning

Salt and freshly ground black pepper, to taste

1 tablespoon extra-virgin olive oil (evoo)

3 shots brandy (about 4 ounces total)

2 tablespoons butter

The grated zest of 1 large navel orange

Parsley sprigs and sliced navel oranges, for garnish

Preheat oven to 400°F.

Make the shrimp: To a small skillet over medium heat, add the evoo and butter. When butter has melted, add celery, onion, and red bell pepper and sauté 5 minutes. Add the crab and season with thyme or poultry seasoning, paprika, salt, and pepper. Fold a few handfuls of diced toasted bread into the stuffing. Stir in parsley, and remove from heat.

Brush a baking dish with melted butter. Butterfly shrimp by cutting along the deveining line, into and almost through the shrimps. Place an open butterflied shrimp in your hand. Dab the shrimp with melted butter and place a rounded spoonful of crab stuffing on the shrimp. Set the shrimp in the baking dish with the stuffing exposed and the tail upright; repeat with remaining shrimp and stuffing. Bake until shrimp are pink and firm and stuffing is browned, 6 to 8 minutes.

Season chicken breasts with ground thyme or poultry seasoning, salt, and pepper. In a second skillet over medium-high heat, add evoo and cook breasts, 5 minutes on each side, then remove to a serving plate. Take the pan off the heat to add brandy; return to heat and cook alcohol off, 1 minute. Add butter and orange zest, and spoon over the chicken, topping each breast with 2 stuffed shrimp. Garnish with sliced oranges and parsley sprigs. ★

✪ ✪ ✪ ✪
MAKES 4 SERVINGS

Fruited White and Wild Rice

2 cups water
1 tablespoon butter
1 teaspoon salt (eyeball it)
1 cup white and wild rice blend
3 tablespoons golden raisins (a handful)
1/2 cup mandarin orange sections, drained and chopped
1 package (2 ounces) sliced almonds (available on the baking aisle)
3 scallions, thinly sliced

Bring water to a boil in a small saucepan, add butter and salt. Add white and wild rice blend and golden raisins, stir, return to a boil. Reduce heat, cover, and simmer until just tender, about 20 minutes. Fluff with a fork. Add chopped oranges, almonds, and scallions. Toss to combine and serve. ★

✪ ✪ ✪ ✪
MAKES 4 SERVINGS

Maple Nut Coffee Ice Cream Dessert

2 pints coffee ice cream
1 cup salted mixed nuts, coarsely chopped
1/2 cup medium to dark amber maple syrup, warmed
Rolled wafer cookies, for garnish

Place 2 scoops of coffee ice cream in each bowl and top with chopped salted mixed nuts. Drizzle nuts and ice cream with warm maple syrup. Garnish with rolled wafer cookies, and serve. ★

Serve this dessert in cocktail or martini glasses for a fancy finish.

A true food lover's menu full of earthy, rich flavors.

✪ ✪ ✪ ✪
MAKES 4 SERVINGS

Sage Veal Chops

4 veal chops, each 1 inch thick
Salt and freshly ground black pepper, to taste
6 sprigs fresh sage, chopped (about 4 tablespoons)
1 tablespoon extra-virgin olive oil (evoo) (once around the pan)
2 tablespoons butter
1/2 cup dry white wine (eyeball it)

Heat a heavy-bottom skillet over medium-high heat. Season chops with salt and pepper and rub them each with about 1 tablespoon chopped sage, rubbing well into both sides of the chops. Add evoo to the pan. Melt butter into the oil and add chops to the pan. Cook 5 minutes on each side, remove to warm platter, and let rest. Add wine to the pan and scrape up the drippings. Spoon over the chops and serve. ★

✪ ✪ ✪ ✪
MAKES 4 SERVINGS

Wild Mushroom Fricassee Over Polenta

POLENTA
3 cups chicken broth
1 cup quick-cooking polenta (found in Italian or specialty foods aisles)
2 tablespoons butter
1/4 cup grated Romano or Parmigiano Reggiano cheese
Salt and freshly ground black pepper, to taste

FRICASSEE
2 tablespoons extra-virgin olive oil (evoo) (twice around the pan)
1 tablespoon butter
4 portobello mushroom caps, halved, then thinly sliced
16 fresh shiitake mushrooms, coarsely chopped
Coarse salt and freshly ground black pepper, to taste
2 tablespoons balsamic vinegar
1/2 cup beef stock or broth
2 scallions, thinly sliced on an angle

To start the polenta, bring chicken broth to a boil in a covered pot.

Sage Veal Chops

Meanwhile, start the fricassee. Heat a large nonstick skillet over medium-high heat. Add evoo and butter. When butter has melted into oil, add mushrooms and season with salt and pepper. Cook, stirring frequently, until mushrooms are all dark and tender, about 10 minutes. Add vinegar and stir to coat. Cook until vinegar cooks away, about 1 minute. Add broth and scallions. Toss to combine.

Stir polenta into boiling chicken broth until it masses. Stir in butter and cheese and season with salt and pepper.

Serve polenta topped with Mushroom Fricassee alongside Sage Veal Chops. ★

✪ ✪ ✪ ✪
MAKES 4 SERVINGS

Arugula Salad with Blue Cheese, Pears, and Apricot Vinaigrette

2 bunches arugula, washed and dried, stems trimmed

1 head Bibb lettuce, washed and torn

The juice of 1/2 lemon

1 ripe pear, thinly sliced

8 ounces blue cheese, such as Maytag, crumbled

DRESSING

1 small shallot, minced

2 tablespoons white wine vinegar

1/4 cup apricot all-fruit spread (found near jams and jellies)

1/3 cup extra-virgin olive oil (evoo) (eyeball the amount)

Salt and freshly ground black pepper, to taste

Combine arugula and lettuce in a salad bowl. Squeeze a little lemon juice over pear slices to keep them from browning. Arrange them on top of the lettuce and arugula. Top with blue cheese crumbles.

To make the dressing, combine shallots, vinegar, and apricot spread in a bowl. Stream in evoo as you whisk. Add to salad, season with salt and black pepper and serve. ★

I often have a salad of arugula, pears, blue cheese, and dried apricots at Thalia in New York. When I make it for myself at home, I put the apricot flavor right into the dressing— delicious with the cheese and fruit in the salad.

174

✪ ✪ ✪ ✪

MAKES 4 SERVINGS

Sea Scallops with Vermouth

3 tablespoons extra-virgin olive oil (evoo)

1 shallot, chopped

2 cans (15 ounces each) quartered artichoke hearts in water, drained

Salt and freshly ground black pepper, to taste

A handful chopped fresh flat-leaf parsley

2 tablespoons capers, drained

16 sea scallops, drained and trimmed

1/2 cup dry vermouth

Heat a large nonstick skillet over medium-high heat. Add about 2 tablespoons evoo (twice around the pan) then the chopped shallots to the pan. Cook 1 minute or so, add artichoke hearts, and toss to heat through. Season with salt and pepper and combine with parsley and capers. Transfer to a serving dish.

Wipe out pan and return to stove, raising heat a bit. Season scallops with salt and pepper. Add 1 turn of evoo to the very hot pan and immediately place the scallops in the pan. Sear the scallops in a single layer, causing them to caramelize, 2 minutes on each side. Add vermouth and cook out the alcohol, 1 to 2 minutes. Arrange over top of the artichokes and serve. ★

30-MINUTE MEALS

MENU

COOKING WITH WINE

1

entree
SEA SCALLOPS WITH VERMOUTH

2

side dish
VEAL SCALOPPINI WITH WINE, MUSHROOMS, AND GREEN OLIVES

3

dessert
RIPE PEACHES WITH PORT

Veal Scaloppini

Sea Scallops with Vermouth

✪ ✪ ✪ ✪
MAKES 4 SERVINGS

Veal Scaloppini with Wine, Mushrooms, and Green Olives

Salt and freshly ground black pepper, to taste

3/4 pound linguini

4 tablespoons extra-virgin olive oil (evoo), plus some for drizzling

3 slices pancetta or bacon, chopped

1 small onion, chopped

16 crimini or white mushrooms, chopped

1 pound veal scaloppini, cut into 1-inch strips

2 cloves garlic, smashed

1 cup dry white wine

16 pitted, large green olives, coarsely chopped

A handful chopped fresh flat-leaf Italian parsley

1 tablespoon butter, cut into pieces

1/3 cup grated Parmigiano Reggiano or Romano cheese (a couple handfuls)

Put a large pot of water over high heat for the pasta. When water boils, add salt and linguini. Cook according to package directions until al dente. Drain.

Meanwhile, preheat a large heavy skillet over medium to medium-high heat. Add 1 tablespoon evoo (once around the pan) and the pancetta or bacon. Cook 1 to 2 minutes, then add onions and cook another 2 to 3 minutes. Add mushrooms and cook, another 3 to 5 minutes.

While vegetables are cooking, season veal strips with salt and pepper. In a second skillet preheated over medium-high heat, add 1 & 1/2 tablespoons evoo and 1 clove smashed garlic. Quick-fry half of the veal, searing each side of the strips, 1 to 2 minutes. Transfer to a plate and repeat. When done, add all of the veal and garlic to the onions and mushrooms, then add wine to the veal pan and scrape up all of the drippings. Cook wine down (and alcohol out), 2 to 3 minutes. Stir in olives and parsley, and serve on a bed of hot linguini tossed with a drizzle of evoo, butter, and grated cheese. ★

✪ ✪ ✪ ✪
MAKES 4 SERVINGS

Ripe Peaches with Port

4 ripe peaches, sliced

2 teaspoons sugar

4 shots (about 6 ounces total) port wine

4 scoops vanilla ice cream

Place peaches in a bowl, sprinkle with sugar and add port. Toss to coat and let stand, 15 minutes. Spoon into dessert dishes and top each with a small scoop of vanilla ice cream. ★

One of my 5 favorite menus. It must be those wines!

✪ ✪ ✪ ✪

MAKES 4 SERVINGS

Everyday Cioppino (Fish Stew)

1/4 cup extra-virgin olive oil (evoo)

1 teaspoon crushed red pepper flakes (eyeball it and crush in your palm)

1 tin flat anchovy fillets, drained

6 cloves garlic, crushed

1 bay leaf, fresh or dried

2 ribs celery

1 medium onion

1 cup good-quality dry white wine

1 container (14 ounces) chicken broth (from a can or paper container, such as Kitchen Basics)

1 can (28 ounces) chunky-style crushed tomatoes

4 sprigs fresh thyme, leaves stripped and chopped

A handful chopped fresh flat-leaf parsley

1 & 1/2 pounds cod, cut into 2-inch chunks

Salt and freshly ground black pepper, to taste

8 large shrimp (ask for deveined, easy-peel, or peel and devein yourself)

8 sea scallops

16 to 20 raw mussels, scrubbed

A loaf of fresh, crusty bread, for mopping

In a large pot over medium heat, combine evoo, red pepper flakes, anchovies, garlic, and bay leaf. Let anchovies melt into the oil. They act as natural salt and will break up into the pepper-infused oil, providing heat in the flavor. Chop celery and onion near stove and add to the pot as you work. Sauté vegetables a couple of minutes until they begin to soften, then add wine. Cook to reduce, 1 minute, then add chicken broth, tomatoes, thyme, and parsley. Bring sauce to a bubble, then reduce heat to medium-low.

Season fish chunks with salt and pepper, add to sauce, and simmer 5 minutes, giving the pot a shake now and then. (Don't stir with a spoon; you'll break the fish up.) Add shrimp, scallops, and mussels, and cover pot. Cook 10 minutes, giving the pot an occasional good shake. Remove lid and discard any unopened mussels. Carefully ladle stew into shallow bowls and pass bread at the table. ★

Everyday Cioppino

✪ ✪ ✪ ✪
MAKES 4 SERVINGS

Mixed Greens and Fennel Salad

2 hearts romaine lettuce
1 medium head radicchio
1 small bulb fennel
A generous drizzle balsamic vinegar
3 tablespoons extra-virgin olive oil (evoo) (3 times around the salad bowl)
Salt and freshly ground black pepper, to taste

Shred romaine and radicchio and discard cores. Trim tops of fennel bulb and quarter lengthwise. Remove core with an angled cut into each quarter. Slice fennel across into thin slices and add to salad. Dress with vinegar, evoo, salt, and pepper. Toss well and serve. ★

✪ ✪ ✪ ✪
MAKES 20 APPLE FRITTER RINGS

Nothin' to Fret About Apple Fritters

Vegetable oil, for frying
4 Red or Golden Delicious apples
2 teaspoons lemon juice
2 cups complete pancake mix
1 & 1/2 cups water
1/2 teaspoon ground or freshly grated nutmeg
1/2 cup confectioners' sugar

Heat 1 inch vegetable oil in a heavy pot or deep skillet over medium to medium-high heat. To test the oil temperature, add a 1-inch cube of bread to the hot oil; if it turns a deep, golden brown by the time you count to 40, the oil is ready.

Core apples with an apple corer. Cut apples crosswise, forming 1/4-inch-thick apple rings. Sprinkle rings with the lemon juice to prevent browning. Combine pancake mix and water; season with nutmeg. Place some paper towels or a brown paper sack on a work surface for draining fritters. Working in small batches of 5 to 6 slices, coat apple rings in batter and fry 2 to 3 minutes, until golden brown. Transfer to paper towels or paper sack to drain. When all the fritters are cooked, turn off oil and allow to cool before discarding.

Top fritters with confectioners' sugar (using a sifter or tea strainer) and transfer to a serving platter. ★

I learned of this fabulous, easy fruit fritter from my friend Rene. After I tried it out at home, she became my good friend Rene. Many thanks!

180

Try this Mother's Day favorite from my own sweet mom.

★ ★ ★ ★
MAKES 4 SERVINGS

Lamb Chops with Mint-Mustard Dipping Sauce

2 cloves garlic, smashed

2/3 cup extra-virgin olive oil (evoo) (eyeball it)

12 loin lamb chops, 1/2 to 3/4 inch thick

Salt and freshly ground black pepper, to taste

3 rounded tablespoons grainy mustard

2 tablespoons white wine vinegar (2 splashes)

1 tablespoon honey (a good drizzle)

1/4 cup mint leaves (a couple handfuls), reserve 4 leaves, for garnish

4 leaves radicchio lettuce

Preheat broiler to high.

Place garlic in a small saucepan, add evoo to cover and heat over low heat for 5 minutes, then remove garlic. Arrange lamb chops on a broiler pan. Drizzle 3 teaspoons garlic oil over the lamb, brushing to coat evenly. Season chops with salt and pepper and set aside.

To make the dipping sauce, place mustard, vinegar, and honey in a food processor or blender and, while processing or blending, stream in remaining garlic and oil. Turn the processor or blender off and add mint to the container. Pulse-grind to incorporate the mint leaves.

Broil lamb chops, 3 minutes on each side, then let them rest for up to 10 minutes, to allow the juices to redistribute. The lamb will be cooked to medium. Serve 3 chops per person with portions of dipping sauce and radicchio leaves set alongside the chops. Garnish with sprigs of mint. Tabouleh-Stuffed Tomatoes and White Beans with Thyme make wonderful side dishes. ★

30-MINUTE MEALS
MENU

MOTHER'S DAY MEAL FROM MOM

1
entree
LAMB CHOPS WITH MINT-MUSTARD DIPPING SAUCE

2
side dishes
TABOULEH-STUFFED TOMATOES

WARM WHITE BEANS WITH THYME

3
dessert
LIMONCELLO DESSERT

✪ ✪ ✪ ✪

MAKES 4 SERVINGS

Tabouleh-Stuffed Tomatoes

3/4 cup bulgur wheat (available in rice section)

1 cup boiling water

The juice of 2 lemons

1 cup chopped fresh flat-leaf parsley (1 bunch)

1/2 cup chopped mint leaves (1/2 bunch)

4 scallions, thinly sliced

1 plum tomato, seeded and diced

2 tablespoons extra-virgin olive oil (evoo) (twice around the bowl)

Salt and freshly ground black pepper, to taste

4 large vine-ripe tomatoes or beefsteak tomatoes

In a medium bowl, cover bulgur wheat (tabouleh) with boiling water and stir. Cover the bowl, place it in the refrigerator, and let stand 20 minutes to soften. Then add lemon juice, parsley, mint, scallions, and chopped plum tomato to the tabouleh and toss to combine. Dress the salad with evoo, salt, and pepper.

To serve, cut a large, ripe tomato into quarters, leaving the skin intact on the bottom so that the tomato resembles an open flower. Season with salt and pepper and pile a generous amount of tabouleh salad on top of the tomato, allowing the salad to spill down and over the wedges of tomato onto the plate. ★

✪ ✪ ✪ ✪

MAKES 4 SERVINGS

Warm White Beans with Thyme

3 tablespoons extra-virgin olive oil (evoo) (three times around the pan)

2 large cloves garlic, chopped

2 tablespoons fresh thyme leaves, chopped, plus 4 extra sprigs for garnish

1/2 cup shredded radicchio lettuce (1/2 head)

1 large can (1 pound, 13 ounces) white cannellini beans, drained well

Salt and freshly ground black pepper, to taste

In a medium skillet, heat evoo and garlic over medium heat, 2 minutes. Add thyme and radicchio and cook 1 minute longer. Add beans, and toss with radicchio and garlic to combine. Season with salt and pepper. Warm beans through, 2 minutes, then serve. Garnish with extra sprigs of fresh thyme. ★

✪ ✪ ✪ ✪
MAKES 4 SERVINGS

Limoncello Dessert

1 pint lemon sorbet

1 pint vanilla ice cream

4 shots Limoncello or any lemon liqueur

The grated zest of 1 lemon

Wafer cookies, for garnish

Place one scoop of lemon sorbet alongside a scoop of vanilla ice cream in each dessert cup or stemmed cocktail glass. Top each serving with 1 shot lemon liqueur and a sprinkle of grated lemon zest. Garnish with wafer cookies placed directly into the ice cream and sorbet scoops, then serve. ★

Limoncello is an Italian lemon liqueur available at any large liquor store.

30-MINUTE MEALS
MENU

**FRENCH
RESTAURANT
DINNER**

1

appetizer
ROQUEFORT,
PEAR, AND
WALNUT TOASTS

2

entree
CHICKEN
PAILLARD ON
BABY GREENS

3

drink
CITRUS WINE
SPRITZER

This meal can serve many or few. It is healthful, and the ingredients for the chicken paillard are items that you can always have on hand: prewashed mixed baby salad greens in a sack, individually portioned chicken cutlets stored in the freezer and quickly defrosted, flour and chicken broth to make the pan gravy.

✪ ✪ ✪ ✪
MAKES 4 SERVINGS

Roquefort, Pear, and Walnut Toasts

1 baguette, thinly sliced on an angle

A wedge of lemon

1 pear, quartered lengthwise and thinly sliced

3/4 pound Roquefort cheese, crumbled

1 cup walnut pieces

Preheat broiler to high.

Arrange 12 baguette slices on a broiler pan in a single layer. Toast lightly on each side. Squeeze lemon juice over the pear slices to keep them from browning. Place a slice of pear on each toast and top with Roquefort crumbles and walnut pieces. Return pan to broiler 6 inches from heat source and broil toasts 2 or 3 minutes to melt cheese and toast walnuts. Transfer to a plate and start snacking! ★

✪ ✪ ✪ ✪
MAKES 4 SERVINGS

Chicken Paillard on Baby Greens

8 chicken breast cutlets

2 tablespoons extra-virgin olive oil (evoo) (twice around the bowl), plus more for drizzling

4 sprigs fresh thyme, leaves stripped and chopped

2 tablespoons chopped fresh flat-leaf parsley (a palmful)

The juice and grated zest of 1 lemon

Coarse salt and freshly ground black pepper, to taste

2 tablespoons butter

2 tablespoons all-purpose flour

2 cups chicken broth

1 sack (5 ounces) mixed baby salad greens

Preheat a large nonstick skillet over medium-high heat. Arrange the chicken

Chicken Paillard

The paillard is my version of a favorite dish at Balthazar and Pastis restaurants in New York City, where I often enjoy brunch. While it's not quite the same thing as being there, you'll find it is just as delicious and much more economical to prepare in your own kitchen. As for the drinks, substitute white grape juice in place of the wine for a nonalcoholic or kid-friendly spritzer "mocktail."

in a shallow dish and drizzle with evoo to just coat the chicken, about 1 & 1/2 tablespoons total. Combine chopped herbs and lemon zest and sprinkle over the chicken. Season with salt and pepper. Using your hands, rub the chicken to coat evenly with the herbs and seasonings. (Wash hands with hot water and soap.) Using tongs, transfer chicken in a single layer to hot skillet and cook 3 or 4 minutes on each side. Remove cooked chicken to a warm serving dish and cover loosely with foil; repeat with remaining cutlets.

Return pan to heat and add butter. When the butter melts, add flour to the butter and cook, stirring with a whisk, 1 or 2 minutes to make a light roux. Whisk in chicken broth and when it thickens to just coat the back of a spoon, remove pan from heat and turn off burner.

Toss salad greens with lemon juice and coarse salt. Drizzle 2 tablespoons evoo around the bowl and retoss greens.

To serve, cover the bottom of a dinner plate with the warm sauce. Top with a small pile of salad greens and 2 grilled chicken cutlets. ★

✪ ✪ ✪ ✪
MAKES 4 SERVINGS

Citrus White Wine Spritzer

Ice
2 thin slices lemon
2 thin slices lime
4 ounces (1/2 cup) dry, crisp white wine, **such as Pinot Grigio**
2 ounces (1/4 cup) lemon–lime seltzer water

In a large stem glass, arrange slices of lemon and lime among ice cubes to fill the glass. Pour the white wine and lemon-lime seltzer down over fruit and ice. Stir with a straw and serve. ★

This dish makes great tailgate party food or a pot luck supper contribution.

✪ ✪ ✪ ✪

MAKES 4 SERVINGS

Beef and Cider Pot

2 tablespoons extra-virgin olive oil (evoo)

1 & 1/2 pounds beef sirloin, cut into bite-size cubes

Worcestershire sauce

Montreal Steak Seasoning by McCormick or coarse salt and freshly ground black pepper, to taste

2 medium white-skinned potatoes, thinly sliced

1 medium yellow onion, chopped

2 carrots, diced

1 turnip, peeled and diced

1/4 cup all-purpose flour (a couple handfuls)

1 & 1/2 cups apple cider

1 tablespoon cider vinegar or white vinegar

A handful chopped fresh flat-leaf parsley

1 cup shredded cheddar or smoked cheddar cheese

Pour 1 tablespoon evoo (once around the pan) into a deep, heavy skillet and heat over high heat. Add beef cubes to pot and brown, 3 to 5 minutes. Sprinkle with Worcestershire sauce and Montreal Seasoning or salt and pepper. Remove the meat and reduce heat a little, to medium-high.

Add another tablespoon evoo. Cover the bottom of the skillet with a layer of about half of the potatoes. Sprinkle with Montreal Seasoning or salt and black pepper. Brown the potatoes for 3 or 4 minutes on each side and remove. Add onions, carrots, and turnips to pan. Cook for 5 minutes. Sprinkle with flour and cook 1 minute. Add cider, vinegar, parsley, and beef cubes to pot. Combine ingredients well.

Preheat the broiler.

Lay remaining potatoes across the top of skillet and cover with lid or foil. Reduce heat to low and simmer for a few minutes, until veggies are all just tender. Uncover and sprinkle the potatoes with cheese. Place skillet under broiler to melt and brown cheese. Serve from the pot, along with crusty bread. ★

30-MINUTE MEALS
MENU

TAKE ALONG MEAL

1
entree
BEEF AND CIDER POT

2
suggested side
CRUSTY BREAD

✪ ✪ ✪ ✪

MAKES 4 SERVINGS

Herb and Goat Cheese Toasts

1 baguette, sliced

12 blades fresh chives

2 sprigs fresh rosemary, leaves stripped from stem

2 handfuls fresh flat-leaf parsley leaves

Coarse freshly ground black pepper, to taste

8 ounces fresh goat cheese

Arrange baguette slices on a cookie sheet or broiler pan. Toast under broiler until lightly golden on each side. Remove and arrange on a serving plate. Chop and combine fresh chives, rosemary, and parsley. Add coarse black pepper to the herb mixture, then roll goat cheese in the herbs to coat evenly. Set alongside toasts to serve, using a butter knife to spread herbed cheese on warm toasts. ★

✪ ✪ ✪ ✪

MAKES 4 SERVINGS

Grilled Balsamic Chicken Cutlets over Spinach Salad with Warm Shallot Vinaigrette

1 & 1/2 pounds (8 pieces) chicken breast cutlets (sometimes marked "thin cut")

2 tablespoons balsamic vinegar, enough to just coat the breast slices

3 tablespoons extra-virgin olive oil (evoo) (eyeball it)

Steak seasoning blend such as Montreal Seasoning by McCormick OR salt and freshly ground black pepper, to taste

4 sprigs fresh rosemary, leaves stripped and finely chopped

SPINACH SALAD

1 pound center-cut bacon, chopped into 1-inch pieces

1 pound fresh spinach leaves, trimmed and cleaned

8 gourmet white stuffing mushrooms, thinly sliced

8 radishes, thinly sliced

4 scallions, thinly sliced on an angle

Salt and freshly ground black pepper, to taste

DRESSING
2/3 cup extra-virgin olive oil (evoo) (eyeball it)
1 large shallot, minced
3 rounded teaspoonfuls Dijon mustard
3 tablespoons balsamic vinegar

Coat chicken with vinegar, evoo, seasonings, and rosemary and set aside.

Brown half the chopped bacon in a skillet over medium-high heat. Transfer the bits to a paper towel–lined plate to drain and repeat with the remaining bacon.

Coarsely chop spinach leaves and place in a salad bowl. Top with mushrooms, radishes, and scallions. Season with salt and pepper.
Preheat another large nonstick skillet over medium-high heat for the chicken. For the dressing, wipe out the bacon pan and return to stove over medium-low heat. Add evoo and shallots and sauté, 3 minutes. Remove from heat.

In a bowl, combine mustard and balsamic vinegar. Stream in shallot oil slowly while whisking the dressing to emulsify it. Pour warm dressing over spinach salad and toss to coat evenly. Add cooked bacon and toss again.

Brown chicken cutlets, 4 minutes on each side, in a single layer in the preheated nonstick skillet. Before serving, slice breasts on an angle. Then pile spinach salad onto dinner plates and top each salad with 2 sliced cutlets. ★

30-MINUTE MEALS
MENU

FAMILY-
STYLE
SUPPER

1
entree
RAVIOLI
VEGETABLE
"LASAGNA"

2
side dish
ROMAINE
HEARTS WITH
LEMON-CHIVE
VINAIGRETTE

3
dessert
FRESH ORANGES
WITH LIME
SORBET

I met a real working mom on a set for a TV commercial who shared a cooking secret. She told me that when she runs short of time, she layers red meat sauce with ravioli, like a lasagna, and adds lots of cheese on top. I thought, GREAT idea for a fast vegetable lasagna, too!

✪ ✪ ✪ ✪
MAKES 4 TO 6 SERVINGS

Ravioli Vegetable "Lasagna"

2 packages (12 ounces each) chopped frozen spinach, defrosted in microwave

2 tablespoons extra-virgin olive oil (evoo), plus a drizzle

4 to 6 cloves garlic, minced

2 cans (15 ounces each) quartered artichokes in water, drained well

Salt and freshly ground black pepper, to taste

2 tablespoons butter

2 tablespoons all-purpose flour

2 cups vegetable or chicken stock

1/2 cup cream or half-and-half

1/2 cup grated Parmigiano Reggiano cheese (a couple handfuls)

1/4 teaspoon freshly grated nutmeg

Salt and freshly ground black pepper, to taste

1 large package (24 to 28 ounces) fresh ravioli, such as Contadina brand, in your favorite filling, such as wild mushroom or 4-cheese

1 pound thin asparagus spears, trimmed of tough ends, cut on an angle into 2-inch pieces

2 cups shredded provolone or Italian 4-cheese blend

Put a large pot of water over high heat for the ravioli.

Meanwhile, drain defrosted frozen chopped spinach by wringing it dry in a kitchen towel, working over a garbage bowl or sink.

Heat a medium skillet over medium heat. Add 2 tablespoons evoo and the garlic and sauté 1 minute, then sprinkle spinach into the garlic oil. Add artichokes and turn to combine and heat through. Season with salt and pepper and remove from heat to a bowl. Place skillet back on the heat and melt butter. Whisk in flour and cook 1 to 2 minutes. Whisk in stock and let it bubble. Whisk in cream and Parmigiano cheese; season with nutmeg, salt, and pepper and thicken 1 to 2 minutes.

Preheat broiler to high. Set rack about 8 inches from heat.

When ravioli water boils, add salt, then ravioli and cook, 4 to 5 minutes. (Ravioli should be less than al dente, still a bit chewy; it will continue cooking when combined with sauce and vegetables.) Place a colander over ravioli as it cooks; add asparagus and cover. Steam the chopped asparagus while pasta cooks, 2 to 3 minutes, until just fork-tender, but still green.

Remove asparagus and add to bowl with spinach and artichokes. Place colander in sink and drain ravioli.

Drizzle a touch of evoo into the bottom of a medium-size oval casserole or a rectangular baking dish and brush to coat evenly. Arrange a layer of cooked ravioli, about 1/3 of the ravioli, in the dish. Layer half of the cooked vegetables over the ravioli. Next, add a few ladles of sauce, another layer of ravioli, then vegetables, then top casserole with the last of the ravioli. Dot top of "lasagna" with any remaining sauce and cover liberally with shredded provolone or 4-cheese blend. Brown in broiler, about 5 minutes, until cheese is golden and "lasagna" is heated through. ★

✪ ✪ ✪ ✪
MAKES 4 SERVINGS

Romaine Hearts with Lemon–Chive Vinaigrette

1/4 cup lemon curd
2 tablespoons white vinegar
10 blades chives, chopped or snipped
1/3 to 1/2 cup extra-virgin olive oil (evoo)
Salt and freshly ground black pepper, to taste
2 hearts romaine lettuce
1/2 pint grape tomatoes, for garnish

In a small bowl, heat lemon curd 15 seconds in microwave. Remove from microwave and whisk in vinegar. Allow mixture to cool 2 minutes, add chives, and whisk in evoo in a slow stream. Season with salt and pepper.

Quarter each heart of romaine lengthwise. Trim core at ends. Place 2 quarters on each salad plate. Halve a few grape tomatoes and place at plates' edges for garnish. Drizzle liberally with vinaigrette and serve. ★

✪ ✪ ✪ ✪
MAKES 4 SERVINGS

Fresh Oranges with Lime Sorbet

2 large naval oranges
1 pint lime, lemon, or other fruit sorbet

Trim a piece of skin off the top and bottom of each orange, then cut in half, across. Section each half as you would a grapefruit. Set oranges upright and top each half orange with sorbet. The halved, sectioned oranges double as the dessert bowls for sorbet. ★

Freshly grated nutmeg really complements the spinach in this "lasagna."

191

✪ ✪ ✪ ✪

MAKES 4 SERVINGS

Southwestern Stuffed Peppers

2 **cups** vegetable broth

1 **tablespoon** butter

1 **cup** white rice

2 **long** mild chile peppers, **red or green** (Italian cubanelle peppers may be substituted)

1 **tablespoon** extra-virgin olive oil (evoo) (once around the pan)

1 **small** onion, chopped

1 **cup frozen** peas

1 **cup mild or medium** taco sauce

Salt **and freshly ground black** pepper, **to taste**

2 **tablespoons chopped** cilantro **or fresh flat-leaf parsley, for garnish**

2 scallions, **thinly sliced, for garnish**

Preheat a grill pan over high heat.

Bring vegetable broth and butter to a boil in a small covered pot. Add rice, reduce heat to low, and cook, covered, until rice is tender and liquid absorbed, 18 to 20 minutes.

Split peppers lengthwise and remove seeds, leaving stems intact. Grill peppers on hot grill pan 3 to 5 minutes on each side. Remove from grill and let cool.

To a medium skillet over medium heat, add evoo and onion, and sauté 2 or 3 minutes. Add cooked rice to the pan and stir in peas and taco sauce. Season with salt and pepper.

Load up pepper halves with seasoned rice. Place on serving dish and top with chopped cilantro or parsley, and scallions. Pile any extra rice on serving plates, nesting the stuffed peppers within. ★

30-MINUTE MEALS

MENU

MEAT-FREE FIESTA MENU

1
appetizer
SOUTHWESTERN STUFFED PEPPERS

2
entree
WILD MUSHROOM QUESADILLAS WITH WARM BLACK BEAN SALSA

3
drink
FRESH STRAWBERRY MARG-ALRIGHTAS

Gently clean your
'shrooms. Clean
mushrooms with a
damp cloth. Do not
run fresh mushrooms
under water, they
will discolor and
toughen.

✪ ✪ ✪ ✪

MAKES 4 SERVINGS

Wild Mushroom Quesadillas with Warm Black Bean Salsa

2 tablespoons extra-virgin olive oil (evoo), plus some for drizzling

16 crimini mushroom caps (baby portobellos) with stems trimmed and thinly sliced or 4 portobello caps, halved and thinly sliced

16 shiitake mushrooms, stems removed and thinly sliced

Salt and coarse freshly ground black pepper, to taste

1 tablespoon fresh thyme, chopped, or 1 teaspoon dried

4 large (12-inch) flour tortillas

2 cups shredded sharp white cheddar cheese

SALSA

1 tablespoon extra-virgin olive oil (evoo) (once around the pan)

1 small onion, finely chopped

2 cloves garlic, minced

1 jalapeño pepper, seeded and chopped

1 can (15 ounces) black beans, drained

1 cup frozen corn kernels

1/2 cup sun-dried tomatoes in oil, chopped

1/2 cup smoky barbecue sauce

Salt and freshly ground black pepper, to taste

Heat a medium nonstick skillet over medium heat. Add 2 tablespoons evoo, then the sliced mushrooms. Season with salt, pepper, and thyme, and sauté until mushrooms are dark and tender, about 10 minutes. Remove from heat and transfer to a dish.

For the salsa, return skillet to the stove over medium heat, and add another turn of olive oil. Add the onions, garlic, and jalapeño pepper and sauté, 2 or 3 minutes, then add the beans and corn. Stir in sun-dried tomatoes and barbecue sauce. Season with salt and pepper, and transfer to a serving dish.

Heat a griddle pan or large nonstick skillet over medium to medium-high heat. Add a drizzle of evoo to the pan and 1 tortilla. Cook tortilla 1 minute, then turn it over. Sprinkle 1/2 cup sharp cheddar over half the tortilla. Cover the cheese with 1/4 of the cooked mushrooms. Fold the plain half of the tortilla over top of the filling and gently press down with a spatula. Cook the filled quesadilla 30 seconds to 1 minute longer on each side to lightly brown and crisp the outside and melt the cheese. Remove the quesadilla to a large cutting board or transfer to a warm oven to hold, then repeat the process for remaining quesadillas.

Cut each quesadilla into wedges and serve with warm salsa for topping. ★

✪ ✪ ✪ ✪
MAKES 4 SERVINGS

Fresh Strawberry Marg-alrightas

2 pints ripe strawberries

The juice of 4 limes

8 rounded tablespoons sugar

1/2 cup orange juice

8 shots good-quality tequila

2 trays of ice cubes

Coarse salt, to rim glasses

1 lime, cut into wedges, for garnish

Reserve 4 strawberries for garnish and split them, keeping their stems intact. Trim remaining strawberries.

To make one drink, add half a pint of strawberries to a blender. Add the juice of 1 lime, 2 rounded tablespoons sugar, a splash of orange juice, and 2 shots tequila. Fill the blender with half a tray of ice and blend on high speed until the drink is icy but smooth.

Rim a cocktail glass with lime juice and salt and scoop in the frozen strawberry-lime drink. Garnish glass with a wedge of lime and a split strawberry. Repeat with remaining ingredients. ★

30-MINUTE MEALS
MΣNU

MAKE IT SNAPPY

1
entree
RED SNAPPER
WITH OLIVE
SALSA

2
side dish
GREEN BEANS
WITH ALMONDS

2
drink
SUNSET
SANGRIA

✪ ✪ ✪ ✪
MAKES 4 SERVINGS

Red Snapper with Olive Salsa and Green Beans with Almonds

SALSA
3 plum tomatoes, seeded and chopped
A handful cilantro leaves, finely chopped (flat-leaf parsley may be substituted)
1/2 small red onion, chopped
12 large green olives, pitted or cracked away from pits with the flat of your knife, then coarsely chopped
The juice of 1 lime
1 teaspoon crushed red pepper flakes

GREEN BEANS
1 & 1/2 pounds fresh green beans, trimmed
1 tablespoon extra-virgin olive oil (evoo) (once around the pan)
1 tablespoon butter
Salt, to taste
Toasted slivered or sliced almonds, for garnish

RED SNAPPER
4 red snapper fillets (8 ounces each)
Extra-virgin olive oil (evoo), for drizzling
1 & 1/2 teaspoons ground cumin (1/3 palmful)
1 & 1/2 teaspoons sweet paprika (1/3 palmful)
1 teaspoon coarse salt
1 teaspoon freshly ground black pepper
1 teaspoon ground coriander

Combine salsa ingredients in a small bowl and allow flavors to combine until ready to serve.

Cook green beans in 1 inch of boiling, salted water, covered, for 5 minutes, then drain. They should be bright green and still crisp. Return pan to heat and toss beans with evoo and butter. Season with a little salt, transfer to a serving plate, and garnish with toasted almonds.

Preheat a grill pan, cast-iron skillet, or indoor electric grill to high heat.

Drizzle snapper with evoo. Combine spices in a small bowl, and rub fish with the mixture. Place fish on hot grill skin side down. After 3 minutes, turn and cook fish 3 to 4 minutes longer.

To serve, place green beans alongside spiced snapper topped with a generous serving of salsa. Sunset Sangria makes a wonderful beverage for this meal. ★

✪ ✪ ✪ ✪

MAKES 4 SERVINGS

Sunset Sangria

3 tablespoons sugar

3 tablespoons spiced dark rum

3 tablespoons orange liqueur, such as Cointreau

1 navel orange, sliced

1 lemon, sliced

2 ripe peaches, cut into wedges

3 ripe plums, cut into wedges

2 cinnamon sticks

1 bottle dry red wine, such as red Rioja

Sparkling soda water

Combine sugar, rum, orange liqueur, fruits, and cinnamon sticks in a large pitcher. Cover with wine and chill sangria several hours. To serve, spoon fruits into glasses or goblets. Pour in the sangria and top off with a splash of soda water. ★

This sangria takes 5 to 10 minutes to assemble in a large pitcher. Prepare it in the morning so it has several hours to develop its fruity flavors. Take it out when dinner is ready to serve that evening.

✪ ✪ ✪ ✪
MAKES 4 SERVINGS

Red Snapper Livornese

4 red snapper fillets (8 ounces each)
Salt and freshly ground black pepper, to taste
1 tablespoon extra-virgin olive oil (evoo) (once around the pan)

SAUCE
1 tablespoon extra-virgin olive oil (evoo) (once around the pan)
3 cloves garlic, minced
1 cup dry white wine
1 can (14 ounces) diced tomatoes in juice
1/4 cup chopped fresh flat-leaf parsley (a couple handfuls)

Heat a large nonstick skillet over medium-high heat. Score the snapper skins in a 1-inch crosshatch with a sharp knife. Season both sides of the fish with salt and pepper. Add evoo to skillet and cook skin side down until skin is crisp, 4 or 5 minutes. Turn fillets and cook on reverse side until fillets are firm and flesh is opaque, about 3 minutes. Transfer to a warm, shallow serving dish.

For the sauce, reduce heat under skillet to medium. Add evoo and garlic and sauté, 2 minutes. Add wine and reduce by half, about 2 minutes. Add tomatoes and parsley and simmer, 2 minutes more. Pour sauce over fish and serve. ★

✪ ✪ ✪ ✪
MAKES 4 SERVINGS

Penne with Parsley and Walnut Pesto

Salt and freshly ground black pepper, to taste
1 pound penne rigate (with lines) pasta
2 cloves garlic, cracked with the flat of a knife
1/2 cup extra-virgin olive oil (evoo) (eyeball it)
2 cups fresh flat-leaf parsley leaves
1/2 cup walnut pieces or 2/3 cup walnut halves, toasted
1/4 teaspoon ground or grated nutmeg
1/2 cup grated Parmigiano Reggiano cheese
1/3 pound fresh green beans, cut into thirds

Put a large pot of water over high heat for the pasta. When the water boils, add salt and penne.

While water is heating, place a small saucepan over medium heat and cook garlic in evoo, 5 minutes; remove pan from heat. Fill the food processor with parsley leaves, loosely packed. Add walnuts and 1/2 of the warm oil and both cloves of garlic to the parsley in the processor. Add nutmeg, salt, and pepper; set lid in place, and pulse-grind the mixture into a thick paste. Add any remaining parsley and pulse to combine. Transfer to a large pasta bowl. Stir in remaining oil and the cheese. Adjust seasonings to taste.

Cook penne to package directions for al dente, keeping an eye on the time. After about 6 minutes, add green beans to the pot to cook along with the pasta for the last 2 or 3 minutes. Drain pasta and beans together in a colander, then transfer to the pasta bowl with the pesto. Toss for 1 to 2 minutes to combine. Serve immediately. ★

✪ ✪ ✪ ✪
MAKES 4 SERVINGS

Cauliflower with Red, Green, and Black Confetti

1 head cauliflower, separated into bite-size florets

2 tablespoons extra-virgin olive oil (evoo) (twice around the pan)

3 to 4 large cloves garlic, chopped

4 anchovy fillets (optional)

1/2 teaspoon crushed red pepper flakes

1 jar (14 ounces) roasted red peppers, drained and diced into small bits

16 oil-cured olives, drained and chopped into small bits

1/2 cup fresh flat-leaf parsley, finely chopped

Salt and freshly ground black pepper, to taste

Cook cauliflower in 1 inch of boiling water, covered, until tender, 6 to 8 minutes. Drain and set cauliflower aside.

Return pan to stove. Set heat at medium and add evoo, garlic, anchovies (optional), and crushed red pepper flakes to the pan. Break up anchovies with the back of a wooden spoon until they melt into oil. Add roasted peppers, olives, and parsley and combine. Add cauliflower and toss to distribute the red, green, and black confetti. Season with salt and pepper and serve. ★

Another of my friend Vicky's creations! The anchovies are optional—unless you are dining with Vicky!

30-MINUTE MEALS
MENU

GROUP TOUR TO SPAIN

1

appetizer
SPANISH CHEESE AND OLIVES

2

entree
PAELLA FOR 8

3

drink
WHITE SANGRIA

✪ ✪ ✪ ✪
MAKES 8 SERVINGS

Spanish Cheese and Olives

1 package of your favorite crackers

1/2 pound assorted Spanish cheeses, such as Manchego, Cabrales Blue, and Mahon

4 ribs celery, halved lengthwise, cut into 4-inch sticks

1 pound Spanish green olives (available in specialty olives case near deli section) or other mixed olives

Arrange crackers, cheeses, celery sticks, and a dish of olives on a cutting board or large serving platter and set out for guests to snack on while dinner cooks. ★

✪ ✪ ✪ ✪
MAKES 8 SERVINGS

Paella for 8

3 tablespoons extra-virgin olive oil (evoo)

3 cloves garlic, crushed

1/2 to 1 teaspoon crushed red pepper flakes

2 cups enriched white rice

1/4 teaspoon saffron threads

1 bay leaf, fresh or dried

1 quart chicken broth

4 sprigs fresh thyme

1 & 1/2 pounds chicken tenders, cut into thirds

Salt and freshly ground black pepper, to taste

1 red bell pepper, seeded and chopped

1 medium onion, chopped

3/4 pound chorizo, casings removed (if preferred) and sliced on an angle

1 pound peeled and deveined large shrimp (about 24 shrimp)

18 mussels, cleaned (green-lipped, if available)

1 cup frozen peas

The grated zest of 2 lemons

1/4 cup chopped fresh flat-leaf parsley, for garnish

4 scallions, chopped, for garnish

Lemon wedges, for garnish

Crusty bread, for passing

A handful fresh flat-leaf parsley, finely chopped

1 lemon, wedged

Turn oven on low and rest a platter on an oven rack. Put a deep pot with a few inches water on high heat. When water boils, add salt and potatoes (water should just cover potatoes), and cook until potatoes are fork-tender, about 12 minutes.

Trim asparagus by holding an asparagus spear at each end, and bend to snap tip away from its tough end; cut remaining spears at about the place where the first one snapped; discard tough ends. After the potatoes have cooked about 6 minutes, place asparagus in a colander and rest colander on top of the potato pot, and cover. Potatoes will be just about done when the last of the trout is going into the skillet (see below). When the potatoes are tender, remove colander with asparagus and drain potatoes; return them to the warm pot. Leave asparagus covered, and set aside. Dress potatoes with chives, a drizzle of evoo, and a little salt. Leave in warm pot until trout is on the table, then transfer to a serving bowl.

While potatoes are cooking, heat a large skillet over medium heat. Combine egg and milk in a pie tin, and beat with a fork. Place a cup of flour in a second pie tin and season well with salt and sparingly with pepper. Coat trout fillets in egg and milk, then in seasoned flour. Collect fillets on a plate until all of them are dredged and ready to be cooked.

To the skillet add 1/2 tablespoon evoo (half a turn of the pan in a slow stream) and 1 & 1/2 tablespoons butter. When butter foams, add 4 trout fillets and gently sauté 2 or 3 minutes on each side, until golden. Transfer trout to warm platter in oven. Return pan to the stove and add remaining 1/2 tablespoon oil and 1 & 1/2 tablespoons butter, and sauté rest of trout. When all of the trout is cooked and added to serving platter, add last tablespoon of butter to the pan. When the butter melts, add almonds and brown until lightly golden, 1 to 2 minutes. Remove trout from oven and pour almonds over the platter. Garnish with chopped parsley, lemon wedges, and steamed asparagus spears. ★

✪ ✪ ✪ ✪
MAKES 4 SERVINGS

Dessert Cheeses and Fresh Fruits

Place rinsed grapes and pears on a cutting board with your favorite dessert cheeses and sweet biscuits for a simple, elegant end to your meal. I like slightly sweet whole wheat biscuits by Carr's crackers and St. André triple-crème cheese. Ask for help from the cheese counter specialist in your market; they'll let you taste your pick of cheeses. ★

Timing Tip:
Set a deep pot half full of water on the stove for your potatoes. It will come to a boil while you prepare the appetizer tray. When choosing your pâté, look in the specialty foods or deli case of your supermarket; choose country or mousse-style, any flavor. Ask for tastings! Enjoy this appetizer spreading the bread rounds with a slather of pâté topped with mushrooms. Ooh la la!

30-MINUTE MEALS
MENU

GROUP
TOUR TO
SPAIN

1

appetizer
**SPANISH CHEESE
AND OLIVES**

2

entree
PAELLA FOR 8

3

drink
WHITE SANGRIA

MAKES 8 SERVINGS

Spanish Cheese and Olives

1 package of your favorite crackers

1/2 pound assorted Spanish cheeses, such as Manchego, Cabrales Blue, and Mahon

4 ribs celery, halved lengthwise, cut into 4-inch sticks

1 pound Spanish green olives (available in specialty olives case near deli section) or other mixed olives

Arrange crackers, cheeses, celery sticks, and a dish of olives on a cutting board or large serving platter and set out for guests to snack on while dinner cooks. ★

✪ ✪ ✪ ✪

MAKES 8 SERVINGS

Paella for 8

3 tablespoons extra-virgin olive oil (evoo)

3 cloves garlic, crushed

1/2 to 1 teaspoon crushed red pepper flakes

2 cups enriched white rice

1/4 teaspoon saffron threads

1 bay leaf, fresh or dried

1 quart chicken broth

4 sprigs fresh thyme

1 & 1/2 pounds chicken tenders, cut into thirds

Salt and freshly ground black pepper, to taste

1 red bell pepper, seeded and chopped

1 medium onion, chopped

3/4 pound chorizo, casings removed (if preferred) and sliced on an angle

1 pound peeled and deveined large shrimp (about 24 shrimp)

18 mussels, cleaned (green-lipped, if available)

1 cup frozen peas

The grated zest of 2 lemons

1/4 cup chopped fresh flat-leaf parsley, for garnish

4 scallions, chopped, for garnish

Lemon wedges, for garnish

Crusty bread, for passing

202

While water is heating, place a small saucepan over medium heat and cook garlic in evoo, 5 minutes; remove pan from heat. Fill the food processor with parsley leaves, loosely packed. Add walnuts and 1/2 of the warm oil and both cloves of garlic to the parsley in the processor. Add nutmeg, salt, and pepper; set lid in place, and pulse-grind the mixture into a thick paste. Add any remaining parsley and pulse to combine. Transfer to a large pasta bowl. Stir in remaining oil and the cheese. Adjust seasonings to taste.

Cook penne to package directions for al dente, keeping an eye on the time. After about 6 minutes, add green beans to the pot to cook along with the pasta for the last 2 or 3 minutes. Drain pasta and beans together in a colander, then transfer to the pasta bowl with the pesto. Toss for 1 to 2 minutes to combine. Serve immediately. ★

✪ ✪ ✪ ✪
MAKES 4 SERVINGS

Cauliflower with Red, Green, and Black Confetti

1 head cauliflower, separated into bite-size florets

2 tablespoons extra-virgin olive oil (evoo) (twice around the pan)

3 to 4 large cloves garlic, chopped

4 anchovy fillets (optional)

1/2 teaspoon crushed red pepper flakes

1 jar (14 ounces) roasted red peppers, drained and diced into small bits

16 oil-cured olives, drained and chopped into small bits

1/2 cup fresh flat-leaf parsley, finely chopped

Salt and freshly ground black pepper, to taste

Cook cauliflower in 1 inch of boiling water, covered, until tender, 6 to 8 minutes. Drain and set cauliflower aside.

Return pan to stove. Set heat at medium and add evoo, garlic, anchovies (optional), and crushed red pepper flakes to the pan. Break up anchovies with the back of a wooden spoon until they melt into oil. Add roasted peppers, olives, and parsley and combine. Add cauliflower and toss to distribute the red, green, and black confetti. Season with salt and pepper and serve. ★

Another of my friend Vicky's creations! The anchovies are optional—unless you are dining with Vicky!

199

30-MINUTE MEALS

MENU

PASSPORT TO FRANCE

1

appetizer
MUSHROOM DUXELLES AND PÂTÉ PLATTER WITH SLICED BAGUETTE

1

entree
TROUT AMANDINE

2

side dishes
STEAMED ASPARAGUS

NEW POTATOES

3

dessert
DESSERT CHEESES AND FRESH FRUITS

✪ ✪ ✪ ✪
MAKES 4 SERVINGS

Mushroom Duxelles and Pâté Platter with Sliced Baguette

1/2 pound crimini mushrooms, coarsely chopped
1 tablespoon extra-virgin olive oil (evoo) (once around the pan)
1 tablespoon butter
1 large shallot, finely chopped
1/2 teaspoon ground thyme
Salt and freshly ground black pepper, to taste
1/2 cup dry sherry
8 ounces pâté
1 baguette, sliced at bread counter
Cornichons
Capers
Chopped fresh flat-leaf parsley, for garnish

Heat a skillet over medium heat. Finely chop mushrooms in a food processor. Add evoo and butter to the skillet, then shallots and mushroom bits. Season with ground thyme, salt, and pepper, and sauté until mushrooms are deep brown, about 6 minutes. Deglaze pan with sherry, scraping up browned bits with a wooden spoon. Transfer mushroom duxelles to a small serving dish, and place on a platter alongside pâté and sliced baguette. Garnish tray with cornichons, capers, and a sprinkle of chopped parsley. ★

✪ ✪ ✪ ✪
MAKES 4 SERVINGS

Trout Amandine, Steamed Asparagus, and New Potatoes

Salt and freshly ground black pepper, to taste
2 pounds small red-skinned potatoes, quartered
1 & 1/4 pounds thin asparagus spears
10 blades fresh chives, snipped or chopped
1 tablespoon extra-virgin olive oil (evoo), plus a drizzle
8 trout fillets (4 to 6 ounces each), lake or rainbow
1 egg
1 cup milk
1 cup all-purpose flour
4 tablespoons (1/2 stick) butter
1 cup (about 6 ounces) whole blanched almonds

Paella for 8

Preheat a very wide skillet or paella pan over medium-high heat. Add 2 tablespoons evoo (twice around the pan), garlic, red pepper flakes, and rice and sauté, 2 or 3 minutes. Add saffron, bay leaf, broth, and thyme and bring to a boil over high heat. Cover with lid or foil and reduce heat to simmer. In a separate nonstick skillet, over medium-high heat, add remaining 1 tablespoon evoo and brown chicken on both sides. Season chicken with salt and pepper. Add red bell pepper and onions to the pan and cook 3 minutes. Add chorizo and cook 2 minutes. Remove pan from heat.

When rice has cooked about 13 minutes, add shrimp and mussels to the paella pan, nesting them in the cooking rice. Pour in peas, scatter lemon zest over the rice and seafood, then cover the pan again. Cook 5 minutes, uncover, and discard any unopened mussels. Stir rice and seafood and lift out bay leaf and thyme stems, now bare of their leaves. Arrange cooked chicken, peppers, onions and chorizo around the paella pan. Sprinkle with parsley and scallions and serve with wedges of lemon and warm bread. ★

✪ ✪ ✪ ✪
MAKES 8 SERVINGS

White Sangria

3 tablespoons sugar

3 shots apple liqueur, such as Calvados

1 lime, sliced

1 lemon, sliced

2 ripe peaches, pitted and cut into wedges

3 ripe green apples, cored and cut into wedges

1 bottle dry white Spanish wine, such as white Rioja

1 pint raspberries

Sparkling soda water, for topping off sangria at table

Combine sugar, apple liqueur, lime, lemon, peaches, and apples in a large pitcher. Cover with wine and chill sangria at least several hours. To serve, spoon fruits into glasses or goblets, adding a few fresh raspberries to each glass. Pour sangria over top of the fruit, topping glasses off with a splash of soda water. ★

For deep fruit flavor, take 5 minutes to prepare sangria in the morning for serving later in the day.

✪ ✪ ✪ ✪

MAKES 6 SERVINGS

Elsa's Sliced Roast Salmon

SALMON SAUCE

1 cup sour cream or reduced-fat sour cream

2 tablespoons tarragon vinegar or white wine vinegar

A few sprigs fresh dill, leaves stripped and chopped

A few blades fresh chives, chopped

A few sprigs fresh tarragon, leaves stripped and chopped

1 tablespoon capers, smashed with side of knife

SALMON

1 whole side of fresh Atlantic salmon, 2 & 1/2 to 3 pounds

Coarse salt, to taste

The juice of 1 lime

8 tablespoons (1 stick) butter, melted

Vegetable oil, for pan

1 English seedless cucumber, peeled and thinly sliced, for serving

12 slices pumpernickel bread, quartered, or 2 loaves cocktail-size sliced pumpernickel, for serving

Combine all ingredients for sauce in a bowl. Transfer to serving dish; cover. Chill for up to 48 hours prior to party.

Cover bottom rack of oven with aluminum foil. Preheat oven to 400°F.

Rinse salmon and pat dry with paper towels. Sprinkle with coarse salt. Place salmon flesh side up in the middle of a carving board. With a very sharp carving or fillet knife, beginning at the tail end, slice salmon into 1/4-inch-thick slices at a steep angle, stopping each cut at skin. Do not cut through the skin, only to the skin. Flip carved meat over to the right as you slice, creating a fanlike effect.

Squeeze lime juice into melted butter; stir to combine. Brush fish with mixture, allowing it to seep in and around the slices.

Turn a cookie sheet upside down. Oil flat surface of pan and carefully place fish on it. You need a pan with no lip whatsoever so that you can slide fish onto a serving platter or board without breaking once it's cooked. The foil-covered rack below will catch the runoff.

Roast salmon on middle rack until fish is firm and opaque (an instant-read thermometer should read 120°F), 8 to 10 minutes.

Remove from oven and let cool. Carefully slide fish onto a platter or board. Serve at room temperature with sauce, sliced cucumbers, and bread for sandwich-making. Cake servers or small spatulas make good utensils for serving fish. Small spatulas allow guests to lift salmon slices away from skin with ease. Serve with tomato and onion salad on the side. ★

30-MINUTE MEALS

MENU

COMPANY'S COMING

1

entree
ELSA'S SLICED
ROAST SALMON

2

suggested side
TOMATO AND
ONION SALAD

NIGHT ON THE TOWN

1

entree
DELMONICO STEAKS WITH BALSAMIC ONIONS AND STEAK SAUCE

2

side dishes
OVEN STEAK FRIES

BLUE CHEESE AND WALNUT SPINACH SALAD WITH MAPLE DRESSING

✪ ✪ ✪ ✪

MAKES 4 SERVINGS

Delmonico Steaks with Balsamic Onions and Steak Sauce

2 teaspoons extra-virgin olive oil (evoo)

4 Delmonico steaks (10 to 12 ounces each), 1 inch thick

Steak seasoning blend such as Montreal Seasoning by McCormick OR salt and freshly ground black pepper, to taste

ONIONS

1 tablespoon extra-virgin olive oil (evoo) (once around the pan)

2 large yellow onions, thinly sliced

1/4 cup balsamic vinegar (eyeball it)

STEAK SAUCE

1 & 1/2 teaspoons extra-virgin olive oil (evoo) (half a turn around the pan)

2 cloves garlic, chopped

1 small white boiling onion, chopped

1/4 cup dry cooking sherry (eyeball it)

1 cup canned tomato sauce

1 tablespoon Worcestershire sauce (eyeball it)

Freshly ground black pepper, to taste

Heat a heavy grill pan or griddle pan over high heat, and wipe it with evoo. Cook steaks 4 minutes on each side for medium, 7 to 8 minutes for medium-well. Season with steak seasoning or salt and pepper and remove to a warm platter.

For the onions: Heat a medium nonstick skillet over medium-high heat. Add evoo and onions and cook, stirring occasionally until onions are soft and sweet, 10 to 12 minutes. Add balsamic vinegar and turn onions until vinegar cooks away and glazes onions a deep brown, 3 to 5 minutes.

For the steak sauce: Heat a small saucepan over medium heat. Add evoo, garlic, and white onions and sauté until tender, 5 minutes. Add sherry and combine with onions. Stir in tomato sauce and Worcestershire and season with black pepper.

To serve, top steaks with onions and drizzle a little steak sauce down over the top, reserving half to pass at table. ★

Guaranteed to
please any guest!

✪ ✪ ✪ ✪
MAKES 4 SERVINGS

Oven Steak Fries

5 russet potatoes, with skins, cut into thin wedges

3 tablespoons extra-virgin olive oil (evoo)

1 teaspoon dried thyme (eyeball it)

1 teaspoon dried oregano (eyeball it)

1 tablespoon steak seasoning blend such as Montreal Seasoning by
    McCormick or salt and freshly ground black pepper, to taste

Preheat oven to 500°F.

Spread potato wedges out on a cookie sheet. Coat potatoes with evoo,
thyme, oregano, and steak seasoning or salt and pepper. Spread potatoes
to the corners of the cookie sheet and cook 25 minutes, turning them once,
halfway through. Serve fries hot from the oven. ★

✪ ✪ ✪ ✪
MAKES 4 SERVINGS

Blue Cheese and Walnut Spinach Salad with Maple Dressing

1 sack (10 ounces) baby spinach

1/3 pound blue cheese, crumbled

1 can (6 ounces) walnut halves, toasted

1/4 cup maple syrup, warmed

1 & 1/2 tablespoons cider vinegar

1/4 cup extra-virgin olive oil (evoo)

Salt and freshly ground black pepper, to taste

Place spinach on a large platter. Top with blue cheese and walnuts. Warm
maple syrup in a small saucepan. Pour vinegar into a small bowl. Whisk
evoo into vinegar in a slow stream, then whisk in maple syrup slowly. Pour
dressing over the salad and serve. Season with salt and pepper.★

30-MINUTE MEALS
MENU

GET
STUFFED

1

entree
SPINACH AND
MUSHROOM
STUFFED
CHICKEN
BREASTS

2

side dish
SPAGHETTI WITH
ZUCCHINI AND
GARLIC

✪ ✪ ✪ ✪
MAKES 4 SERVINGS

Spinach and Mushroom Stuffed Chicken Breasts

4 boneless, skinless chicken breasts (6 ounces each)

Large plastic food storage bags or waxed paper

1 package (10 ounces) frozen chopped spinach, defrosted (in microwave)

2 tablespoons butter

12 small mushroom caps, crimini or white

2 cloves garlic, cracked with the flat of a knife

1 small shallot, quartered

Salt and freshly ground black pepper, to taste

1 cup part-skim ricotta cheese

1/2 cup grated Parmigiano Reggiano or Romano cheese (a couple handfuls)

1/2 teaspoon freshly grated or ground nutmeg

Toothpicks

3 tablespoons extra-virgin olive oil (evoo) (three times around the pan)

SAUCE
2 tablespoons butter

2 tablespoons all-purpose flour

1/2 cup white wine

1 cup chicken broth

Place chicken in a plastic food storage bag or between 2 large sheets of waxed paper. Pound the chicken from the center outward using a heavy-bottomed skillet or mallet.

Place spinach in a kitchen towel and wring it out until very dry. Transfer to a medium mixing bowl.

Place a nonstick skillet over medium heat. When skillet is hot, add butter, mushrooms, garlic, and shallot. Season with salt and pepper and sauté, 5 minutes. Transfer to a food processor. Pulse-grind the mushrooms and add to the spinach in the mixing bowl. Add ricotta, grated cheese, and nutmeg to the bowl and stir to combine.

Return skillet to the stove over medium-high heat. Place a mound of stuffing on each chicken breast and roll breast over the stuffing. Secure with toothpicks. Add 3 tablespoons evoo to the pan, add breasts, and brown on all sides, 10 to 12 minutes. The meat will cook quickly because it is thin. Remove stuffed chicken to a warm platter.

To make the sauce, add butter and flour to the pan and cook for 1 minute, then whisk in wine and cook to reduce, 1 minute. Whisk in broth and return chicken to the pan. Reduce heat and simmer until ready to serve. Serve the stuffed chicken breasts whole, or slice on an angle and fan out on dinner plates. Top with generous spoonfuls of the sauce. ★

✪ ✪ ✪ ✪

MAKES 4 SERVINGS

Spaghetti with Zucchini and Garlic

Salt and freshly ground black pepper, to taste

1 pound spaghetti

2 small to medium zucchini

1/4 cup extra-virgin olive oil (evoo) (4 times around the pan)

4 cloves garlic, minced

1/2 cup grated Parmigiano Reggiano or Romano cheese

Put a large pot of water over high heat for the pasta. When water boils, add salt and spaghetti. Cook according to package directions to al dente.

Meanwhile, pile up 2 or 3 layers of paper towels on a work surface. Using a box grater, hold the zucchini at an angle and shred onto the towels.

Heat a large skillet over medium heat. Add the evoo, then the garlic. When garlic sizzles, add shredded zucchini and season with salt and pepper. Sauté, 7 to 10 minutes. Add hot, drained pasta to the pan, and toss with zucchini. Add a couple of handfuls of grated cheese. Adjust seasonings and serve. ★

I am not much for gadgets and tools. My food processor is my most exotic kitchen accessory, and I only started using one in the late '90s! I am a kitchen minimalist by practice and of necessity. I have a tiny kitchen in my cabin in the woods. Tiny kitchens have tiny cabinets. No room for clutter.

As you bite into the burgers, you will find a smoky, cheesy surprise inside.

✪ ✪ ✪ ✪
MAKES 6 SERVINGS

Outside-In Bacon Cheeseburgers with Scallion Mayo

6 slices bacon, chopped
4 scallions, cleaned and trimmed
Extra-virgin olive oil (evoo), for drizzling
1 & 3/4 pounds ground beef sirloin
1 & 1/2 tablespoons Worcestershire sauce (eyeball it)
1 & 1/2 tablespoons steak seasoning blend, such as Montreal by McCormick OR coarse salt and freshly ground black pepper
3/4 pound extra-sharp white cheddar cheese, crumbled
1 cup mayonnaise or reduced-fat mayonnaise
1 teaspoon ground cumin
Salt and freshly ground black pepper, to taste
6 crusty Kaiser rolls, split
6 leaves crisp romaine lettuce

Preheat a grill pan over high heat.

In a medium pan over medium-high heat, brown bacon and drain on a paper towel-lined plate.

Brush scallions with a little evoo and grill on hot grill pan 2 or 3 minutes on each side. Remove from heat to cool.

Make the burgers: Combine ground beef with Worcestershire and steak seasoning or salt and pepper. Divide meat into 6 equal parts. Combine cheese crumbles and cooked bacon. Take a portion of the ground meat in your hand and make a well in the center of it. Pile in cheese and bacon, then carefully form the burger around the cheese and bacon filling. Make sure the fillings are completely covered with meat. When all 6 large patties are formed, drizzle burgers with evoo and place on hot grill pan. Cook 2 minutes on each side over high heat, reduce heat to medium-low and cook burgers 7 or 8 minutes longer, turning occasionally. Do not press down on burgers. Transfer to a plate and let them rest 5 minutes before serving.

Make the mayonnaise: Chop cooled, grilled scallions and place in a food processor. Add mayonnaise and cumin and pulse-grind to combine. Season with salt and pepper.

Place burgers on buns and top with crisp lettuce leaves and a slather of scallion mayonnaise. ★

Outside-In Bacon Cheeseburgers

At Peter Luger's Steak House in Brooklyn, you can order sliced beefsteak tomatoes and thick-cut Vidalia onions. Then you can pour Luger Sauce all over everything—including this salad. This recipe is a quick salad dressing that tastes like tangy steak sauce. Try it on this salad or your next steak!

✪ ✪ ✪ ✪

MAKES 6 SERVINGS

Beefsteak Tomato and Vidalia Onion Salad with Steak Sauce Dressing

1/4 cup red wine vinegar (eyeball it)

3 rounded tablespoons brown sugar

1 tablespoon Worcestershire sauce (eyeball it)

1 teaspoon freshly ground black pepper (eyeball it)

1 cup canned tomato sauce

2 tablespoons extra-virgin olive oil (evoo) (eyeball it)

4 beefsteak tomatoes, sliced 1/2 inch thick

1 large Vidalia onion, peeled and sliced across, 1/2 inch thick

Salt, to taste

3 tablespoons chopped parsley, for garnish

Make the dressing: In a small saucepan over medium heat, combine vinegar, brown sugar, Worcestershire, and pepper. Allow sugar to dissolve in vinegar and liquids to come to a bubble. Remove sauce from heat and whisk in tomato sauce, then evoo. Serve warm or chilled.

Arrange sliced tomatoes and onions on a serving platter. Season with salt. Pour dressing over salad and garnish with chopped parsley. ★

✪ ✪ ✪ ✪

MAKES 24 COOKIES

Kahlúa Chocolate Chunk Cookies

1 package (17 & 1/2 ounces) dry chocolate chip cookie mix (found on baking aisle)

7 tablespoons butter, softened

1 large egg, beaten

1/4 cup coffee liqueur, such as Kahlúa

3 tablespoons instant espresso powder or instant coffee crystals

1 tablespoon ground coffee beans

1 cup bittersweet chocolate chunks, such as Ghirardelli brand

4 ounces broken walnut pieces

Preheat oven to 375°F.

Place racks in center of oven. Pour cookie mix into a mixing bowl and make a well in the center. Add softened butter, egg, Kahlúa, instant espresso, ground coffee, chocolate chunks, and walnuts. Mix well to combine all ingredients into cookie dough. Using a small scoop or a heaping teaspoon, drop cookies 2 inches apart on an ungreased nonstick cookie sheet or sheets. Bake cookies in batches until crisp and browned at edges, 9 to 11 minutes. Transfer to a wire rack to cool. ★

✪ ✪ ✪ ✪

MAKES 8 SERVINGS

Smoked Salmon Rounds

4 slices pumpernickel bread
2 tablespoons chopped or snipped fresh chives
4 ounces (half a brick) cream cheese, softened
1/2 pound smoked salmon, thinly sliced
2 ounces (1 small jar) salmon roe (optional)
3 tablespoons fresh dill (a handful)

Lightly toast bread slices. Using a shot glass, a spice jar cap, or other round shape, cut 4 rounds out of each bread slice to make 16 rounds total.

Mix chives into softened cream cheese. Spread cream cheese on bread rounds in a thin layer. Top each round with a slice of smoked salmon; pile it like a ribbon or roll the slice. Garnish salmon rounds with a dot of salmon roe, if desired, and a sprig of dill. Arrange rounds on a plate. ★

✪ ✪ ✪ ✪

MAKES 8 SERVINGS

Tea Party Club Sandwiches

12 slices white sandwich bread
3/4 cup (1 & 1/2 sticks) unsalted butter, softened
10 to 12 sprigs tarragon, leaves stripped and chopped
1/2 English (seedless) cucumber, very thinly sliced
1 bunch watercress, leaves stripped (1 & 1/2 cups)
4 plum tomatoes, very thinly sliced
Salt and freshly ground black pepper, to taste

Trim crusts off of the bread. Mix butter and tarragon with a rubber spatula. Spread tarragon butter on one side of all 12 slices of bread.

On 4 buttered slices, arrange cucumber slices and watercress in thin layers. Top with 4 slices bread, buttered side down. Butter the tops of the 4 completed single-layer sandwiches. Top butter with a layer of sliced tomatoes and season tomatoes with salt and pepper. Complete club sandwiches by setting the remaining 4 slices of bread, buttered side down, on top.

Cut each sandwich twice, corner to corner, making 16 triangles. Arrange on a serving plate. ★

✪ ✪ ✪ ✪

MAKES 16 SCONES

Quick Cream-Currant-Cranberry Scones and Devonshire-ish Cream

SCONES
2 packages (7.5 ounces each) complete biscuit mix, such as Bisquick (3 cups total)

1 cup light cream or half-and-half

1/2 teaspoon grated or ground nutmeg (eyeball it)

1/3 cup currants (2 handfuls)

1/2 cup dried sweetened cranberries, such as Craisins by Ocean Spray

1/3 cup sugar

4 tablespoons (1/2 stick) butter, melted, for brushing

CREAM
1 brick (8 ounces) cream cheese, softened

1 teaspoon vanilla

1/4 cup sugar

1/4 cup sour cream

1/4 cup light cream or half-and-half

1 small package edible flowers (available in fresh herbs section of produce department in larger markets) (optional)

Preheat oven to 450°F.

For the scones, mix biscuit mix, cream, nutmeg, currants, cranberries, and sugar in a medium bowl. Drop 8 scones each onto 2 nonstick or greased cookie sheets in 2 & 1/2-inch mounds. Brush with melted butter and bake until lightly golden all over, 8 to 11 minutes.

For the Devonshire-ish Cream, beat cream cheese, vanilla, sugar, sour cream, and light cream together in a medium bowl with a hand mixer. Beat in torn bits of edible flowers, if desired. Transfer to a serving dish. Garnish with additional edible flowers, if desired. Serve scones with cream alongside for spreading. ★

Optional accompaniments: Lemon curd (available on jam and preserves aisle) and fresh strawberries.

Every person I know with an Italian woman in their family tree—mamma, zia, or nona—remembers this dish from childhood as being their favorite. Chicken, potatoes, rosemary: simple food that has filled the stomachs and fed the souls of countless children for generations. Hot peppers may be omitted. Use 1 cup white wine, rather than pepper juice, to deglaze pan. Try this recipe on a night when you have more than 30 minutes to spare.

✪ ✪ ✪ ✪

MAKES 9 TO 10 SERVINGS

Chicken in the Oven

Extra-virgin olive oil (evoo), for drizzling

24 small white- or red-skinned potatoes

Coarse salt and freshly ground black pepper, to taste

1 bunch (8 to 10 sprigs) rosemary, leaves stripped from stem and finely chopped

8 jarred, pickled hot cherry peppers, thinly sliced

16 cloves garlic, crushed and popped from skin

4 chickens (2 & 1/2 to 3 pounds each), split into halves by butcher

1 cup juice from jarred, pickled hot cherry peppers

Preheat oven to 350°F.

Coat the bottom of two roasting pans with evoo. Cut potatoes into wedges and add to pans in single layers. Drizzle potatoes with enough oil to coat them, then season with salt and pepper and a little of the chopped rosemary. Sprinkle peppers and half of the garlic (8 cloves) on top of the potatoes.

Rinse chickens and pat dry. Make a paste on your cutting board by mincing the remaining garlic with rosemary, salt, and pepper. Rub the paste all over the chickens, top and bottom. Place birds, skin side up, on top of the potatoes. Cover pans with aluminum foil and place in oven.

Roast, basting occasionally with pan juices, until a meat thermometer in chicken reads 165°F, or until juices run completely clear when skin is pricked at thickest part of thigh, and potatoes are tender. Roasting time will be about 1 hour. Remove pans from oven and turn oven up to 400°F. Uncover and drizzle pepper juice over chicken. Return to oven to darken and crisp chicken skin, 12 to 15 minutes.

Serve with a big tossed salad and lots of crusty bread. ★

PARTIES

30-MINUTE MEALS
MENU

CHILDHOOD FAVORITE

1
entree
CHICKEN IN THE OVEN

2
suggested sides
GREEN SALAD AND CRUSTY BREAD

217

✪ ✪ ✪ ✪
MAKES 4 SERVINGS

Pâté and Toast with Accessories

4 slices whole-grain or dark bread, toasted
1/2 pound mousse pâté, any variety
1 large shallot, very thinly sliced
3 tablespoons capers
1 jar (12 ounces) cornichons or baby gherkin pickles

Spread each slice of toast liberally with mousse pâté. Cut each toast diagonally into 4 triangles. Top each triangle with sliced shallots and capers. Arrange toasts on a serving plate with cornichons or baby gherkins. ★

✪ ✪ ✪ ✪
MAKES 4 SERVINGS

Roasted Butterflied Cornish Hens

4 Cornish hens, butterflied by butcher
Salt and freshly ground black pepper, to taste
4 or 5 sprigs fresh rosemary, leaves stripped and chopped
3 tablespoons fresh thyme, chopped
3 tablespoons extra-virgin olive oil (evoo)

Evenly space 2 racks in oven and preheat to 500°F.

Place birds in a large bowl and coat with salt, pepper, herbs, and evoo. Arrange the birds on 2 shallow baking trays, breast side down. Roast birds 10 minutes. Reduce heat to 400°F, flip the birds, and roast 15 minutes longer. Remove from oven, fold birds over and serve 1 per person. ★

✪ ✪ ✪ ✪
MAKES 4 SERVINGS

White and Wild Rice with Chives

2 cups chicken broth
3 tablespoons wild rice
1 cup enriched white rice
2 tablespoons butter
3 tablespoons chopped chives

Place broth in a saucepan with a tight-fitting lid and bring to a boil. Add wild and white rice and butter. Return broth to a boil and cover; reduce heat to medium-low. Simmer rice until tender, 20 minutes. Add chives and fluff rice with a fork, then serve. ★

218

✪ ✪ ✪ ✪
MAKES 4 SERVINGS

Broccoli Florets with Red Bell Peppers

1 pound broccoli florets (available in ready-to-cook bags in produce department)

2 tablespoons extra-virgin olive oil (evoo) (twice around the pan)

1 red bell pepper, seeded, quartered lengthwise, then thinly sliced

Salt and freshly ground black pepper, to taste

Place 1 inch water in a skillet and bring to a simmer. Add broccoli florets and cover. Simmer 3 minutes. Drain broccoli and remove from skillet. Return pan to the stovetop over medium heat. Add evoo to the pan and sauté sliced red bell peppers, 2 or 3 minutes. Add the broccoli back to the pan and toss to combine with peppers. Season with salt and pepper to taste, then remove from heat and serve. ★

✪ ✪ ✪ ✪
MAKES 4 SERVINGS

Nutkins (Frozen Drinks with Ice Cream and Nut-Flavored Liqueurs)

2 ounces Frangelico hazelnut liqueur

2 pints vanilla ice cream

6 ounces (4 shots) Amaretto di Sorrona

1 pint half-and-half

8 ice cubes

Nutmeg, freshly grated or ground, for garnish

In a blender combine 1 ounce Frangelico (just over half a shot), 4 scoops ice cream, 3 ounces (2 shots) Amaretto, 1 cup half-and-half, and 4 ice cubes. Blend until smooth. Pour into 2 large cocktail glasses, garnish with a sprinkle of freshly grated or ground nutmeg, and repeat with remaining ingredients. ★

✪ ✪ ✪ ✪
MAKES 10 SERVINGS

Select Soft Cheese Board

2 tins (10 ounces each) smoked almonds
1/2-pound wedge brie with herbs
1/2-pound wedge Saga blue cheese
1 log (6 ounces) goat cheese, any variety
1 baguette, sliced at bakery counter
1 package assorted crackers, such as Carr's
1 pound grapes, black, red, or green, separated into small bunches

Pour nuts into a large brandy snifter and set on cheese board. Arrange cheeses with baguette slices and crackers. Decorate with clusters of grapes. Place a few spreaders near cheeses and set out where guests will gather. ★

✪ ✪ ✪ ✪
MAKES 10 SERVINGS

Balsamic Pork Tenderloins

4 & 1/2 pounds pork tenderloin (2 packages with 2 tenderloins each)
Balsamic vinegar, for drizzling (about 3 tablespoons)
Extra-virgin olive oil (evoo), for drizzling
8 cloves garlic, cracked with the flat of a knife
Steak seasoning blend such as Montreal Seasoning by McCormick OR
    coarse salt and freshly ground black pepper, to taste
4 sprigs fresh rosemary, leaves stripped and finely chopped
4 sprigs fresh thyme, leaves stripped and finely chopped

Preheat oven to 500°F.

Trim silver skin or connective tissue off tenderloins with a thin, very sharp knife. Place tenderloins on a nonstick cookie sheet with a rim. Coat tenderloins with a few tablespoons balsamic vinegar, rubbing vinegar into meat. Drizzle tenderloins with evoo, just enough to coat. Cut small slits into meat and disperse chunks of cracked garlic cloves into meat. Combine steak seasoning blend or coarse salt and pepper with rosemary and thyme and rub meat with blend. Roast in hot oven 20 to 25 minutes. Let meat rest, transfer to a carving board, slice, and serve. ★

✪ ✪ ✪ ✪
MAKES 10 SERVINGS

Roasted Ratatouille Vegetables

1 large red bell pepper, seeded and cut lengthwise into 1-inch strips

1 medium onion, sliced

1 medium eggplant, sliced into 1/2-inch pieces, slices piled and quartered

1 zucchini, sliced 1/2 inch thick

4 plum tomatoes, seeded and quartered lengthwise

6 cloves garlic, crushed

Extra-virgin olive oil (evoo), to coat

4 sprigs fresh rosemary, leaves stripped and chopped

Coarse salt and freshly ground black pepper, to taste

Preheat oven to 500°F.

Working on a cookie sheet, combine vegetables and garlic. Drizzle liberally with evoo and season with rosemary, salt, and pepper. Toss to coat vegetables evenly. Roast until just tender, 15 minutes. Transfer to a serving platter. ★

✪ ✪ ✪ ✪

MAKES 10 SERVINGS

Tortellini with Spinach-Walnut Pesto

2 pouches (2 ounces each) chopped walnuts (from baking aisle)

Salt and freshly ground black pepper, to taste

2 family-size packages (18 ounces each) cheese- or mushroom-and-cheese-filled fresh tortellini (sold on dairy aisle)

1 cup chicken broth

1 package (10 ounces) baby spinach, a few leaves reserved for garnish

2 cloves garlic

2/3 cup grated Parmigiano Reggiano or Romano cheese

1/4 teaspoon ground or freshly grated nutmeg

1/4 cup extra-virgin olive oil (evoo) (eyeball it)

Edible flowers, for garnish (optional)

Toast walnut pieces in a small pan or toaster oven until lightly browned. Remove to cool.

Place a large pot of water on to boil for the pasta. Add salt and tortellini; cook tortellini according to package directions. Drain.

Meanwhile, heat chicken broth to a boil and remove from heat.

Working in batches with a food processor, grind spinach with walnuts, chicken broth, and garlic. Transfer to a large bowl. Stir in cheese, nutmeg, evoo, salt, and pepper to taste. Toss hot, cooked tortellini with sauce, then turn pasta out onto a serving platter and garnish with a few baby spinach leaves and edible flowers, if desired. ★

The seeds of the eggplant look like caviar. In my family, this spread is sometimes called Poor Man's Caviar.

✪ ✪ ✪ ✪
MAKES 10 SERVINGS

Eggplant "Caviar"

1 medium, firm eggplant

1 clove garlic, cracked away from the skin with the flat of a knife

2 pinches ground allspice

Coarse salt and freshly ground black pepper, to taste

A handful of fresh flat-leaf parsley leaves

A drizzle of extra-virgin olive oil (evoo)

1 whole-grain baguette or other long crusty bread, sliced at bread counter

Preheat oven to highest setting, 500°F.

Cut 2 or 3 slits into one side of a whole eggplant. Place eggplant directly on the oven rack in the middle of the oven and roast until eggplant is tender, about 20 minutes. Keep the slits facing up so that the eggplant does not lose liquid as it roasts.

The roasted eggplant will look like a flat tire when you remove it from the oven. Let cool enough to handle. Using a sharp utility knife, carefully peel skin away from eggplant flesh, discarding skin. Add cooked eggplant flesh and juice to food processor and combine with garlic, allspice, salt, pepper, parsley, and evoo. Pulse-grind the eggplant into a paste and transfer to a serving dish.

To serve, surround a bowlful of spread with crusty bread rounds. ★

30-MINUTE MEALS
MENU

ANOTHER TAKE ON COOKING FOR 10 IN 30

1
appetizer
EGGPLANT "CAVIAR"

2
entree
TUSCAN-STYLE CHICKEN WITH ROSEMARY

3
side dishes
WILD MUSHROOM RISOTTO

MIXED GREENS SALAD

✪ ✪ ✪ ✪

MAKES 10 SERVINGS

Wild Mushroom Risotto

6 ounces dried porcini mushrooms (found in produce department)

1 quart beef stock

1 quart water

2 tablespoons extra-virgin olive oil (evoo) (twice around the pan)

1 tablespoon butter

2 shallots, finely chopped

2 cups Arborio rice

1/2 cup dry sherry or 1/4 cup cognac

8 sprigs fresh thyme, leaves stripped and chopped

3/4 cup Parmigiano Reggiano cheese (eyeball it)

Salt and freshly ground black pepper, to taste

Place dried porcini mushrooms, stock, and water in a saucepan and bring to a boil, then reduce heat to low and let simmer.

In a large skillet, heat evoo and butter over medium to medium-high heat. Add shallots and sauté, 2 minutes. Add Arborio rice and sauté, 2 or 3 minutes more. Add sherry or cognac and cook the liquid completely out. Add several ladles of the hot beef stock and reduce heat slightly. Simmer, stirring frequently until liquid is absorbed.

Remove mushrooms from stock, reserving stock. Coarsely chop the mushrooms and add them to the rice. Continue to ladle stock into rice, stirring mixture each time you add broth. Wait until the liquid is absorbed before adding more broth. When the rice is cooked to al dente, stir in thyme and cheese. Season with salt and pepper. The ideal total cooking time for perfect risotto is 22 minutes. The consistency should be creamy from the starch of the rice. ★

✪ ✪ ✪ ✪
MAKES 10 SERVINGS

Tuscan-Style Chicken with Rosemary

2 pounds boneless, skinless chicken thighs

1 & 1/2 pounds chicken tenderloins

Salt and freshly ground black pepper, to taste

3 tablespoons extra-virgin olive oil (evoo)

6 cloves garlic, crushed

2 tablespoons white wine vinegar (2 splashes)

2 tablespoons butter

2 shallots, chopped

6 sprigs fresh rosemary, leaves stripped and finely chopped

2 tablespoons all-purpose flour

1 cup dry white wine

2 cups beef broth (yes, beef broth)

Heat a large, deep skillet over medium-high heat. Season chicken with salt and pepper. Add 2 tablespoons evoo (twice around the pan), half the chicken pieces, and a couple of cloves of crushed garlic. Brown chicken 2 minutes on each side and remove from pan. Add the remaining tablespoon evoo (another single turn of the pan), the remaining chicken pieces, and the remaining garlic. Brown chicken 2 minutes on each side and remove.

Add vinegar to the pan; let it cook off. Add butter, shallots, and rosemary to the pan and cook 2 minutes. Add flour and cook 1 minute more. Whisk in wine; reduce 1 minute. Whisk in broth and bring liquids up to a bubble. Return chicken to the pan and simmer over medium heat, 7 to 8 minutes to finish cooking chicken through. ★

✪ ✪ ✪ ✪
MAKES 10 SERVINGS

Mixed Greens Salad

2 sacks (10 ounces each) ready-to-use mixed greens

3 tablespoons balsamic vinegar

1/4 cup extra-virgin olive oil (evoo)

Salt and freshly ground black pepper, to taste

Edible flowers, for garnish (available in produce department near the herbs)

Place greens in a large salad bowl. Toss with balsamic vinegar and evoo; season with salt and pepper. Scatter flowers across salad bowl to garnish.★

Fill out menu with Italian cheeses and olives, bread sticks, and an Italian cookie or mini-pastry tray (store-bought).

225

30-MINUTE MEALS
MENU

30-MINUTE THANKFUL FEAST

1

entree
TURKEY CUTLETS WITH MUSHROOM-WATER CHESTNUT STUFFING AND PAN GRAVY

- - - -

2

side dishes
BROWN RICE WITH HAZELNUTS

- - - -

SUGAR SNAP PEAS AND CHIVES

- - - -

✪ ✪ ✪ ✪

MAKES 6 SERVINGS

Turkey Cutlets with Mushroom-Water Chestnut Stuffing and Pan Gravy

6 slices marble rye bread

4 tablespoons (1/2 stick) butter, softened

2 & 1/2 pounds turkey breast cutlets

Salt and freshly ground black pepper, to taste

3 teaspoons poultry seasoning

4 tablespoons extra-virgin olive oil (evoo)

1 quart turkey broth, such as College Inn brand, or chicken broth, such as Kitchen Basics brand

2 tablespoons all-purpose flour

1 pound white mushrooms, chopped

2 ribs celery, from the heart, with greens, chopped

1 can (8 ounces or 1 cup) water chestnuts, drained and chopped

1/2 red bell pepper, seeded and chopped

3 scallions, chopped

2 tablespoons fresh thyme leaves, chopped

2 tablespoons chopped fresh flat-leaf parsley (a palmful)

Preheat broiler to high and toast bread on both sides. Use 2 tablespoons of the butter to spread liberally on the toast. Switch oven to "bake" and preheat to 375°F.

Season turkey cutlets with salt, pepper, and 2 teaspoons of the poultry seasoning . In a large skillet over medium-high heat, heat 2 tablespoons evoo; brown turkey cutlets in evoo, about 2 minutes on each side. Transfer cutlets to a shallow baking dish and add 1 cup broth to keep meat moist. Tent cutlets loosely with aluminum foil and transfer to oven.

For the gravy, add the remaining 2 tablespoons butter to the same skillet and let it melt over medium heat. Add flour and cook 1 to 2 minutes more. Whisk in 2 cups broth and allow gravy to thicken, 5 minutes. Season with salt and pepper and the remaining 1 teaspoon poultry seasoning.

Preheat a second skillet over medium-high heat and add the remaining 2 tablespoons evoo. Add mushrooms and brown 5 minutes, stirring frequently. Season mushrooms with salt and pepper. Add celery, water chestnuts, and bell pepper. Continue to cook until veggies are all tender, another 5 minutes. Add scallions, thyme, and parsley. Cut toast into cubes and add to skillet. Moisten stuffing with remaining 1 cup broth. Transfer to a serving dish. Use an ice cream scoop to portion out the stuffing at the table. Top mounds of stuffing with turkey cutlets and gravy. ★

Mushroom–Water Chestnut Stuffing

Turkey Cutlets

This menu can turn any day into Thanksgiving day.

✪ ✪ ✪ ✪
MAKES 6 SERVINGS

Brown Rice with Hazelnuts

1 cup chopped hazelnuts, such as Diamond brand (available on baking aisle)

3 cups chicken broth

2 tablespoons butter or extra-virgin olive oil (evoo)

1 & 1/2 cups brown rice

2 tablespoons chopped fresh flat-leaf parsley (a palmful)

Toast nuts in a small skillet over low heat for a few minutes, then remove from heat and reserve.

Put broth and butter or evoo in a medium saucepan over high heat and bring to a boil. Add rice, stir, and return to a boil; cover and reduce heat. Simmer until tender and liquid is absorbed, 17 to 18 minutes. Remove from heat. Add nuts and parsley as you fluff rice with a fork. Transfer to serving dish. ★

✪ ✪ ✪ ✪
MAKES 6 SERVINGS

Sugar Snap Peas and Chives

1 & 1/2 pounds sugar snap peas, strings removed

Salt, to taste

1 teaspoon sugar

2 tablespoons butter

3 tablespoons chopped or snipped fresh chives

Place peas in a pot and add 1 inch water. Add a little salt, the sugar, and butter to the pot. Bring water to a boil. Reduce heat to simmer. Cover and cook until peas are tender but still bright green, 7 to 8 minutes. Remove from heat and add chives. Transfer peapods to a serving dish. ★

✪ ✪ ✪ ✪

MAKES 4 TO 6 SERVINGS

Lemon-Thyme Chicken with Sweet Gnocchi

SWEET GNOCCHI

Salt, to taste

1 pound potato gnocchi (found in frozen foods section)

2 tablespoons butter

1/2 teaspoon cinnamon (a couple pinches)

2 tablespoons sugar

Grated Parmigiano Reggiano cheese

CHICKEN

1/4 cup all-purpose flour (a handful)

1/2 teaspoon coarse salt (a couple pinches)

Freshly ground black pepper, to taste

1/2 teaspoon poultry seasoning (a couple pinches)

1 & 1/2 pounds boneless skinless chicken breasts

3 tablespoons extra-virgin olive oil (evoo) (3 times around the pan)

2 tablespoons butter

1 medium onion, chopped

1 cup no-fat, low-sodium chicken broth

The juice of 2 lemons

6 to 8 sprigs fresh thyme, leaves stripped from stem and chopped

Put a large pot of water over high heat for the pasta. When water boils, add salt and pasta. Cook according to package directions, until al dente. Drain.

Meanwhile, start the chicken: Dump flour, salt, pepper, and poultry seasoning in a big plastic bag. Pat chicken dry and drop into bag. Give the chicken a good shake to lightly coat the breasts. Remove chicken from the bag and set aside, saving the flour.

Heat evoo over medium-high heat in a big nonstick skillet. Add chicken and cook 5 minutes, flip, and cook another 5 minutes. Remove chicken and add 1 tablespoon butter and the onions to the pan. Cook 2 or 3 minutes, stirring frequently. Add reserved flour and cook 1 minute more to incorporate flour. Add broth and bring sauce to a boil. Reduce heat to medium-low and squeeze lemon juice into sauce. Add thyme and the remaining 1 tablespoon butter. Add chicken back to pan and let simmer until gnocchi is done.

Toss hot gnocchi with 2 tablespoons butter. Combine cinnamon and sugar. Sprinkle cinnamon-sugar over gnocchi and toss. Top with a generous sprinkling of Parmigiano Reggiano cheese and serve alongside lemon-thyme chicken breasts. Steamed baby carrots make a nice accompaniment. ★

30-MINUTE MEALS

MENU

THYME ON YOUR SIDE!

1
entree
LEMON-THYME CHICKEN

2
side dish
SWEET GNOCCHI

3
suggested side
STEAMED BABY CARROTS

30-MINUTE MEALS
MENU

FANCY FISH

1

menu one
BAKED STUFFED
FLOUNDER

2

side dish
LONG-GRAIN
AND WILD RICE
WITH
ARTICHOKES

★ ★ ★ ★

MAKES 6 SERVINGS

Baked Stuffed Flounder

1 tablespoon extra-virgin olive oil (evoo) (once around the pan)

2 slices bacon, chopped

1 medium onion, finely chopped

1 shallot, finely chopped

2 cloves garlic, chopped

1/4 red bell pepper, finely chopped

1 rib celery with greens, finely chopped

Salt and freshly ground black pepper, to taste

1/2 teaspoon ground thyme

3 tablespoons chopped fresh flat-leaf parsley

6 ounces crabmeat, flaked

4 tablespoons (1/2 stick) butter, cut into pieces

4 large flounder fillets (1 & 1/3 pounds total)

1 lemon, cut into wedges

1/2 cup bread crumbs

A sprinkle of sweet paprika, for garnish

Preheat oven to 400°F.

Heat a medium skillet over medium-high heat; add evoo and bacon and cook until bacon begins to crisp, 2 to 3 minutes. Add onion, shallot, garlic, bell pepper, celery, salt, pepper, thyme, and 2 tablespoons parsley. Sauté 2 minutes. Stir in crabmeat and remove from heat.

Heat a second medium skillet over medium heat. Add butter and let it melt. Season flounder with salt and squeeze a little lemon juice on both sides. Turn fish in melted butter and set on a shallow baking pan or sheet pan. Add bread crumbs to the melted butter and cook, stirring, until brown. Add the crab and vegetable mixture to the bread crumbs and combine. Mound stuffing on half of each flounder fillet and fold fillets over to wrap and seal the stuffing.

Bake until fish is opaque, about 20 minutes. Serve with remaining lemon wedges, garnished with the remaining tablespoon parsley and a sprinkle of paprika. ★

✪ ✪ ✪ ✪
MAKES 4 SERVINGS

Long-Grain and Wild Rice with Artichokes

1 & 3/4 cups chicken broth
1 tablespoon extra-virgin olive oil (evoo)
1 tablespoon butter, cut in half
1 package (6 ounces) long-grain and wild rice, such as Near East brand
1 clove garlic, crushed
1 can (15 ounces) small artichoke hearts, drained and halved
Salt and freshly ground black pepper, to taste
2 tablespoons chopped fresh flat-leaf parsley (a handful)

Place chicken broth, half a tablespoon evoo (eyeball it), and half a tablespoon butter in a small pot; bring to a boil. Add spice packet and rice and return to a boil. Cover, reduce heat to simmer, and cook 17 minutes.

To a small skillet over medium heat, add remaining half tablespoon each evoo and butter. Add garlic and cook a minute, then add artichokes, season with a little salt and pepper, and cook 5 minutes. Portion out cooked rice on dinner plates and top with artichokes and a generous sprinkling of parsley. Serve alongside flounder. ★

BIG CITY BISTRO

1
entree
COD WITH BURST GRAPE TOMATOES, PARSLEY-MINT PESTO BROTH

2
side dish
FINGERLING POTATO CRISPS WITH HERBS

3
suggested side
GREEN SALAD

You could get $40 a head for this plate! Nice!

✪ ✪ ✪ ✪
MAKES 2 SERVINGS

Cod with Burst Grape Tomatoes, Parsley-Mint Pesto Broth, and Fingerling Potato Crisps with Herbs

POTATO CRISPS

2 large fingerling potatoes

1 tablespoon extra-virgin olive oil (evoo)

Salt and freshly ground black pepper, to taste

1 tablespoon chopped fresh tarragon or 1 teaspoon dried

1 tablespoon chopped fresh chives or 1 teaspoon dried

1 tablespoon chopped fresh flat-leaf parsley

FISH

1 pound thick, center-cut cod fillet, cut into 2 portions

The juice of 1/4 lemon

Salt and freshly ground black pepper, to taste

Extra-virgin olive oil (evoo), for drizzling

1/2 pint whole grape tomatoes

BROTH

1/3 cup fresh flat-leaf parsley leaves (a big handful)

1/4 cup mint leaves (a handful)

1 cup chicken broth

1 small shallot or 1/2 large shallot, coarsely chopped

Salt and freshly ground black pepper, to taste

3 tablespoons olive or vegetable oil, for frying

3 cloves garlic, gently cracked from skin with the flat of a knife and very thinly sliced

Preheat oven to 400°F.

Preheat a medium oven-safe skillet over high heat. (If your skillet doesn't have an oven-safe handle, wrap it in two layers of foil to protect it.)

Start the potatoes: Prick the potatoes 3 or 4 times each with a fork and cook them in the microwave for 5 minutes on high.

Meanwhile, for the fish, pat cod dry, squeeze a little lemon juice over it, and season with salt. Drizzle fish with evoo.

When potatoes are just cool enough to handle, slice them lengthwise into 1/4-inch pieces. Coat them with evoo and salt and pepper. Arrange them on a cookie sheet in a single layer and roast them in the oven, 20 minutes. Do

232

not move or turn them as they cook. Combine tarragon, chives, and parsley in a small bowl and set aside.

Add cod, seasoned side down, to preheated, very hot skillet and sear for 3 minutes. Do not flip the cod. Drizzle tomatoes with evoo and season with salt and pepper. Add tomatoes to the fish and sear for 1 minute. Transfer pan to the oven and roast until fish is firm and opaque and tomatoes have all burst, about 8 minutes.

For the broth, place parsley, mint, chicken broth, and shallots in a food processor or blender, and puree. Transfer to small saucepan and bring to a simmer. Season the broth with salt and pepper.

Heat the frying oil in a small skillet over medium heat. Add sliced garlic to the hot oil and let it fry until crisp and golden brown, 3 to 5 minutes. Remove garlic chips and drain on paper towel.

When the potatoes are very brown and crisp on the bottom side and tender on top, remove. Coat sliced potatoes liberally with the chopped tarragon, chives, and parsley.

Ladle warm pesto broth onto each dinner plate. Remove the fish from the oven. The bottom should be crisp and brown. Place the fish crispy-side up in pools of broth. Arrange the herb potato slices and tomatoes decoratively around the fish. Top the dish off with a scattering of garlic crisps. Serve with green salad on the side. ★

Dinner in Agrigento at the Baglio Della Luna as the kitchen was closing: "I'll take anything you have left," I said in very bad Italian. This fantastic dish was what I got.

✪ ✪ ✪ ✪
MAKES 4 SERVINGS

Baglio Della Luna Marinara

Salt and freshly ground black pepper, to taste

1 pound penne

3 tablespoons extra-virgin olive oil (evoo) (3 times around the pan)

4 cloves garlic, minced

3 pinches crushed red pepper

2 cans (6 ounces each) Italian tuna in oil, drained or 2 cans (6 ounces each) Albacore tuna, drained

1 cup dry red wine (a few good glugs)

1 can (14 ounces) diced tomatoes

1 can (14 ounces) crushed tomatoes

16 to 20 oil-cured black olives, pitted and coarsely chopped

2 tablespoons capers, smashed with flat of knife

A handful fresh flat-leaf parsley, chopped

Put a large pot of water over high heat for the pasta. When water boils, add salt and penne. Cook according to package directions, until al dente. Drain.

In a deep skillet, heat evoo, garlic, and crushed red pepper over medium heat until garlic sizzles. Add tuna and sauté 1 to 2 minutes. Add wine, bring to a boil, and reduce liquid by half. Add crushed tomatoes, olives, capers, parsley, and a few grinds of black pepper. Bring to a bubble, reduce heat, and simmer 10 minutes.

Toss pasta in two-thirds of sauce and transfer to platter. Serve with remaining sauce for passing, along with salad and bread. ★

30-MINUTE MEALS
MENU

LEFTOVER DINNER

1
entree
BAGLIO DELLA LUNA MARINARA

2
side dish
GREEN SALAD AND CRUSTY BREAD

✪ ✪ ✪ ✪

MAKES 4 SERVINGS

Crab-Stuffed Portobellos and Citrus-Mustard Dressed Greens

1/4 cup extra-virgin olive oil (evoo) (eyeball it)

4 large portobello mushroom caps, wiped clean with damp cloth

Grill seasoning, such as Montreal Steak Seasoning by McCormick

3 tablespoons butter, softened

1 bay leaf

2 ribs celery from heart of stalk, chopped

1 small onion, chopped

1 small red bell pepper, seeded and chopped

Salt and freshly ground black pepper, to taste

2 teaspoons Old Bay seasoning (a palmful) or 1 teaspoon poultry seasoning plus 1 teaspoon paprika

2 teaspoons cayenne pepper sauce, such as Frank's Red Hot or Tabasco (eyeball it)

6 ounces lump crabmeat (available in 6-ounce tubs in fresh seafood section)

3 slices white bread, toasted

1 cup chicken broth

A handful of chopped fresh flat-leaf parsley

SALAD

1 rounded tablespoon lemon curd (available in jars near jams and jellies)

2 tablespoons white wine vinegar (eyeball it)

2 teaspoons Dijon mustard

1/3 cup extra-virgin olive oil (evoo) (eyeball it)

Salt and freshly ground black pepper, to taste

1 sack (10 ounces) mixed baby greens (available on produce aisle)

For the mushrooms, heat a grill pan or large nonstick skillet over medium-high heat. Pour evoo into a small dish. Using a pastry brush, coat mushroom caps with oil. Grill until tender, about 10 minutes, and season with grill seasoning blend.

Preheat a medium skillet over medium-high heat. Add remaining evoo (from brushing mushroom caps) to skillet and combine with 2 tablespoons butter. Let butter melt into oil and add bay leaf, celery, onions, and bell pepper; season with salt, pepper, and Old Bay seasoning or poultry seasoning and paprika, and cook until almost tender, 3 to 5 minutes. Add hot sauce to vegetables. Run your fingers through the crab to make sure there are no pieces of shell in the meat. Break up crabmeat with fingertips and mix into veggies. ★

Butter toasted bread with remaining 1 tablespoon butter; cut toast into small dice. Add toast to veggies and moisten stuffing with chicken broth. Adjust seasonings. Top cooked portobello caps with stuffing. Garnish with chopped parsley.

Make the salad dressing: In a small bowl, whisk together lemon curd with vinegar and mustard. Whisk in evoo in a slow stream and season with salt and pepper. Pour lettuce into a bowl and drizzle dressing over the top. Serve mushroom caps with greens on the side. ★

✪ ✪ ✪ ✪
MAKES 4 SERVINGS

Tiny Trifles

4 individual (3-inch) sponge cakes
4 tablespoons orange or almond liqueur
1/2 cup seedless raspberry all-fruit spread or preserves
2 individual cups (4 ounces each) prepared vanilla pudding (available on dairy aisle)
1/4 cup sliced almonds
4 large strawberries, hulled and sliced
1 kiwi, peeled and diced

Douse cakes with liqueur. Spread with fruit spread. Top with a layer of vanilla pudding and sprinkle pudding with sliced almonds. Arrange berries and kiwi over the pudding and nuts. ★

Clean all greens, veggies, and herbs when you bring them home from the market. Your produce will be ready to use—no fuss, no mess, no wasted time.

✪ ✪ ✪ ✪
MAKES 4 SERVINGS

Mediterranean Succotash: Butter Beans, Corn, and Bell Peppers

2 tablespoons extra-virgin olive oil (evoo) (twice around the pan)
2 cloves garlic, chopped
2 bell peppers, yellow, red, or green, seeded and chopped
2 cups frozen corn kernels
1 can (15 ounces) butter beans, drained
Salt and freshly ground black pepper, to taste
A handful chopped fresh flat-leaf parsley

Heat a medium skillet over medium-high heat. Add evoo, garlic, and peppers. Sauté, stirring frequently, 5 minutes. Add corn, cook 2 or 3 minutes longer. Add beans and heat them through, 1 or 2 minutes. Season with salt and pepper, then stir in parsley. Transfer to individual dinner plates or a serving bowl. ★

✪ ✪ ✪ ✪
MAKES 4 SERVINGS

Poached Grouper with Tomato and Basil

4 grouper fillets (6 to 8 ounces each)
Salt and freshly ground black pepper, to taste
1 tablespoon extra-virgin olive oil
1 clove garlic, crushed
1 shallot, sliced
1/2 cup white wine (eyeball it)
1 can (14 ounces) diced tomatoes, well drained
The juice of 1/4 lemon
20 leaves fresh basil, torn, or rolled and shredded with your knife

Season fish with salt and pepper. To a large skillet with a tight-fitting lid, add the evoo and fish, turning fish to coat lightly in the oil. Then add garlic, shallots, and wine. Top each fillet with 1/4 of the tomatoes. Place the pan on the stovetop and bring the liquid to a boil over medium-high heat. Cover, and reduce heat to medium. Cook fish until opaque and flaky, but not dry, 8 to 10 minutes. Carefully transfer fish topped with tomatoes to dinner plates or serving plate with a thin spatula. Spoon pan juices over the fish. Squeeze lemon over the fish and top with lots of torn or shredded basil. Serve immediately. ★

✪ ✪ ✪ ✪

MAKES 4 SERVINGS

Melon with Sorbet and Berries

1 cantaloupe, quartered and seeded
1 pint mango or strawberry sorbet
1/2 pint raspberries
1/2 pint strawberries, hulled and sliced
2 teaspoons sugar

Cut a thin slice from the skin side of each melon wedge to give it a stable base on the plate. Top each melon "boat" with a scoop of mango or strawberry sorbet. Toss berries with a little sugar and spill them down and over the sorbet and melon. ★

Juice lemons with cut side facing up, letting juice spill over the sides of the lemon. The seeds will stay with the lemon and not fall into your food.

239

30-MINUTE MEALS
MENU

FINE FRENCH TOAST

1

entree
MORNING
MONTE CRISTOS

2

suggested sides
FRESH FRUIT
AND YOGURT

MAKES 5 SERVINGS

Morning Monte Cristos

2 jumbo eggs

1 cup sugar

1 tablespoon cornstarch

2 or 3 drops vanilla extract

1 cup milk or lowfat milk

2 or 3 pinches ground nutmeg

10 slices firm white toasting bread, crusts trimmed

5 teaspoons all-fruit apricot jam

10 thin slices Golden Delicious apple

5 slices baked ham (from the deli counter)

One brick (8 ounces) smoked cheddar cheese, thinly sliced

Butter, for frying

Confectioners' sugar, for topping

Beat eggs 2 to 3 minutes with an electric mixer. Add the sugar and continue to beat. Add cornstarch and vanilla and beat in. When well mixed, add milk and nutmeg and mix well again.

Preheat oven to 150°F.

Pour 1/8 inch batter into a 9x13-inch baking dish. Spread 5 slices bread with 1 teaspoon apricot jam each and set them, jam side up, in dish. Top each with 2 thin slices of apple, a slice of ham folded to fit bread, and a thin layer of cheese. Top with remaining 5 slices bread and pour the rest of the batter over the tops of the sandwiches. Lift sandwiches out of batter and transfer to a separate dish to keep bread from getting too soggy.

Fry sandwiches in a lightly greased nonstick skillet over medium heat until golden on each side, adding a little butter to pan as needed. Keep sandwiches warm in oven until all are completed. Cut sandwiches in half diagonally and arrange on a platter. Sprinkle with a touch of powdered sugar and serve warm with fresh fruit and yogurt on the side. ★

30-MINUTE MEALS
MENU

**STOUP: IN
BETWEEN
SOUP AND
STEW**

1

entree
**ZUPPA OSSO
BUCO**

2

suggested side
CRUSTY BREAD

✪ ✪ ✪ ✪

MAKES 4 SERVINGS

Zuppa Osso Buco

VEAL DUMPLINGS

1 pound ground veal

1 large egg, beaten

1/3 cup Italian bread crumbs

1/4 cup grated Parmigiano Reggiano or Romano cheese (a generous handful)

1/4 to 1/2 teaspoon freshly grated nutmeg (eyeball it)

Salt and freshly ground black pepper, to taste

STOUP

2 carrots

2 ribs celery with greens

1 medium onion

2 tablespoons extra-virgin olive oil (evoo) (twice around the pot)

Salt and freshly ground black pepper, to taste

1 fresh or dried bay leaf

1/2 cup white wine

1 can (14 ounces) cannellini (white beans), drained

1 can (15 ounces) diced tomatoes in puree or coarsely ground tomatoes

3 cups chicken broth

2 cups beef stock or broth

1 cup egg pasta, such as egg fettucine (broken into pieces) or medium egg noodles

GREMOLATA

2 cloves garlic, cracked away from skins with the flat of a knife

6 to 8 anchovies (1 tin flat fillets; 2 ounces), drained

1/4 cup loosely packed fresh flat-leaf parsley leaves (a handful)

The grated zest of 1 lemon (2 tablespoons)

Crusty bread, to pass at table

Start the dumplings: Combine veal, egg, bread crumbs, cheese, nutmeg, salt, and pepper in a bowl; reserve. Wash your hands.

Make the stoup: Heat a medium soup pot over medium heat. Chop veggies while pot heats up: dice carrots into 1/4-inch pieces, chop celery and onion. Add evoo to hot pot, then add carrots. Turn carrots to coat them in oil and add celery and onions. Season with salt and pepper; add bay leaf. Stir and cook to begin to soften, about 5 minutes. Do not let vegetables brown; reduce heat if necessary. Add wine, beans, tomatoes, chicken broth, and beef stock to the pot. Put a lid on the pot and raise heat to high.

Start rolling dumpling mixture into 1-inch balls. When soup boils, about 3 minutes, add dumplings directly to the pot. Stir in egg noodles. Simmer to cook noodles and meat dumplings, 6 minutes. Adjust seasonings and turn the heat off, then let stoup stand a couple of minutes.

Make gremolata: Pile garlic, anchovies, parsley, and lemon zest on a cutting board and finely chop together, then transfer to a small dish.

Serve stoup in shallow bowls with a couple of teaspoonfuls of gremolata on top. Let everyone stir the gremolata throughout their stoup; pass crusty bread at the table for dipping and mopping. ★

This "stoup" tastes like osso buco: slow-braised veal shanks and vegetables, topped with gremolata—a lemon, anchovy, and garlic topping that adds a bright, nutty flavor. In 30 minutes, you won't believe the slow-cooked flavor of this "stoup!"

30-MINUTE MEALS
MENU

BIG FLAVOR BRUNCH

1
entree
HASH IT OUT:
COWBOY HASH
AND EGGS

2
side dishes
TEXAS TOAST

YELLOW
TOMATO SALSA

✪ ✪ ✪ ✪
MAKES 4 SERVINGS

Cowboy Hash and Eggs, Texas Toast, and Yellow Tomato Salsa

HASH, EGGS, AND TEXAS TOAST

8 small red-skinned potatoes

3 slices applewood- or hickory-smoked bacon, chopped

2 tablespoons extra-virgin olive oil (evoo) (twice around the pan)

12 medium white mushrooms, quartered

1 green bell pepper, seeded and diced

1/2 medium red onion, chopped

2 teaspoons grill seasoning, such as Montreal Steak Seasoning OR salt and freshly ground black pepper

Cayenne pepper sauce, such as Frank's Red Hot or Tabasco, to taste

2 cups (8 ounces) shredded sharp cheddar, pepper Jack, or smoked cheddar cheese

3 tablespoons butter

4 extra-large eggs

4 thick-cut slices white, whole wheat, or crusty farmhouse bread, 1 to 1 & 1/2 inches thick

1 clove garlic, cracked from skin with the flat of a knife

1/2 teaspoon cayenne pepper or several more drops Frank's Red Hot or Tabasco

Chopped fresh flat-leaf parsley, for garnish

YELLOW TOMATO SALSA

3 medium or 2 large yellow tomatoes, seeded and chopped

1/2 medium red onion, finely chopped

1 serrano or jalapeño pepper, seeded and finely chopped

2 tablespoons chopped fresh cilantro or parsley

Salt, to taste

Start the hash: Pierce potatoes with a fork and microwave on high for 5 minutes. Remove potatoes from microwave and cool 5 minutes to handle.

While potatoes are cooking, add chopped bacon to a large skillet over medium-high heat and brown until crisp. Remove to paper towels to drain; wipe pan and return to heat.

Preheat the broiler to high.

Chop or wedge potatoes. Add evoo to the skillet you cooked the bacon in, then add potatoes. Cook potatoes until brown and crisp, 2 minutes on each side.

Make the salsa: Combine ingredients in a small bowl.

Back to the hash: Add mushrooms to potatoes. Brown mushrooms 1 or 2 minutes, then add peppers and onions and season mixture with grill seasoning blend or salt and pepper, then hot sauce. Cook until veggies are just tender and potatoes are cooked through, 3 to 5 minutes longer. Turn off heat and add bacon back to the pan. Combine bacon with the veggies then add cheese to the pan to evenly cover the mixture. Tent the skillet with aluminum foil to gently melt cheese over vegetables and potatoes and to retain heat.

Fry the eggs: Heat a nonstick griddle pan over medium heat. Add about 1 tablespoon butter to warm pan and let it melt. Crack eggs onto griddle and fry to desired doneness. Eggs may, of course, be cooked over easy or scrambled as well—as you like.

Make the toast: Place bread slices under broiler and toast 6 inches from heat on both sides. Place 2 tablespoons butter in a small cup with a clove of garlic and the cayenne pepper or a few drops of hot sauce. Melt in microwave 30 seconds. Brush toast with garlic-cayenne butter and sprinkle with parsley.

Transfer vegetable and bacon hash to plates. Top each portion with a single fried egg or arrange the eggs evenly over the platter. Serve with Texas garlic toast and salsa on the side. ★

Similar to scrambles, my hashes are easy-to-make jumbles of meats and vegetables combined with eggs. What's the difference? The hashes are heavy on the jumbled ingredients and easy on the eggs; 1 large egg per serving.

30-MINUTE MEALS

MENU

SOUTHERN
COMFORTS
BRUNCH

1

entree
SPIRAL-SLICED
HAM WITH
JEZEBEL SAUCE
AND CHEESE
BISCUITS

2

side dishes
BRAISED
MUSTARD
GREENS

FRIED GREEN
TOMATOES

MASHED SWEET
POTATOES

✪ ✪ ✪ ✪
MAKES 8 SERVINGS

Spiral-Sliced Ham with Jezebel Sauce and Cheese Biscuits

HAM AND SAUCE

1 spiral-sliced cooked ham
1 can (15 ounces) crushed pineapple
1 jar (10 ounces) apricot all-fruit preserves
3 tablespoons dry mustard
1/2 cup prepared horseradish (from dairy aisle)
1 teaspoon freshly ground black pepper

BISCUITS

2 boxes (8 ounces each) biscuit mix, such as Jiffy brand, mixed (but not baked) to package directions
1 cup shredded cheddar cheese
1/4 teaspoon ground or freshly grated nutmeg (a couple pinches)

Preheat oven to 425°F.

Remove ham from packaging and cover loosely in aluminum foil. Bake to warm ham through, 25 to 30 minutes.

For the sauce, combine pineapple, apricot preserves, mustard, horseradish, and pepper in a bowl.

For the biscuits, combine biscuit batter with cheddar cheese and nutmeg. Bake biscuits on a nonstick cookie sheet according to package directions. Serve with warmed ham and sauce. ★

✪ ✪ ✪ ✪
MAKES 6 SERVINGS

Braised Mustard Greens

4 slices bacon, chopped
2 pounds mustard greens, trimmed and chopped
2 tablespoons white vinegar
2 teaspoons sugar
Coarse salt, to taste
2 cups chicken broth

In a large skillet over medium-high heat, brown bacon and render the fat. Add chopped greens to the pan in bunches and turn until they wilt. When all of the greens are in the pan, add vinegar and cook 1 minute. Season greens with sugar and salt. Add chicken broth and cover. Reduce heat to medium-low and simmer greens 15 to 20 minutes, then serve. ★

Spiral-Sliced Ham

Cheese Biscuits

Braised Mustard Greens

Look for green tomatoes with a pinkish hue—they will be the juiciest.

✪ ✪ ✪ ✪
MAKES 6 SERVINGS

Fried Green Tomatoes

1/2 cup of both chili sauce and sour cream

1 cup all-purpose flour

2 eggs, beaten

1/4 cup milk

1 cup cornmeal

1 teaspoon curry powder (eyeball it)

1 teaspoon sweet paprika

1 teaspoon salt

1/4 teaspoon cayenne pepper

6 green tomatoes, sliced

3 to 4 tablespoons vegetable oil

Mix chili sauce with sour cream and set aside. Preheat a skillet over medium-high heat. Place 1/2 cup flour in a pie plate. Beat eggs and milk together in a second pie plate or shallow dish. Combine the remaining 1/2 cup flour, the cornmeal, and spices in a third shallow dish. Coat sliced tomatoes in flour, then egg, then seasoned cornmeal.

Add 2 tablespoons (twice around the pan) vegetable oil to the hot skillet. When oil is hot, fry half of the tomato slices until crisp and golden brown, 2 to 3 minutes on each side; repeat with remaining tomatoes. Serve hot with chili sauce mixed with sour cream, or your favorite condiment. ★

✪ ✪ ✪ ✪
MAKES 6 SERVINGS

Mashed Sweet Potatoes

3 pounds sweet potatoes, peeled and cut into chunks

4 tablespoons (1/2 stick) butter

1/2 banana, sliced

The grated zest and juice of 1 orange

1 cup chicken broth

1/2 cup packed brown sugar

1/2 teaspoon nutmeg

Salt and freshly ground black pepper, to taste

Place potatoes in a large pot and add water to just cover them. Set heat to high and boil potatoes until tender; drain.

Return the empty pot to the stovetop over medium heat. Add butter and bananas to the pot. Cook bananas 5 minutes and add the juice of 1 orange to the pot (reserve the zest). Allow the juice to cook out, 1 minute. Add potatoes to the pot and the broth and sugar. Mash potatoes, banana, broth, and sugar together until well combined. Season with nutmeg, salt, pepper, and orange zest to taste. Mash to combine spices and serve. ★

30-MINUTE MEALS
MƎNU

RISƎ AND SHINE BRUNCH

1
entree
SWEET ITALIAN CHICKEN-SAUSAGE PATTIES

- - - -

2
side dishes
PASTA SALAD WITH LEMON-PESTO DRESSING

BIRDS IN A NEST

- - - -

✪ ✪ ✪ ✪
MAKES 6 TO 8 SERVINGS

Pasta Salad with Lemon-Pesto Dressing

Salt and freshly ground black pepper, to taste

1 pound cavatappi or other corkscrew pasta or medium shells

1 cup store-bought pesto sauce (available in refrigerated section)

The grated zest and juice of 1 lemon

1/4 cup chopped fresh flat-leaf parsley

1 cup grape tomatoes, halved

4 scallions, chopped

20 fresh basil leaves, torn or cut into thin strips

3/4 pound ricotta salata, chopped and crumbled (available in specialty cheese case) or 1 (1-pound) tub bocconcini (mini balls of mozzarella), drained and halved

Put a large pot of water over high heat for the pasta. When water boils, add salt and pasta. Cook according to package directions to al dente. Meanwhile, make the dressing: Place pesto, lemon zest, lemon juice, parsley, tomatoes, scallions, basil, and cheese in a large bowl.

Drain pasta and chill it down under cold running water. Drain well. Add to bowl with dressing. Combine and season with salt and pepper. ★

✪ ✪ ✪ ✪
MAKES 6 SERVINGS

Sweet Italian Chicken-Sausage Patties

1 & 1/3 to 1 & 1/2 pounds ground chicken breast

3 cloves garlic, chopped

3 tablespoons chopped fresh flat-leaf parsley

1/4 cup grated parmesan, Parmigiano Reggiano, or Romano cheese

1 teaspoon fennel seeds

1 teaspoon freshly ground black pepper

3/4 teaspoon salt (eyeball it)

2 tablespoons extra-virgin olive oil (evoo) (twice around the pan)

Mix chicken with garlic, parsley, cheese, fennel, pepper, and salt. Form 6 large, thin patties, 4 to 5 inches in diameter, or 12 small patties, 2 to 3 inches. Wash your hands.

Preheat a large, nonstick skillet over medium heat and fry patties in evoo until done, 3 to 4 minutes on each side. ★

✪ ✪ ✪ ✪

MAKES 6 SERVINGS

Birds in a Nest

1/2 cup extra-virgin olive oil (evoo) (eyeball it)

1 large clove garlic, cracked from skin with the flat of a knife

6 thick slices crusty Italian semolina bread

6 extra-large eggs

1 small jar (6 ounces) roasted red peppers

Salt and freshly ground black pepper, to taste

1/2 cup grated parmesan, Parmigiano Reggiano, or Romano cheese

Preheat a 2-burner nonstick griddle or very large nonstick skillet over medium heat. Pour evoo into a small bowl or dish and add garlic. Microwave oil on high for 30 seconds.

Using a small knife or just your fingers, cut out or pull away a small amount of bread from the center of each slice, making a hole. Brush garlic oil on bread and arrange the pieces on the griddle. Crack each egg and drop it into its "nest," or the hole in each slice of bread. Drain and slice red peppers. Add a strip or two of red pepper to each nest. Season with salt and pepper and sprinkle a little cheese into each nest. Tent the pan with aluminum foil and let the eggs sit in their nests 5 minutes, then transfer them to a platter and serve with chicken-sausage patties. ★

Birds in a nest, or fried egg in bread, is my favorite late-night snack, and I make that bird sing many different tunes, depending on what's in the fridge!

✪ ✪ ✪ ✪

MAKES 6 SERVINGS

Ham and Fontina Frittata

1 pound ham steak (from packaged meats case)
1 tablespoon extra-virgin olive oil (evoo) (once around the pan)
2 tablespoons butter
12 extra-large eggs
1/2 cup milk or half-and-half
Salt and freshly ground black pepper, to taste
8 to 10 ounces fontina cheese, shredded (2 cups)

Preheat oven to 400°F.

Trim any connective tissue and all fat off ham steak. Mince the meat into very small bits and set aside.

Heat a 12-inch nonstick skillet with ovensafe handle over medium heat. (If you only have a rubber-handled skillet, double-wrap the handle in aluminum foil.) Add evoo and 1 tablespoon butter to the skillet and coat sides and bottom of pan evenly with melted-butter-and-oil mixture. Add ham bits to the pan and sauté 3 minutes to brown them a bit and cook out some of the moisture in the meat.

Whisk together eggs and milk. Break off tiny pieces of remaining 1 tablespoon butter and drop them into beaten eggs. Season eggs with a little salt and pepper and whisk again to combine. Pour eggs into skillet over ham. Stir eggs gently to evenly distribute bits of ham throughout the eggs. As eggs set, lift up bottom skin that's formed and allow uncooked eggs to settle. Keep doing this as eggs brown until the egg pie begins to set and take form.

Transfer to the oven and cook until golden on top, about 10 minutes. Add a generous layer of cheese to the frittata and leave in oven until cheese is melted and begins to bubble and brown, 3 to 5 minutes. Serve frittata wedges directly from the skillet with a pie server. ★

✪ ✪ ✪ ✪
MAKES 6 SERVINGS

Swiss Chard with Golden Raisins

1 & 1/2 tablespoons extra-virgin olive oil (evoo) (1 & 1/2 times around the pan)

1/8 pound (2 slices) pancetta or bacon, chopped

1 small yellow onion, chopped

1 & 1/4 to 1 & 1/2 pounds red Swiss chard, stems trimmed, greens coarsely chopped

1/4 cup golden raisins (2 handfuls)

1 container (14 ounces) chicken broth

Salt, to taste

1/8 teaspoon nutmeg

Heat a large skillet over medium-high heat. Add evoo, pancetta, and chopped onion to the pan and cook until onions begin to soften and pancetta is lightly browned, 2 or 3 minutes. Add chopped chard to pan in large bunches, adding remaining chard as the greens wilt. Sprinkle in raisins, pour in broth, and season with salt and nutmeg. Bring liquid to a boil, reduce heat and simmer greens until greens are no longer bitter and you are ready to serve, 10 to 15 minutes. ★

Complete the menu with assorted sweet rolls with jams (store-bought).

These corn cakes
are a savory side
dish—drizzled with
honey.

✪ ✪ ✪ ✪
MAKES 12 SMALL CORN CAKES

Corn Cakes with Walnuts and Sage

4 tablespoons (1/2 stick) butter, plus more for pan and for serving

1 & 1/2 cups water

1 cup cornmeal

2 large eggs

1/2 cup sugar

1/2 cup milk

1 teaspoon salt (1/2 palmful)

1 cup all-purpose flour

4 sprigs fresh sage, leaves stripped and slivered

2 ounces walnut halves or pieces (a couple handfuls) (found in the bulk bins)

Honey, for serving

Heat a nonstick griddle or nonstick skillet over medium heat. In a small saucepan, melt butter and transfer to a small mixing bowl. Wipe out pan and return to heat with 1 & 1/2 cups water. Bring water to a boil over high heat. Add cornmeal to large mixing bowl and scald it with the boiling water; stir to combine. Beat eggs, sugar, and milk with melted butter and stir this mixture into cornmeal. Sprinkle a little salt into bowl. Pour flour into a sieve or a sifter. Knock sieve to add flour into corn cake mix. Add sage to batter and stir to combine.

Nest a pat of butter in a paper towel and wipe butter across the griddle pan to grease it. Pour small ladles of corn cake batter onto grill; make cakes 3 inches wide and allow a bit of space between them. Drop a few walnut pieces into wet batter as the cakes begin to cook. Cook cakes 2 to 3 minutes on each side, until golden brown. Serve cakes with softened butter and honey for drizzling. YUMMY! ★

✪ ✪ ✪ ✪
MAKES 6 SERVINGS

Sugared Peaches

4 or 5 ripe or slightly underripe peaches, pitted and sectioned into wedges

Sugar, for sprinkling

Arrange peaches in a spiral on a plate. Sprinkle with sugar and serve. ★

✪ ✪ ✪ ✪

MAKES 6 SERVINGS

Roasted Red New Potatoes with Sweet Paprika Butter and Parsley

3 pounds small red-skinned new potatoes

1 tablespoon extra-virgin olive oil (evoo), for drizzling

4 tablespoons (1/2 stick) butter

2 teaspoons sweet paprika

1/4 cup parsley leaves, chopped (a couple handfuls)

Salt and freshly ground black pepper, to taste

Preheat oven to 450°F.

Sort potatoes: Those that are 2 inches or less in diameter can be left whole; halve larger potatoes. Place them in a roasting pan and coat very lightly with a drizzle of evoo. Roast until just tender, 20 to 25 minutes.

Melt butter in a small pan with paprika. Transfer potatoes from the oven to a bowl. Pour melted paprika butter over the potatoes. Sprinkle in parsley and season the potatoes with salt and pepper. Toss the potatoes with paprika butter to coat evenly. Adjust salt and pepper and serve. ★

✪ ✪ ✪ ✪

MAKES 6 SERVINGS

Scrambled Eggs with Smoked Salmon

1/4 pound sliced smoked salmon

12 eggs

1/2 cup heavy cream

12 to 15 blades of fresh chives, finely chopped

Salt and freshly ground black pepper, to taste

2 tablespoons butter

Reserve 2 slices of salmon for garnish; chop the rest into very small pieces.

Whisk eggs and cream together. Add half of the chopped chives and season eggs with salt and pepper. Preheat a large nonstick skillet over medium heat. Melt butter in the pan and add eggs. Scramble eggs with a wooden spoon, taking care not to cook them dry. When eggs have come together but remain wet, stir in chopped salmon. Remove pan from the stove and place on a trivet. Garnish the eggs with remaining salmon slices and chives, and serve right out of the warm pan. ★

30-MINUTE MEALS

MENU

EASY YET
ELEGANT
SUNDAY
BRUNCH

1

entree
SCRAMBLED
EGGS WITH
SMOKED
SALMON

- - - - - -

2

side dishes
ROASTED RED
NEW POTATOES
WITH SWEET
PAPRIKA BUTTER
AND PARSLEY

- - - - - -

ELSA'S HAM AND
ASPARAGUS
TOASTS

3

dessert
BROILED CITRUS
SALAD WITH
COINTREAU,
BROWN SUGAR,
AND MINT

A platter of store-bought fruit-filled Danish pastries will complete your elegant brunch. Allow one Danish per person, but halve them so that guests can mix and match varieties.

✪ ✪ ✪ ✪
MAKES 6 SERVINGS

Elsa's Ham and Asparagus Toasts

1 pound thin asparagus spears, trimmed

Salt and freshly ground black pepper, to taste

1 loaf chewy, crusty farmhouse-style bread, cut into 1-inch slices

4 tablespoons (1/2 stick) butter, softened

2 tablespoons Dijon or grainy mustard

1 & 1/4 pounds boiled, baked, or smoked ham (order thick slices at deli counter)

1 pound fontina cheese, shredded or sliced

Bring a pot of water to a boil. Add salt and asparagus. Simmer asparagus, 3 minutes. Drain and reserve.

Preheat the broiler. Toast thick slices of bread under broiler, 6 inches from heat. Combine butter and mustard. Spread the toasted bread with mustard butter.

Cut sliced ham into smaller pieces to process. Grind ham in a food processor. Spread the toast with ground ham. Arrange steamed asparagus spears on top of the ham. Top each toast with a few grinds of black pepper and a mound of fontina cheese. Place toasts on a broiler pan and return to oven under broiler; broil until cheese melts and lightly browns at edges. Arrange on a platter and serve. ★

✪ ✪ ✪ ✪
MAKES 6 SERVINGS

Broiled Citrus Salad with Cointreau, Brown Sugar, and Mint

2 quarts jarred citrus salad, drained

3 ounces orange liqueur, such as Cointreau

1/3 cup packed brown sugar (3 handfuls)

Several sprigs fresh mint, torn or chopped, for garnish

Preheat the broiler to high.

Arrange drained citrus in a casserole dish. Douse fruit with liqueur. Sprinkle brown sugar evenly over the top. Place casserole under hot broiler 6 inches from heat until sugar just begins to brown and bubble, 7 or 8 minutes. Garnish warm casserole with fresh mint leaves and serve. ★

Broiled Citrus Salad

Scrambled Eggs with Smoked Salmon

Elsa's Ham and Asparagus Toasts

RACHAEL RAY
CLASSIC
30-MINUTE MEALS

DATE NIGHTS

I published a version of this entrée in my original *30-Minute Meals* cookbook. A fan of the show wrote to say that she made this menu for her boyfriend who had seconds just before he proposed. Really. He said it was the second helping that did it. Ain't love grand! The dessert recipe is a no-bake pôts de crème, no kidding. Make it first to allow the chocolate cups to set and chill.

★ ★ ★ ★

MAKES 4 SERVINGS IN DEMITASSE CUPS, 2 IN TEACUPS

Decadent Duo for Decadent Duos: Chocolate Cups with Whipped Cream

2/3 cup whole milk

1 egg

2 tablespoons sugar

Pinch salt

1 cup semisweet chocolate chips

2 tablespoons Frangelico (hazelnut liqueur) or dark rum

4 demitasse cups

1 cup whipping cream

2 tablespoons sugar

Edible flowers (found in produce department) or candied violets, for garnish (optional)

Heat milk in a small pan over medium heat until it comes to a boil. In a blender or food processor combine egg, sugar, a pinch of salt, chocolate chips, and liqueur, using the low setting. Pour in boiling milk in a slow stream while blending. The hot milk will cook the egg and melt the chocolate. Process or blend 1 minute, until smooth. Spoon into 4 demitasse cups and chill.

After dinner, beat cream until soft peaks form. Add sugar and beat to combine. Top chocolate cups with a dollop of cream and garnish each cup with an edible flower or candied violet. Place cups on saucers and serve with demitasse spoons. ★

This recipe will make enough for two couples. If you plan a romantic evening where more than two's a crowd, reserve half the sauce to refrigerate or freeze for another supper (omit the basil, adding fresh when you reheat later), and only cook 1/2 to 2/3 pound of penne.

✪ ✪ ✪ ✪

MAKES 4 SERVINGS (MAKE IT FOR 2 WITH SECONDS IN MIND)

You-Won't-Be-Single-For-Long Vodka Cream Pasta

Coarse salt and freshly ground black pepper, to taste

12 ounces pasta, such as penne rigate

1 tablespoon extra-virgin olive oil (evoo) (once around the pan)

1 tablespoon butter

2 cloves garlic, minced

2 shallots, minced

1 cup vodka

1 cup chicken broth

1 can (28 ounces) crushed tomatoes

1/2 cup heavy cream

20 leaves fresh basil, shredded or torn

Crusty bread

Put a large pot of water over high heat for the pasta. When water boils, add salt and penne. Cook according to package directions to al dente. Drain.

Meanwhile, heat a large skillet over medium heat. Add evoo, butter, garlic, and shallots. Gently sauté garlic and shallots, 3 to 5 minutes, to develop their sweetness. Add vodka and cook to reduce by half, 2 or 3 minutes. Add chicken broth and tomatoes. Bring sauce to a bubble, then reduce heat to simmer. Season with salt and pepper.

Stir cream into the vodka sauce. When sauce returns to a bubble, remove from heat. Toss hot pasta with sauce and basil leaves. Serve immediately, along with crusty bread. ★

You-Won't-Be-Single-For-Long
Vodka Cream Pasta

The soft, mellow flavors of these recipes make it a great romantic date meal! The veal is an Italian staple that takes under 15 minutes to prepare, start to finish. End the evening with a real Venetian treat! Sgroppino, or Champagne Freeze. Be careful. It goes straight to your head, and it gets results!

✪ ✪ ✪ ✪
MAKES 2 SERVINGS

Veal Medallions with Lemon on a Bed of Spinach

2 tablespoons extra-virgin olive oil (evoo) (twice around the pan)
1 tablespoon butter
2 tablespoons all-purpose flour
1/2 cup chicken broth
1/2 pound thinly sliced veal scallops
Salt and freshly ground black pepper, to taste
The juice and grated zest of 1 lemon
A handful fresh flat-leaf parsley, finely chopped
1/4 cup water
1 sack (10 ounces) baby spinach
1/4 to 1/2 teaspoon freshly grated or ground nutmeg

In a skillet over medium heat, combine evoo, butter, and flour. Cook 2 or 3 minutes. Whisk in broth. Turn sliced veal in thickened sauce, 3 or 4 minutes and transfer veal to a warm platter. Season with salt and pepper. Add lemon zest, lemon juice, and chopped parsley to the remaining sauce in the pan and remove from heat.

In a second skillet over medium-high heat, wilt spinach in a splash of water. Drain and season with salt, pepper, and nutmeg.

To assemble, divide spinach between 2 dinner plates and top with veal and pan sauce. ★

✪ ✪ ✪ ✪
MAKES 2 SERVINGS

Champagne Freezes

4 scoops lemon sorbet
2 ounces chilled vodka, citrus vodka, or Limoncello (Italian lemon liqueur)
2 ounces sparkling wine, such as Prosecco, or champagne
2 sprigs fresh mint

Blend lemon sorbet on low speed and pour in vodka or lemon liqueur in a slow stream. Add Prosecco or champagne. Pour into chilled martini glasses and serve, garnished with a sprig of mint. ★

One of my favorite restaurants in Florence, Italy, is Trattoria Garga. When I dine at Garga, I must have this pasta, created by the owner, so I'm told. It is called Magnifico, and it is! The flavors are intoxicating: cream, citrus, mint, basil. Unreal! I have tried many times to make it at home, on special nights. This recipe is as close as I've ever gotten to the original.

★ ★ ★ ★
MAKES 2 SERVINGS

Pasta with Citrus Cream Sauce

1/2 teaspoon coarse salt, plus more for pasta water

1/2 pound linguini, or 3/4 pound fresh linguini

1 cup heavy cream

2 tablespoons cognac or dry sherry

The grated zest of 1 lemon

The grated zest of 1 large navel orange

2 tablespoons chopped fresh mint (about 3 sprigs)

12 fresh basil leaves, shredded or torn

1/2 cup grated Parmigiano Reggiano cheese

Put a large pot of water over high heat for the pasta. When water boils, add salt and linguini. Cook according to package directions to al dente. Drain.

Meanwhile, in a skillet over medium-low heat, warm cream. Stir in cognac or sherry, zests of lemon and orange, and salt. Simmer, 7 to 10 minutes. Add mint and basil. Toss hot, drained pasta with sauce and grated cheese. Transfer to serving dish or dinner plates. ★

30-MINUTE MEALS
MENU

MAGNIFICO!

1
appetizer
PASTA WITH CITRUS CREAM SAUCE

2
entree
VEAL MEDALLIONS WITH LEMON ON A BED OF SPINACH

3
drink
CHAMPAGNE FREEZES

The soft, mellow flavors of these recipes make it a great romantic date meal! The veal is an Italian staple that takes under 15 minutes to prepare, start to finish. End the evening with a real Venetian treat! Sgroppino, or Champagne Freeze. Be careful. It goes straight to your head, and it gets results!

✪ ✪ ✪ ✪
MAKES 2 SERVINGS

Veal Medallions with Lemon on a Bed of Spinach

2 tablespoons extra-virgin olive oil (evoo) (twice around the pan)

1 tablespoon butter

2 tablespoons all-purpose flour

1/2 cup chicken broth

1/2 pound thinly sliced veal scallops

Salt and freshly ground black pepper, to taste

The juice and grated zest of 1 lemon

A handful fresh flat-leaf parsley, finely chopped

1/4 cup water

1 sack (10 ounces) baby spinach

1/4 to 1/2 teaspoon freshly grated or ground nutmeg

In a skillet over medium heat, combine evoo, butter, and flour. Cook 2 or 3 minutes. Whisk in broth. Turn sliced veal in thickened sauce, 3 or 4 minutes and transfer veal to a warm platter. Season with salt and pepper. Add lemon zest, lemon juice, and chopped parsley to the remaining sauce in the pan and remove from heat.

In a second skillet over medium-high heat, wilt spinach in a splash of water. Drain and season with salt, pepper, and nutmeg.

To assemble, divide spinach between 2 dinner plates and top with veal and pan sauce. ★

✪ ✪ ✪ ✪
MAKES 2 SERVINGS

Champagne Freezes

4 scoops lemon sorbet

2 ounces chilled vodka, citrus vodka, or Limoncello (Italian lemon liqueur)

2 ounces sparkling wine, such as Prosecco, or champagne

2 sprigs fresh mint

Blend lemon sorbet on low speed and pour in vodka or lemon liqueur in a slow stream. Add Prosecco or champagne. Pour into chilled martini glasses and serve, garnished with a sprig of mint. ★

You-Won't-Be-Single-For-Long
Vodka Cream Pasta

✪ ✪ ✪ ✪
MAKES 4 SERVINGS

Heart-y Salad: Hearts of Romaine, Palm, and Artichoke

1 heart romaine lettuce, shredded

1 cup fresh flat-leaf parsley leaves (half a bundle)

1 can (14 ounces) hearts of palm, drained

1/4 pound prosciutto di Parma

1 can (15 ounces) quartered artichoke hearts in water, drained

1/4 pound wedge Pecorino, Romano, or Asiago cheese

Balsamic vinegar, for drizzling

Extra-virgin olive oil (evoo), for drizzling

Salt and freshly ground black pepper, to taste

Place romaine on a platter and toss with parsley. Wrap hearts of palm in prosciutto and cut into bite-size pieces on an angle. Arrange palm and artichoke hearts over the romaine greens. Shave cheese with a vegetable peeler into short ribbons, working over the salad plate. Drizzle with vinegar and evoo; season with salt and pepper. ★

✪ ✪ ✪ ✪
MAKES 2 SERVINGS

Asparagus Velvet Soup

1 bundle (about 20 spears) thin spears asparagus

1/2 cup dry white wine

1/2 cup water

2 tablespoons butter

2 tablespoons all-purpose flour

1 & 1/2 cups good-quality vegetable stock (available on soup aisle)

Salt, to taste

White pepper, to taste

1/2 cup heavy cream

1 tablespoon chopped fresh tarragon or chives, for garnish (optional)

Edible flowers, for garnish (optional)

Trim asparagus by holding a spear at both ends and allowing it to snap. Use this spear as a guide to cut away the tough ends of the rest.

Bring wine and water to a simmer in a medium saucepan; add asparagus. Cook, covered, until tender, about 5 minutes. Drain asparagus liquid into a food processor. Cut tips off asparagus on an angle and reserve them. Cut the remaining spears into 1-inch pieces and puree in food processor with cooking liquid.

In a medium saucepan, melt butter over medium heat. Whisk in flour and cook 2 minutes. Whisk in stock and bring liquid to a bubble. Whisk in asparagus stock and return soup to a bubble. Season soup with salt and white pepper and stir in cream. Cook to thicken soup slightly. Adjust seasonings and serve hot in small or shallow bowls topped with reserved asparagus tips, chopped herbs, and/or edible flowers for garnish. ★

30-MINUTE MEALS
MENU

SEDUCTIVE SUPPER

1
appetizer
ASPARAGUS VELVET SOUP

2
entree
LOBSTER TAILS THERMIDOR

3
dessert
BERRY-MI-SU

To make this dish with jumbo shrimp, cut up peeled, deveined raw shrimp. Sauté the shrimp in butter, as with cooked lobster. Cook until pink and firm and proceed with recipe. Place the shrimp and sauce into a small casserole, then spoon completed shrimp thermidor over bed of greens and parsley leaves.

✪ ✪ ✪ ✪

MAKES 2 SERVINGS

Lobster Tails Thermidor

2 packaged lobster tails (8 ounces each), OR 1 pound jumbo shrimp or prawns (see sidebar)

4 tablespoons (1/2 stick) butter

1/2 small white onion, finely chopped

2 tablespoons all-purpose flour

A splash of dry white wine or dry sherry

1/2 cup milk (eyeball it)

1/3 cup grated white cheddar cheese

1/2 teaspoon paprika or Old Bay seasoning

Salt and freshly ground black pepper, to taste

2 tablespoons Parmesan cheese

2 tablespoons bread crumbs

2 cups baby greens

A handful fresh flat-leaf parsley leaves

1 lemon, cut into wedges, for garnish

Bring a pot of water, 3 or 4 inches deep, to a boil. Add lobster tails to the water and boil 7 to 8 minutes. Drain and shock under cold water to cool. Use kitchen scissors to cut away soft underside of tails. Save the shells, arranging them in a shallow casserole dish. Remove meat and chop it on an angle into chunks.

Preheat the broiler to high.

Heat a small saucepan and a medium skillet over medium heat. In the small saucepan, melt 2 tablespoons butter. Add onion and cook until very soft, 3 to 5 minutes. To the skillet, add the remaining 2 tablespoons butter. When the butter has melted, add chopped lobster meat and sauté.

Add flour to saucepan with onions and cook together 1 to 2 minutes. Whisk in wine or sherry, then milk. Remove sauce from heat and stir in cheddar cheese and paprika or Old Bay. Season sauce with salt and pepper. Pour sauce over lobster meat and stir to combine.

Pour lobster into and over the shells in a casserole dish and top with Parmesan cheese and bread crumbs. Broil on high until golden, 2 or 3 minutes. Serve each tail, spilling over with lobster bits in sauce, on a bed of mixed baby greens and parsley with wedges of lemon alongside. ★

✪ ✪ ✪ ✪

MAKES 2 SERVINGS

Berry-Mi-Su (Berry-Me-Up)

1/2 package ladyfingers sponge cakes

1 cup raspberries

4 large strawberries, sliced

1/2 cup fresh blackberries (a couple handfuls)

The juice of 1 lemon

2 tablespoons sugar

1 cup mascarpone cheese (available in specialty cheese case)

1/3 cup heavy cream

1/3 cup confectioners' sugar

Open the ladyfingers and separate them. Combine raspberries with sliced strawberries and blackberries. Toss with lemon juice and sugar.

Line 2 large martini glasses or glass dessert bowls with a single layer of ladyfingers, letting the cakes overlap a bit at the stem. Press the cakes down a bit to fit the lines of the glass. Cover the cake with berries.

With a hand mixer, beat cheese with cream and sugar on low, 2 minutes. Spoon sweetened cheese over berries. Spoon more berries over sweetened cheese. Top glasses off with a cap of the ladyfingers dotted with berry juice and more mixed berries. ★

✪ ✪ ✪ ✪

MAKES 2 SERVINGS

Portobello Mushroom "Fries"

3 large portobello mushroom caps

1/4 cup extra-virgin olive oil (evoo), plus more for drizzling

Steak seasoning blend, such as Montreal Seasoning by McCormick OR coarse salt and freshly ground black pepper, to taste

1/4 cup fresh flat-leaf parsley, chopped

1 cup Italian bread crumbs

1/2 cup shredded or grated Parmesan cheese

2 eggs, beaten

Preheat a grill pan over medium-high to high heat.

Scrape the gills off the underside of the portobello mushroom caps with a spoon. Brush caps gently with a damp cloth to clean. Drizzle caps with evoo to keep from sticking to the grill pan, and season the caps with steak seasoning or salt and pepper.

Grill mushrooms until just tender, 3 or 4 minutes on each side, under a loose aluminum foil tent. Remove from heat and cool, 5 minutes.

Combine parsley, bread crumbs, and cheese. Slice grilled caps into 1/2-inch strips. Turn strips in beaten egg, then coat in parsley mixture. Coat a nonstick skillet with a thin layer evoo and place over medium-high heat. Cook "fries" until brown, 2 or 3 minutes on each side. ★

✪ ✪ ✪ ✪

MAKES 2 SERVINGS

Sirloin Bourguignonne Burgers

3/4 to 1 pound ground sirloin

1/4 cup Burgundy

2 tablespoons fresh thyme, chopped

1 shallot, finely chopped

2 teaspoons steak seasoning blend, such as Montreal Seasoning by McCormick, OR salt and freshly ground black pepper

Extra-virgin olive oil (evoo), for drizzling

2 crusty Kaiser rolls, split and toasted

1/4 pound (1/2-inch slice) mousse-style pâté (available near specialty cheeses in large markets)

4 cornichon pickles or baby gherkins, thinly sliced lengthwise

4 pieces red leaf lettuce

Grainy mustard or Dijon-style mustard, to spread on buns

Preheat a grill pan or grill to medium-high heat.

If using a charcoal grill, prepare coals. Combine ground sirloin with wine, thyme, shallot, and steak seasoning or salt and pepper. Form meat into 2 large patties, 1 to 1 & 1/2 inches thick. Drizzle patties with evoo to keep them from sticking to grill or grill pan. Cook patties 5 minutes on each side for medium-rare, 8 minutes on each side for medium-well.

Toast rolls under a hot broiler or in toaster oven. Spread mousse pâté on the bun bottoms. Top with burger, cornichons, and lettuce. Spread the bun tops with mustard and set on burgers. ★

✪ ✪ ✪ ✪
MAKES 2 SERVINGS

Mixed Greens with Tarragon Vinaigrette

5 ounces (half a 10-ounce sack) mixed baby greens

2 scallions, thinly sliced on an angle

2 tablespoons fresh tarragon leaves, chopped

1/2 teaspoon grainy or Dijon-style mustard

2 teaspoons white wine vinegar (2 splashes)

2 tablespoons extra-virgin olive oil (evoo) (eyeball it)

Salt and freshly ground black pepper, to taste

Place greens and scallions in a medium bowl. Whisk tarragon, mustard, and vinegar together and add evoo in a slow stream while whisking. Pour dressing on greens and toss with tongs. Season salad with salt and pepper. ★

30-MINUTE MEALS
MENU

ROOFTOP SUPPER FOR 4

1
appetizer
VEGETABLE ANTIPASTO-STUFFED BREAD

2
entree
GRILLED ROSEMARY TUNA STEAKS

3
side dish
EGGPLANT AND ZUCCHINI SALSA

4
dessert
BERRIES AND SWEET CREAM

✪ ✪ ✪ ✪

MAKES 4 SERVINGS

Vegetable Antipasto-Stuffed Bread

1 loaf crusty bread, 9 to 12 inches in length/diameter

1/4 cup fresh flat-leaf parsley, chopped (a couple handfuls)

1/4 cup (half a small jar) sun-dried tomatoes in olive oil, drained, chopped

1/4 cup black pitted Kalamata or oil-cured olives, chopped

1/2 cup pesto, store-bought or homemade

1/4 pound deli-sliced provolone cheese

1 jar (14 ounces) roasted red peppers, drained

1 can (15 ounces) quartered artichoke hearts in water, drained

1 cup chopped giardiniera (pickled vegetables: hot peppers, cauliflower, carrots) (available on the Italian foods aisle or in bulk bins near deli section with bulk olives)

1/2 a sack mixed greens, from produce section (5 ounces; 3 loosely packed cups)

The juice of 1/2 lemon

Coarse salt and freshly ground black pepper, to taste

Extra-virgin olive oil (evoo), for drizzling

Cut the top off a loaf of crusty bread. Hollow out the inside of the bread.

Mix parsley, sun-dried tomatoes, olives, and pesto. Spread the mixture evenly across the bottom of the hollowed-out bread. Layer the cheese into the loaf. Layer the roasted red peppers on top of the cheese. Coarsely chop the artichoke hearts and add them in a layer over the red peppers. Sprinkle in the giardiniera. Coat the greens with lemon juice, salt, pepper, and a generous drizzle of evoo. Pile the greens on top of the filled loaf and replace the top. Cut the stuffed loaf into pieces and serve. ★

✪ ✪ ✪ ✪
MAKES 4 SERVINGS

Grilled Rosemary Tuna Steaks with Eggplant and Zucchini Salsa

4 tuna steaks (6 to 8 ounces each)

1 & 1/2 tablespoons balsamic vinegar (enough to lightly coat steaks)

6 sprigs fresh rosemary, leaves stripped and chopped (about 3 tablespoons)

Steak seasoning blend such as Montreal Seasoning by McCormick OR coarse salt and freshly ground black pepper, to taste

Extra-virgin olive oil (evoo), for drizzling (about 2 tablespoons)

SALSA

2 tablespoons extra-virgin olive oil (evoo) (twice around the pan)

4 cloves garlic, chopped

1 medium onion, chopped

1 small zucchini

1 small yellow squash

1 small, firm eggplant

6 sprigs fresh thyme, leaves stripped and chopped

Salt and freshly ground black pepper, to taste

2 small vine-ripe tomatoes, seeded and diced

Prepare the fish: Preheat a grill pan to high or preheat grill or charcoal. Coat tuna in vinegar and rub with rosemary, and steak seasoning blend or salt and pepper. Drizzle fish with evoo, coating lightly on both sides.

Make the salsa: Preheat a medium nonstick skillet over medium-high heat. Add evoo. Add garlic and onion, and sauté, 2 or 3 minutes. Dice zucchini and squash while the onion begins to soften. Add zucchini and squash to the pan and turn to coat and combine with garlic and onion.

Slice eggplant into strips and dice, then add to the pan. Turn to combine all of the vegetables. Add thyme, salt, and pepper to season the mixture. Cook over medium-high heat, stirring frequently, 10 minutes, until vegetables are just fork-tender.

Grill tuna 2 to 3 minutes on each side for rare, up to 6 minutes on each side for well done. When tuna is done and vegetables are fork-tender, stir chopped tomatoes into eggplant and zucchini mixture and remove vegetables from heat.

Serve wedges of Vegetable Antipasto-Stuffed Bread alongside tuna steaks topped with vegetable salsa. Extra antipasto slices and vegetables should be passed at the table. ★

Add a candle or two, and this is a romantic Mediterranean get-together that you can make any night of the week.

273

A nice chilled
Sicilian rosé
makes a fine
beverage
companion.

✪ ✪ ✪ ✪
MAKES 4 SERVINGS

Berries and Sweet Cream

1/2 pint blackberries
1/2 pint raspberries or sliced strawberries
2 teaspoons sugar
2 ounces anisette (licorice-flavored liqueur), such as Sambuca Romano
1 pint vanilla ice cream
1 canister real whipped cream (from dairy aisle of market)
8 pizzelle cookies (found on packaged cookies aisle), or wafer cookies

Combine berries with sugar and liqueur. Spoon berries into cocktail glasses
or dessert cups, reserving a few for garnish. Top with small scoops of ice
cream and a rosette of whipped cream. Garnish with a few remaining
berries and serve with pizzelle or wafer cookies. ★

This menu is a jazzed-up home version of a great date John and I had out at a Mexican restaurant in NYC. When we make it ourselves, it's even more romantic; it's like getting away to Baja for the evening.

✪ ✪ ✪ ✪
MAKES 2 SERVINGS

Heck of a Jicama Salad

1/2 bulb jicama root, peeled and sliced into thick matchsticks
1/2 teaspoon salt, plus more to taste
2 teaspoons sugar
The juice of 2 limes
2 hearts of romaine lettuce, chopped
2 tablespoons finely chopped cilantro (a handful of leaves)
1/2 teaspoon cumin (eyeball it in the palm of your hand)
3 tablespoons extra-virgin olive oil (evoo) (eyeball it)
Freshly ground black pepper, to taste

Place jicama in a bowl, sprinkle with salt and sugar, then cover with cold water. Add the juice of 1 lime. Let jicama stand 15 minutes, then drain well. While jicama soaks, work on the rest of the meal.

Arrange lettuce on a serving plate. Top with drained jicama. Juice 1 lime into a small bowl; add cilantro and cumin. Whisk in evoo in a slow stream. Pour dressing over salad and season with salt and pepper. ★

✪ ✪ ✪ ✪
MAKES 2 SERVINGS

Chorizo and Shrimp Quesadillas with Smoky Guacamole

GUACAMOLE

2 ripe Haas avocados
The juice of 1 lime
A couple pinches salt
1/4 cup sour cream (3 rounded tablespoonfuls)
2 chipotle peppers in adobo (available in cans on specialty food aisle or in Mexican section)

QUESADILLAS

1/2 pound chorizo sausage, thinly sliced on an angle
1 tablespoon extra-virgin olive oil (evoo), plus some for drizzling
1 clove garlic, crushed

Mussels in Mexican Beer

12 large shrimp, peeled and deveined, tails removed (ask for easy-peels at seafood counter of market)

Salt and freshly ground black pepper, to taste

4 flour tortillas (12 inches)

1/2 pound shredded pepper Jack cheese (2 cups)

Make the guacamole: Cut avocados all the way around with a sharp knife. Scoop out pit with a spoon, then spoon avocado flesh away from skin into a food processor. Add lime juice, salt, sour cream, and chipotles in adobo. Pulse guacamole until smooth. Transfer to a serving bowl.

For the quesadillas, heat a 12-inch nonstick skillet over medium-high heat. Brown chorizo 2 to 3 minutes, then remove from pan. Add evoo and garlic, then shrimp. Season shrimp with salt and pepper, and cook shrimp until pink, 2 or 3 minutes. Transfer shrimp to a cutting board and coarsely chop. Add a drizzle of oil to the pan, then a tortilla. Cook tortilla 30 seconds, then turn. Cover half of the tortilla with a couple handfuls of cheese. Arrange a layer of chorizo and shrimp over the cheese, and fold tortilla over. Press down gently with a spatula and cook tortilla a minute or so on each side to melt cheese and to crisp. Remove quesadilla to a large cutting board and repeat with remaining ingredients. Cut each quesadilla into 5 wedges and transfer to plates with a spatula. Top wedges of quesadillas with liberal amounts of smoky guacamole. ★

✪ ✪ ✪ ✪
MAKES 2 SERVINGS

Mussels in Mexican Beer

2 tablespoons extra-virgin olive oil (evoo) (twice around the pan)

4 cloves garlic, cracked away from skin with the flat of a knife and crushed

1 small onion, chopped

1 jalapeño, seeded and chopped

A couple pinches salt

2 dozen mussels, scrubbed

1/2 cup dark Mexican beer, such as Negro Modelo or Dos Equis Amber

1 can (15 ounces), diced tomatoes, drained

2 tablespoons chopped fresh flat-leaf parsley or cilantro

In a deep skillet with a cover preheated over medium-high heat, add evoo, garlic, onion, and jalapeño. Season with salt. Sauté 2 minutes. Arrange mussels in the pan. Pour in beer and tomatoes and shake the pan to combine. Cover pan and cook until mussels open, 3 to 5 minutes. Discard any unopened mussels. Remove from heat and spoon sauce down into shells. Garnish with parsley or cilantro. Serve immediately from the pan. ★

Simple, delish, and ready in less than 10 minutes, this recipe may be made first if you enjoy mouthfuls of mussels while you cook. John and I make it last, right before we sit down. We feast and snuggle our way through date nights all week long. Spoiled rotten, we are.

✪ ✪ ✪ ✪

MAKES 2 SERVINGS

Pâté Bites and Herb Brie Board

2 slices dark bread, such as pumpernickel or German whole grain, lightly toasted

Whole-grain mustard, for spreading

1/4 pound country pâté or mousse pâté

1/4 red onion, finely chopped

1/4 cup capers, drained

Red seedless grapes

1/3 pound herb brie

Water crackers

Cornichons or baby gherkin pickles

Spread toasted bread lightly with mustard. Arrange pâté in a thin layer on top of mustard. Top with chopped onions and capers. Cut each slice of pâté-covered bread into 4 quarters, cutting from corner to corner. Arrange pâté bites on a cheese board with a wedge of herb brie, served at room temperature with crackers, small bunches of grapes, and cornichons or pickles. ★

✪ ✪ ✪ ✪

MAKES 2 SERVINGS

Chicken in Tarragon Cream Sauce, White and Wild Rice with Walnuts

1 package (5 to 7 ounces) white and wild rice, chicken or herb flavors, such as Uncle Ben's or Near East brands

2 tablespoons extra-virgin olive oil (evoo) (twice around the pan)

1 pound boneless, skinless chicken breasts

Salt and freshly ground black pepper, to taste

1/4 cup balsamic vinegar (eyeball it)

1/4 cup water (eyeball it)

1 tablespoon tomato paste

1/3 cup heavy cream, half-and-half, or sour cream

4 or 5 sprigs fresh tarragon, leaves stripped and chopped

1 package (2 ounces or 1/4 cup) chopped walnuts, available in baking section, toasted

2 tablespoons chopped fresh flat-leaf parsley

Start cooking rice according to package directions.

Meanwhile, heat a large skillet over medium-high heat. Add evoo, then chicken, and season with salt and pepper. Brown and cook chicken 5 minutes on each side. Transfer chicken to a plate and cover. Reduce heat under skillet a bit. Add vinegar and water; scrape up pan drippings. Stir in tomato paste, cream, and tarragon. Remove skillet from heat.

Toss cooked rice with nuts and parsley. Slice chicken on an angle and arrange on a bed of rice. Top with sauce and serve. ★

✪ ✪ ✪ ✪
MAKES 2 SERVINGS (WITH A LITTLE BIT OF LEFTOVERS)

Triple Chocolate Parfaits

1/2 cup hot fudge sauce, any brand
2 shots chocolate liqueur
1/2 pint chocolate ice cream
1 canister real whipped cream (found on dairy aisle)
Cinnamon or cocoa powder, for garnish
Maraschino cherries

Heat hot fudge sauce in microwave according to package directions (remember to remove metal lid).

In two tall glasses or cocktail glasses, layer chocolate liqueur with chocolate ice cream. Top with hot fudge, whipped cream, cinnamon or cocoa powder, and cherries. ★

Try serving this with Champagne, or French or Sicilian rosé wine.

✪ ✪ ✪ ✪

MAKES 2 BIG GUY SERVINGS

Steak Pizzaola with the Works

1 porterhouse or rib-eye steak (1 & 1/2 to 2 pounds)

Salt and freshly ground black pepper, to taste

3 tablespoons extra-virgin olive oil (evoo)

4 cloves garlic, cracked away from the skin with the flat of a knife

1 teaspoon crushed red pepper flakes

12 mushrooms, sliced

1 small onion, sliced

1 green bell pepper, seeded and sliced

1/3 stick pepperoni, casing removed, then chopped (optional)

1/2 cup dry red wine (eyeball it)

1 can (28 ounces) crushed tomatoes

1 teaspoon dried oregano or 2 teaspoons chopped fresh oregano

1/4 cup grated Parmigiano Reggiano or Romano cheese

Heat a large nonstick skillet over high heat. Season the steak with salt and pepper. Add 2 tablespoons evoo to the pan (twice around the pan), then add the steak. Brown 3 minutes on each side and remove. Add remaining tablespoon evoo to the pan and reduce heat to medium-high. Add garlic, pepper flakes, mushrooms, onions, bell peppers, and pepperoni, if using. Cook mixture 5 minutes, then add wine and scrape up any bits from the bottom of the skillet. Add tomatoes, oregano, salt, and pepper.

Slide steak back in and reduce heat to medium. Cover pan and cook 5 or 6 minutes for medium-rare, 10 to 12 minutes for medium-well. Remove meat; cut away from bone or divide into 2 large portions. Cover steaks with sauce and top with grated cheese. ★

Serve this meal
with a dry martini
and pillows to rest
your heads on, if
you make it through
eating all of this!

✪ ✪ ✪ ✪
MAKES 2 SERVINGS

Big Mussels with Garlic and Dry Vermouth

2 tablespoons extra-virgin olive oil (evoo) (twice around the pan)
2 cloves garlic, cracked away from skin with the flat of a knife
1 pound mussels (buy them scrubbed)
1/2 cup dry white vermouth
2 tablespoons chopped fresh flat-leaf parsley
Salt and freshly ground black pepper, to taste

Heat a medium pan over medium-high heat. Add evoo and garlic, then
mussels. Arrange mussels in a single layer. Add vermouth to the pan and
cover. Cook until mussels open, 3 to 5 minutes. Discard any unopened
shells. Transfer mussels to a bowl. Pour juice from pan over mussels and
sprinkle with parsley, salt, and pepper. Serve with a second bowl, for
shells. ★

✪ ✪ ✪ ✪
MAKES 2 BIG GUY SERVINGS

Romaine Salad with Blue Cheese Vinaigrette

2 hearts romaine, chopped
1 clove garlic, chopped
1/2 teaspoon dried oregano
2 teaspoons sugar
2 tablespoons red wine vinegar
1/4 cup extra-virgin olive oil (evoo)
1/4 pound blue cheese crumbles (available in specialty cheese section
  of market)
Salt and freshly ground black pepper, to taste

Place romaine in a big bowl. In a small bowl, combine garlic, oregano, sugar,
and vinegar. Add evoo to dressing in a slow stream while mixing with a
whisk or fork. Stir in blue cheese. Pour dressing over salad and toss. Season
with salt and pepper, and serve. ★

281

✪ ✪ ✪ ✪
MAKES 2 YUMMY IN THE TUMMY BIG SERVINGS

Pork Chops with Brandied Cherry Sauce, Zucchini with Walnuts

PORK CHOPS

20 to 24 fresh bing cherries or 1 cup canned, drained black pitted
 cherries in natural juices

2 rounded teaspoonfuls sugar (for fresh cherries only)

2 large boneless center-cut pork chops, 1 to 1 & 1/2 inches thick

Salt and freshly ground black pepper, to taste

2 tablespoons extra-virgin olive oil (evoo)

1 large shallot, finely chopped

3 ounces (2 shots) brandy

1/2 cup chicken broth

1 tablespoon butter, cut into pieces

2 tablespoons finely chopped fresh mint

ZUCCHINI

2 ounces (1/4 cup) chopped walnuts (found in small sacks on baking
 aisle)

1 tablespoon extra-virgin olive oil (evoo) (once around the pan)

1 tablespoon butter, cut into small pieces

1 medium zucchini, sliced into 1/4-inch-thick disks

1/4 teaspoon freshly grated nutmeg, or a pinch of ground

Salt and freshly ground black pepper, to taste

Preheat oven to 375°F.

Pull stems off clean, fresh cherries. Pop pits away from cherries by placing the flat of your kitchen knife on top of a cherry or two at a time and giving the cherries a whack with the heel of your hand, just like cracking garlic from its skin. Discard pits and place fruit in a small bowl. Sugar cherries and let stand until ready to cook.

Heat an ovenproof skillet over medium-high to high heat. If you don't have an ovenproof skillet, cover the handle of a rubber-handled pan with aluminum foil. Season chops with salt and pepper. Add 1 tablespoon evoo (once around the pan) to hot skillet. Place chops in skillet and sear meat on both sides to caramelize. Place a loose foil tent over the pan and transfer the chops to oven to finish off until meat is firm to touch, but not tough, 7 or 8 minutes.

While chops are in oven, make the zucchini: Place a second skillet over medium-high heat. Toast nuts 1 to 2 minutes, shaking pan frequently. Remove nuts to cool and add evoo and butter. Add zucchini, season with nutmeg, salt, and pepper, and cook until tender, tossing occasionally, 6 or 7 minutes.

Remove meat from oven and transfer to dinner plates. Cover chops with foil to keep warm. Place chop skillet back on stove over medium heat. Add remaining 1 tablespoon evoo. Add shallots and sauté, 1 to 2 minutes. Add cherries and warm through. Add brandy by removing the pan from the burner to add the alcohol, then carefully flame the pan. Burn off alcohol for 1 minute, then add broth. Cook to reduce broth 1 minute, then add butter in small pieces. Toss sauce to combine and sprinkle in mint. Pour sauce down over chops and serve the zucchini alongside, with a generous topping of toasted walnuts. ★

✪ ✪ ✪ ✪
MAKES 2 SERVINGS

Black Cherry Ice Cream with Chocolate Sauce

1 pint black cherry ice cream
2 ounces cherry liqueur, **such as Kirsch (optional)**
1/4 cup chocolate sauce

Place 2 scoops black cherry ice cream in each of 2 cocktail glasses. Top with a splash of cherry liqueur, if desired, and a drizzle of chocolate sauce. ★

Teriyaki Beef and Scallions

Edamame

Gyoza with Dipping Sauce

✪ ✪ ✪ ✪

MAKES 4 SERVINGS

Edamame, Gyoza with Dipping Sauce, Short-Grain Rice, and Teriyaki Beef and Scallions

GYOZA, RICE, AND EDAMAME

3/4 cup short-grain rice

2 cups edamame (soybeans) (from the frozen vegetables section of large markets)

Coarse salt and freshly ground black pepper, to taste

1 & 1/2 cups shredded Napa cabbage, plus 1 large whole leaf

1/4 pound ground pork

1/4 cup 300-count baby shrimp (a handful), chopped

1 tablespoon sake, mirin may be substituted (a splash)

1 inch fresh gingerroot, peeled and minced

1 scallion, finely chopped

1 tablespoon tamari (dark aged soy) (available on Asian food aisle)

12 wonton wrappers

BEEF

2 fillet of beef steaks (6 ounces each), 1 inch thick

1 teaspoon steak seasoning blend such as Montreal Steak Seasoning or salt and freshly ground black pepper

1/3 cup teriyaki sauce or 1/4 cup tamari mixed with 2 tablespoons dry sherry

1 tablespoon light oil (wok, peanut, or vegetable oil)

4 scallions, chopped on an angle into 1-inch pieces

DIPPING SAUCE

3 tablespoons tamari (eyeball it)

1 teaspoon hot sweet mustard (from Asian foods aisle), or other prepared mustard

2 teaspoons rice vinegar or white vinegar

Place 2 pots of water on to boil: one medium saucepan with 1 & 1/2 cups water in it, one pasta pot with a few inches of water in it. Cover both pots and bring all the water to a boil.

When the saucepan with 1 & 1/2 cups of water comes to a boil, stir in rice and return water to a boil. Reduce heat to simmer. Place a colander over the pot and add the edamame to it. Place the pot cover over the edamame, nesting it in the colander. Steam the edamame 5 minutes, then remove them to 2 small bowls. Stir rice and return lid to rice pot. Salt edamame and cover bowls with plastic or aluminum foil to keep warm.

30-MINUTE MEALS

MENU

PASSPORT TO JAPAN: BENTO BOXES

1
appetizers
EDAMAME

GYOZA WITH DIPPING SAUCE

2
entree
TERIYAKI BEEF AND SCALLIONS

3
side dish
SHORT-GRAIN RICE

While the edamame are steaming, make the gyoza: Add 1/2 cup (a couple handfuls) cabbage to the second pot of water. Blanch the shredded cabbage 1 minute and remove with a spider or tongs to paper towels to drain and cool (leave heat on under water). Chop shredded blanched cabbage. Combine pork, chopped shrimp, sake, ginger, scallion, tamari, a few grinds fresh black pepper, and the cooled, chopped cabbage in a bowl. Place 2 teaspoons of filling onto each wonton wrapper. Wet your fingertips to help seal them; fold wontons in half diagonally; the gyoza should look like small half moons.

Place a whole cabbage leaf into the bottom of the colander. The leaf will prevent the dumplings from sticking to the colander. Arrange dumplings on cabbage leaf in colander and steam over second, larger pot of simmering water. Cover and steam, 10 to 12 minutes. While you are working on this, go back and forth with the edamame as necessary per above directions.

While the dumplings cook, make the steaks: Slice them thinly across the grain. Toss with seasoning and teriyaki or tamari and sherry. Heat a nonstick skillet over high heat. Add oil and the meat, and stir-fry. When meat browns at edges, add scallions and cook 2 minutes more, stirring frequently.

Use remaining raw shredded cabbage as a bed to serve your dumplings on. Plate all of your items on little dishes and in small bowls and fit them into your boxes.

Mix a dipping sauce of tamari, mustard, and vinegar for the gyoza, and set out alongside dumplings. ★

✪ ✪ ✪ ✪

MAKES 2 SERVINGS

Tournedos with Mushroom Caps, Red Wine Sauce, Duchess-Style Potatoes, and Steamed Broccoli Spears

POTATOES

1 pound russet potatoes (2 medium-large potatoes)

Salt and freshly ground black pepper, to taste

2 egg yolks

2 tablespoons butter

2 tablespoons grated cheese, such as Parmesan

2 teaspoons extra-virgin olive oil (evoo)

BROCCOLI

2 clusters of broccoli tops, cut into spears OR 1 pound of broccolini, trimmed

TOURNEDOS

1/2 tablespoon butter

1 tablespoon extra-virgin olive oil (evoo)

2 large stuffing mushroom caps, wiped with damp towel, stems removed

2 beef fillets, 1 inch thick

Salt and freshly ground black pepper, to taste

SAUCE

1 tablespoon butter

1 tablespoon all-purpose flour

1/2 cup dry red wine

1/2 cup beef stock

Preheat oven to 450°F.

Make the potatoes: Peel potatoes and cut into chunks. Boil them until tender in salted water, about 10 minutes. Mix a little cooking water into 1 beaten egg yolk. Drain potatoes and transfer to a food processor. Add egg yolk mixture, butter, and cheese. Process until smooth and add salt to taste. Scrape potatoes into a pastry bag or a cone made from rolled up waxed or parchment paper, a disposable alternative to a pastry bag. Pipe potatoes into conical shapes on a nonstick cookie sheet or greased baking sheet.

Make a wash: Beat the remaining egg yolk with evoo and brush potatoes with wash. Bake potatoes until golden, about 10 minutes.

While the potatoes cook, steam the broccoli and make the tournedos.

30-MINUTE MEALS
MENU

MEAT AND POTATOES À DEUX

1
entree
TOURNEDOS WITH MUSHROOM CAPS AND RED WINE SAUCE

2
side dishes
DUCHESS-STYLE POTATOES

STEAMED BROCCOLI SPEARS

3
dessert
BLACK-AND-WHITE ICE CREAM SANDWICHES

Steam broccoli in 1 inch of water, covered, 3 minutes. Remove from heat. Drain, but leave covered in pan for another 5 minutes. The broccoli will continue to cook, but not lose all of its color.

Make the tournedos: In a small skillet, heat butter and evoo over medium-high heat. Cook mushroom caps until just golden, 3 or 4 minutes; turn them and set to sides of pan. Season meat with salt and pepper and add to skillet. Cook 3 minutes on each side for medium-rare, 5 minutes on each side for medium-well. Remove steaks and caps from the pan and tent loosely with foil to keep warm and let juices distribute.

Make the sauce: Add butter and flour to the meat pan, cook for a few minutes, and whisk in wine. Scrape up drippings, reduce wine for half a minute, then whisk in a little beef stock. Thicken sauce another 30 seconds, then remove from heat.

To serve, top each steak with a mushroom cap and pour a little sauce down over the top. Serve the potato cones and broccoli tops alongside. Makes a dinner fit for a king and a queen. ★

✪ ✪ ✪ ✪
MAKES 2 SERVINGS

Black-and-White Ice Cream Sandwiches

1/2 pint fudge swirl ice cream, softened
4 chocolate cookies OR thin chocolate brownie bars (3 inches diameter) (from baked goods section)
1/2 cup chopped walnuts

Place a large scoop of ice cream between 2 cookies or thin brownies and squish the ice cream out to the edges. Repeat with remaining ice cream and cookies. Roll edges of the ice cream sandwiches in chopped walnuts and serve. ★

Tournedos with Mushroom Caps and Red Wine Sauce

✪ ✪ ✪ ✪

MAKES 2 SERVINGS

Quick Ginger Peach Cobbler

1 can (14 & 1/2 ounces) sliced peaches in juice, drained

1 inch fresh gingerroot, peeled and minced, or 1/2 teaspoon ground ginger

1 tablespoon butter, softened

2 tablespoons brown sugar

1/2 cup granola cereal with raisins and nuts

1 egg white, beaten

1 canister real whipped cream (from dairy aisle)

Preheat oven to 400°F.

Mix drained peaches with ginger. Place sliced peaches in small ovenproof bowls.

Combine butter and sugar with a fork, then mix with granola. Fold in beaten egg white. Mound the topping on top of the peaches. Place dishes on a small baking sheet and bake, 10 to 12 minutes. Remove and cool cobbler while you enjoy dinner.

After dinner, serve warm cobbler with whipped cream. ★

✪ ✪ ✪ ✪

MAKES 2 SERVINGS

Salisbury Steak with Wild Mushroom Gravy, Smashed Potatoes with Garlic & Herb Cheese and Chives, and Creamed Spinach

POTATOES

1 pound russet potatoes (2 large potatoes), peeled and chunked

Salt and freshly ground black pepper, to taste

1/4 cup half-and-half or cream (eyeball it)

3 ounces (1/3 cup or half of one small container), garlic and herb cheese, such as Boursin

2 tablespoons chopped chives (6 blades), or 1 scallion, thinly sliced

MEAT AND GRAVY

3/4 pound ground beef sirloin

2 teaspoons Worcestershire sauce (eyeball it)

1/2 small onion, finely chopped

1 teaspoon steak seasoning blend, such as Montreal Seasoning by McCormick OR coarse salt and freshly ground black pepper, to taste

2 tablespoons extra-virgin olive oil (evoo)

1 tablespoon butter

6 crimini or baby portobello mushrooms, sliced

6 shiitake mushrooms, chopped

Salt and freshly ground black pepper, to taste

1 tablespoon all-purpose flour

1/2 cup beef stock

SPINACH

1 box (10 ounces) chopped spinach, defrosted in microwave

1 tablespoon butter, cut into pieces

1/4 cup half-and-half or heavy cream

Salt and freshly ground black pepper, to taste

Start the potatoes: Place them in a pot with water. Cover pot, bring to a boil, and lightly salt. Leave uncovered and cook at rolling boil until tender, 8 to 10 minutes.

While potatoes cook, make the steaks: Combine meat, Worcestershire, onion, and steak seasoning or salt and pepper. Form 2 large, oval patties, 1 inch thick. Preheat a large nonstick skillet over medium-high heat. Add 1 tablespoon evoo (once around the pan) and meat patties to hot pan. Cook 6 minutes on each side until meat is evenly caramelized on the outside and juices run clear. Remove meat and cover loosely with aluminum foil to keep warm. Add 1 more tablespoon evoo and the butter to the pan, then the mushrooms. Season with salt and pepper, and sauté until tender, 3 to 5 minutes.

While mushrooms cook, make the spinach: Wring spinach dry in a clean kitchen towel. To a small skillet, add butter and cream and heat to a bubble over medium heat. Add spinach and salt and pepper. Cook until cream thickens, 3 to 5 minutes.

To mushrooms, add a sprinkle of flour to the pan and cook 2 minutes more. Whisk in stock and thicken 1 minute.

While sauce thickens, drain potatoes and return them to hot pot. Smash potatoes with a little half-and-half or cream and garlic and herb cheese. Smash and incorporate chives. Add salt and pepper to taste.

To serve, pour gravy over steak. Serve potatoes and creamed spinach alongside the steaks. Now that's a TV dinner, DELUXE! ★

This meal is a tribute dinner that John and I came up with in honor of our friend and inspiration, chef Jon Young, of Kitch'n on Roscoe in Chicago. Jon is our age and has this too-groovy restaurant that serves upscale versions of familiar foods. He makes Twinkie tiramisu and psychedelic TV dinners. This gourmet-made-everyday Salisbury steak dinner is a winner. Enjoy it while watching "Starsky & Hutch" reruns or Shaft videos with someone you love.

30-MINUTE MEALS
MENU

EXPRESS
LANE
DINNER
DATE:
10 ITEMS
OR LESS

1

entree
ROSEMARY
CHICKEN
BREASTS

2

side dishes
BROWN BUTTER
AND BALSAMIC
RAVIOLI

TOMATO AND
ONION SALAD

✪ ✪ ✪ ✪

MAKES 2 SERVINGS

Rosemary Chicken Breasts, Brown Butter and Balsamic Ravioli, Tomato and Onion Salad

CHICKEN

2 boneless, skinless chicken breasts (6 to 8 ounces each)

1 tablespoon balsamic vinegar, just enough to coat chicken lightly (eyeball it)

2 tablespoons extra-virgin olive oil (evoo)

2 stems rosemary, leaves stripped and chopped

Salt and freshly ground black pepper, to taste

2 cloves garlic, cracked away from skin with the flat of a knife

RAVIOLI

Salt and freshly ground black pepper, to taste

1 package (12 to 16 ounces) fresh ravioli, any flavor filling

3 tablespoons butter, cut into small pieces

2 tablespoons balsamic vinegar

2 handfuls grated Parmigiano Reggiano cheese

1/4 cup fresh flat-leaf parsley leaves, chopped (a couple handfuls)

SALAD

4 vine-ripe tomatoes, seeded and chopped

1/2 small white onion, thinly sliced

1/4 cup fresh flat-leaf parsley leaves, chopped (a couple handfuls)

2 tablespoons extra-virgin olive oil (evoo) (eyeball it)

Salt and freshly ground black pepper, to taste

Marinate the chicken: Coat chicken in balsamic vinegar, then evoo. Season chicken with rosemary, salt, and pepper and let stand, 10 minutes.

Start the ravioli: Bring a large pot of water to a boil. Salt water and drop ravioli in water. Cook 6 to 8 minutes or until raviolis expand and float to top of water and are al dente. Drain.

Heat a medium nonstick skillet over medium-high heat. Add chicken breasts and cracked garlic to the pan. Cook chicken until juices run clear, 10 to 12 minutes, turning occasionally. The balsamic vinegar will produce a deep brown, sweet finish on the chicken as it cooks.

When the chicken has cooked midway, 5 or 6 minutes, start to prepare butter for ravioli: To a cold skillet, add butter and turn on medium heat. Let the butter brown. If you start with a cold pan, the butter should be lightly browned by the time it comes to a bubble. When the butter for the ravioli has browned, add cooked ravioli to the pan and turn in butter to heat through. Add balsamic vinegar to the ravioli and cook 1 to 2 minutes longer to reduce the vinegar and glaze the ravioli. The vinegar will become thick and syruplike. Add cheese, parsley, salt, and pepper to the pasta and remove the pan from the heat.

Make the salad: Combine tomatoes, onions, parsley, evoo, salt, and pepper. Toss to coat salad evenly with oil and to mix in salt and pepper. Adjust seasonings.

Slice cooked chicken on an angle and serve with ravioli and salad alongside. ★

Even when you shop and cook together, it's still a date. This menu is great for busy couples: three courses from ten items, so you can hit the express lane at your market. The menu is especially romantic to me because it combines recipes of John's and mine. We eat this meal often.

✪ ✪ ✪ ✪
MAKES 2 SERVINGS

Herb-Cheese-Tipped Endive and Artichoke Hearts with Lemon and Parsley

1 head endive
3 ounces soft herb cheese, such as Boursin
2 tablespoons chopped chives
1 can (15 ounces) whole artichoke hearts in water, drained
1/2 cup fresh flat-leaf parsley leaves, coarsely chopped
The grated zest of 1 lemon
The juice of 1/2 lemon
1 & 1/2 tablespoons extra-virgin olive oil (evoo) (eyeball it)
Salt and freshly ground black pepper, to taste
Edible flowers, for garnish (optional)

Trim endive and separate leaves. Pick out 6 leaves, wrap the leftover endive to add to salad another evening. Spread a rounded teaspoonful of cheese onto the firm end of each leaf. Sprinkle the cheese-tipped ends with chives.

Halve artichoke hearts top to bottom and combine with parsley, lemon zest, and lemon juice. Coat with evoo, toss, and season with salt and pepper. Divide the artichokes between 2 plates and garnish each plate with 3 cheese-filled pieces of endive and a few edible flowers. ★

✪ ✪ ✪ ✪
MAKES 2 SERVINGS

Rice with Asparagus Tips

1 tablespoon extra-virgin olive oil (evoo) (once around the pan)
1 shallot, chopped
1 can (14 ounces) chicken broth
1 cup long-grain white rice
1 bundle (3/4 pound) thin asparagus spears

Preheat a medium saucepan over medium heat. Add evoo and shallot. Sauté shallot, 1 or 2 minutes. Add broth and bring to a boil. Add rice and stir. When broth returns to a boil, cover and reduce heat to simmer. Cook 18 minutes, until rice is tender.

Trim asparagus of tough bottoms and cut tops into 1-inch pieces on an angle. Steam in 1 inch of water, 3 minutes; drain. Remove rice from heat, fluff with fork, combine with asparagus, and serve. ★

Herb-Cheese-Tipped Endive

✪ ✪ ✪ ✪
MAKES 2 SERVINGS

Salmon with Champagne-Vanilla Sauce

2 salmon fillets (6 ounces each)
Salt and freshly ground black pepper, to taste
2 tablespoons extra-virgin olive oil (evoo)
1 large or 2 small shallots, finely chopped
1 split dry champagne (a 6- to 6.5-ounce bottle)
1 whole vanilla bean
1/2 cup heavy cream
2 tablespoons chopped fresh flat-leaf parsley

Heat a nonstick skillet over medium-high heat. Season fish with salt and pepper. Add 1 tablespoon evoo (once around the pan) to the pan, then add fish. Cook salmon, 3 minutes on each side, 5 minutes if you like your fish well done. Transfer fish to a serving plate or dinner plates and cover with foil to keep warm.

Add remaining tablespoon of evoo to the pan. Add shallots and cook, 2 minutes. Add champagne to the pan and cook to reduce by half. Split the vanilla bean in half lengthwise and scrape the seeds into champagne. Add cream to the pan and reduce heat to low. Simmer 5 minutes. Pour sauce over fish, garnish with parley, and serve. ★

✪ ✪ ✪ ✪
MAKES 2 SERVINGS

Raspberry Sorbet Desserts

4 sprigs fresh mint
1 pint raspberry sorbet
1/2 pint fresh raspberries
2 ounces Chambord raspberry liqueur (optional)
Piroline or other rolled dessert cookies

Chop the leaves from 2 of the mint sprigs. Scoop sorbet into large cocktail glasses or dessert cups. Top with fresh raspberries, Chambord (if desired), and chopped mint. Garnish with remaining sprigs of mint and rolled cookies. ★

MAKES 4 SERVINGS

Chicken Salad with Figs and Prosciutto

4 boneless, skinless chicken breasts

1 can (14 ounces) no-fat, low-sodium chicken broth

A handful hazelnuts

4 ounces mixed baby salad greens (a couple handfuls, from the bulk bin in the produce department)

6 fresh figs, trimmed and quartered, or 8 dried figs, reconstituted by simmering in water for 10 minutes, then draining and halving

1/4 pound prosciutto di Parma, sliced thin at the deli, then cut into short, wide strips, working across the slices of prosciutto

1 teaspoon currant or seedless blackberry jam or all-fruit spread

3 tablespoons extra-virgin olive oil (evoo) (a couple of glugs)

A splash balsamic vinegar

Freshly ground black pepper

Preheat oven to 300°F.

Place chicken in a skillet and cover with broth. Place skillet over high heat to bring to a boil. Reduce heat to medium-low. Cover and simmer 12 minutes to poach chicken through. Drain and let stand at room temperature.

While chicken is cooking, toast hazelnuts in a cake pan or on a cookie sheet in oven until golden brown. Pour nuts onto a slightly damp towel and rub off skins. Transfer nuts to a plastic bag and give them a whack with a blunt instrument to break them up a bit.

Chunk the chicken. Combine in a shallow bowl with greens, figs, and prosciutto. Mix jam, evoo, and vinegar with a fork. Drizzle over the salad and lightly toss to coat. Sprinkle with nuts and black pepper. Serve with crusty bread. ★

30-MINUTE MEALS

MENU

SWEET SALAD

1

entree
CHICKEN SALAD WITH FIGS AND PROSCIUTTO

2

suggested side
CRUSTY BREAD

30-MINUTE MEALS

MENU

SUPPER EXPRESS

1

entree
LINGUINI WITH WHITE CLAM SAUCE
- - - - - -

2

side dish
GREENS 'N BEANS SALAD
- - - - - -

✪ ✪ ✪ ✪

MAKES 2 SERVINGS

Linguini with White Clam Sauce

Salt and freshly ground black pepper, to taste

1/2 pound linguini

1/4 cup extra-virgin olive oil (evoo) (eyeball it)

4 to 6 cloves garlic, minced

1 tin flat anchovy fillets (6 or 7 fillets), drained

4 or 5 sprigs fresh thyme, leaves stripped and chopped, or 1 & 1/2 teaspoons dried thyme

1 cup dry white wine

1 can (15 ounces) fancy whole baby clams with juice

The grated zest of 1 lemon

2 tablespoons chopped fresh flat-leaf parsley

Crusty bread, to pass at table

Put a large pot of water over high heat. When water boils, add salt and pasta. Cook pasta until slightly underdone, 6 to 7 minutes. Drain.

Meanwhile, heat a large, deep skillet over medium heat. Add evoo, garlic, and anchovies and cook until anchovies have melted into evoo. Add thyme and wine. Simmer wine to reduce, 1 minute. Stir in clams with their juice and the lemon zest.

Add pasta to skillet and toss with sauce; cook 2 to 3 minutes, until pasta is al dente and has absorbed some of the sauce and flavor. Add parsley, salt, and pepper and serve with bread for mopping up remaining juices. ★

✪ ✪ ✪ ✪
MAKES 2 SERVINGS

Greens 'n' Beans Salad

1/2 head escarole, chopped

1/2 head green or red leaf lettuce, chopped

1 can (15 ounces) cannellini, drained

1/4 red onion, chopped

1 clove garlic, minced

1 teaspoon sugar

1 tablespoon lemon juice

1 tablespoon red wine vinegar

3 tablespoons extra-virgin olive oil (evoo)

Salt and freshly ground black pepper, to taste

Arrange greens on a large platter or in a salad bowl. Top with beans and red onions. In a small bowl, blender, or food processor, combine garlic, sugar, lemon juice, and vinegar. Mix in evoo. Pour dressing evenly over the salad. Season salad with salt and pepper, toss, and serve. ★

30-MINUTE MEALS
MENU

15-MINUTE
MEAL—FOR
REAL

1

entree
VICKI'S
CHICKEN AND
GRAPES WITH
CREAMY
MUSTARD SAUCE
AND COUSCOUS

2

suggested side
GREEN SALAD

Vicki Cusimano makes this for her husband, Andy. They have been married 40 years and are sickeningly in love. I am going to keep making this for my husband, John. He's their son. I hope it brings me 40 happy years, too—and many more!

✪ ✪ ✪ ✪
MAKES 2 SERVINGS (WITH LEFTOVERS)

Vicki's Chicken and Grapes with Creamy Mustard Sauce and Couscous

3 tablespooons all-purpose flour
1 tablespoon extra-virgin olive oil (evoo) (once around the pan), plus a drizzle
2 tablespoons butter, cut into pieces
2 packages (1 & 1/4 to 1 & 1/2 pounds total) chicken tenders
Salt and freshly ground black pepper, to taste
1/3 cup white wine (eyeball it)
1 cup half-and-half
1/4 cup grainy stone-ground mustard
1 cup seedless red grapes, halved
2 cups chicken broth
2 cups couscous

Place flour in a shallow bowl. Place a large skillet over medium to medium-high heat; add 1 tablespoon evoo and the butter. Dredge chicken in flour; season with salt and pepper. Add chicken to skillet and cook until browned, 7 or 8 minutes. Add wine and scrape up browned bits as wine comes to a bubble; cook the liquid down, 30 seconds to 1 minute. Combine half-and-half and mustard and pour the mixture over the chicken. Add grapes to the pan and shake to coat chicken and grapes in sauce. Reduce heat to low and simmer 3 to 5 minutes more.

Meanwhile, make the couscous: Bring chicken broth and a drizzle evoo to a boil. Add couscous. Remove pan from heat and cover. Let couscous sit 5 minutes, then fluff with a fork.

Serve mounds of couscous with chicken and grapes alongside or over the top. Add a green salad for a complete meal. ★

Vicki's Chicken and Grapes with Creamy Mustard Sauce

30-MINUTE MEALS
MENU

JOHN'S
FAVORITE
FISH
DINNER

1

entree
HADDOCK WITH
BACON,
ONIONS, AND
TOMATOES

2

side dish
WILTED SPINACH
WITH BUTTER
AND WINE

✪ ✪ ✪ ✪

MAKES 2 SERVINGS

Haddock with Bacon, Onions, and Tomatoes

1 pound haddock fillet, cut into 2 equal portions

1 tablespoon lemon juice (the juice of 1 small wedge)

Salt, to taste

Extra-virgin olive oil (evoo), for drizzling

1/2 tablespoon butter, softened

3 slices smoky bacon, chopped

3 or 4 cippolini (small flat Italian sweet onion), peeled and thinly sliced (a small to medium yellow onion, quartered then thinly sliced, may be substituted)

1/2 cup Italian bread crumbs

2 to 3 tablespoons chopped fresh flat-leaf parsley (a handful)

1 plum tomato, seeded and chopped

Preheat oven to 400°F.

Rinse fish and pat dry. Sprinkle fish with lemon juice and salt. Coat an oven-safe skillet with a drizzle of evoo and the softened butter. If your skillet doesn't have an oven-safe handle, wrap the handle in tin foil twice and it should be fine in oven. Set fish into skillet.

Heat a small skillet over medium-high heat. Add a drizzle of evoo and the bacon. Render the bacon fat, 3 minutes, then add onions. Cook onions until softened, 10 minutes. Remove pan from heat. Add bread crumbs to the pan and turn to coat them in drippings. Add parsley and combine. Top fish with coating of onions, bacon, and bread crumbs. Bake 15 minutes. Transfer fish to dinner plates, top with chopped tomato, and serve. ★

✪ ✪ ✪ ✪

MAKES 2 SERVINGS

Wilted Spinach with Butter and Wine

2 tablespoons butter

1 sack (1 pound) triple-washed spinach, tough stems removed, coarsely chopped

1/2 cup dry white wine

Salt and freshly ground black pepper, to taste

Heat a medium skillet over medium heat. Melt butter in pan. Add spinach in bunches, adding more as it wilts down. When all of the spinach is wilted, add wine and turn to coat. Let wine cook down 1 or 2 minutes. Season with salt and pepper and serve. ★

My sweetie and I eat a lot of fish. This is a recipe my mother first made for both of us, and I continue to make for him, as it has become a favorite! The spinach takes only 5 minutes to prepare, so begin preheating the skillet 6 to 7 minutes before you are ready to sit down and eat.

✪ ✪ ✪ ✪

MAKES 2 SERVINGS

Salad with Strawberries and Balsamic Vinegar

1 head green leaf lettuce, chopped or torn

12 ripe strawberries, hulled and thinly sliced

3 tablespoons balsamic vinegar, aged for 6 or more years (available on specialty foods aisle)

3 tablespoons extra-virgin olive oil (evoo) (eyeball it)

Salt and freshly ground black pepper, to taste

Place lettuce in a salad bowl. Place sliced berries in a small bowl, cover with balsamic and let stand 15 minutes. Remove berries with a slotted spoon and add to the salad. Whisk evoo into remaining balsamic vinegar and season with salt and pepper. Dress and toss salad just before serving. ★

✪ ✪ ✪ ✪

MAKES 2 SERVINGS

Anchovy and Potato Appetizers

2 large fingerling potatoes or thin, oval-shaped white potatoes

Extra-virgin olive oil (evoo), for drizzling

Salt and freshly ground black pepper, to taste

6 stems rosemary, leaves stripped and coarsely chopped

1 jar (4 ounces) anchovies or 2 tins (2 ounces each), drained

2 small plum or Roma tomatoes, seeded and chopped

Preheat oven to 425°F.

Slice potatoes lengthwise into thin 1/8- to 1/4-inch-thick slices. Coat potatoes with evoo, salt, and pepper and place on a cookie sheet. Top potatoes liberally with chopped rosemary. Rest 1 large anchovy or 2 small anchovies on each slice of potato: It will cover the potato slice from end to end. Top anchovies with chopped tomato and an additional drizzle of evoo. Roast potatoes and anchovies until potatoes are tender, 15 to 18 minutes. Remove from oven and serve hot. ★

✪ ✪ ✪ ✪

MAKES 2 SERVINGS (NO LEFTOVERS IN OUR HOUSE, BUT YOU MIGHT HAVE SOMETHING LEFT FOR LATE-NIGHT SNACKING)

Tuna Marinara with Ravioli

Salt and freshly ground black pepper, to taste

1 package (12 to 16 ounces) fresh ravioli

2 tablespoons extra-virgin olive oil (evoo) (twice around the pan)

3 cloves garlic, peeled and minced

1 can (6 ounces) Italian tuna in water or oil, drained

1/4 medium onion, finely chopped

3 to 4 tablespoons chopped pitted black olives, such as Kalamata (available in deli section)

3 to 4 tablespoons finely chopped fresh flat-leaf parsley leaves (a handful)

1 can (15 ounces) crushed tomatoes

8 to 10 leaves fresh basil, shredded or torn

Put a large pot of water over high heat for the ravioli. When water boils, add salt and pasta. Cook 5 to 6 minutes until they float and are al dente. Drain carefully or remove the ravioli with a slotted spoon or a spider strainer.

Meanwhile, make the sauce: Heat a deep skillet over medium heat. Add evoo, then garlic. Cook garlic 1 minute, then add tuna. Break tuna up and mash it into the oil with the back of a wooden spoon. Add onions and cook 3 to 5 minutes. Add olives and parsley, and stir in tomatoes. Season with a pinch of salt (if needed) and lots of pepper. Reduce heat to simmer.

Add cooked ravioli to sauce and turn gently, then transfer to plates. Top with remaining sauce left in the skillet and garnish with lots of basil. ★

This is my kind of supper. It is a meal that I shared with my true love when we were travelling in Italy. The sauce on the pasta was actually a mussel sauce, but the tuna sauce is our at-home adaptation, simpler and faster than shucking a mountain of mussels!

30-MINUTE MEALS
MENU

party ideas
KIDS' COOKING
PARTY POINTERS
AND TABLE TIPS

Tableart

Call up your local newspaper and ask them if you can come by and pick up the ends of their paper rolls. Most newspapers will be only too glad to give you hundreds of feet of scrap-paper-on-a-roll. Cover any dining table, big coffee table, or picnic table with long sheets torn from the paper roll and tape edges down to secure. Let kids decorate their table by drawing on the paper table cover with crayons or washable markers. For an easy seating idea, surround your coffee table with big pillows.

Cupcake Toppings Party

For a fun and edible party craft, buy
• Bulk candies: different shapes and sizes
• Small tubes of prepared icing (so little hands can draw with them)
• Thin licorice whips, cut into strips.

Place all the toppings on a tray and let kids make up faces and creatures on the tops of frosted cupcakes. Halloween cupcakes can be turned into spiders and goblins. Christmas cupcakes can look like ornaments. Birthday cupcakes can be turned into favorite animals. Cream cheese frosting, homemade or store-bought, makes a good canvas for the toppings.

Use spice cake mix, made to low-fat directions on the box by adding applesauce, to make a nice cupcake that appeals to everyone. This will help avoid fights over the last chocolate or the last vanilla cupcake.

Keep it Clean!

Helpers and kids should always wash hands, utensils, and work surfaces after handling raw meats. This is very important. The heat from cooking can kill any bad germs growing on the meat, but using the same utensils or using dirty hands to handle or chop things that will not be cooked will transfer the bad germs from the meat to the other foods.

Make it Fun!

A little music adds to any party and relaxes every cook. Mix it up! Play a little samba and swing along with kids' favorites. Kids can bring their own chart-topping tapes or disks to the gathering and take turns sharing their tastes. (After-dinner dancing is also highly recommended.)

30-MINUTE MEALS
MENU

MEXICAN TAKEOUT AT HOME

1
entree
MEXICAN RICE BOWL

2
suggested side
TORTILLA CHIPS AND SALSA

✪ ✪ ✪ ✪
MAKES 4 SERVINGS

Mexican Rice Bowl

For ages 7 and up, with a Grown-up Helper

1 tablespoon extra-virgin olive oil (evoo) (once around the pan)

2 tablespoons butter (tablespoons are marked on the wrapper)

3/4 pound chicken tenders, cut into bite-size pieces

Salt and freshly ground black pepper, to taste

2 cups white rice

1 quart chicken broth

1 tablespoon Sazon seasoning blend by Goya (available in Mexican and Spanish foods section)

1/2 cup tomato salsa or taco sauce

1/4 cup drained chopped olives and pimentos (salad olives)

2 tablespoons chopped fresh flat-leaf parsley (a handful)

Blue or red corn tortilla chips and salsa, for serving (optional)

Heat a medium pot over medium heat; add evoo and butter. When butter has melted into oil, add cut-up chicken tenders. (Your GH, or Grown-up Helper, can chop for you if you are not comfortable enough with your knife yet. Remember: All fingers should be tucked under; keep knife blade tilted away from your body; use a knife that matches your size and skill level. Wash your hands after handling the raw chicken pieces.) Season the chicken with salt and pepper. Sauté the chicken, stirring, until lightly browned. Add the rice and cook another 1 to 2 minutes. Add chicken broth to the pot and Sazon seasoning. Raise the heat to high to bring the broth to a quick boil, 2 or 3 minutes. When the liquid boils, reduce heat to simmer and put the lid on. Cook until rice is tender but still a little chewy in the center, 13 to 15 minutes.

Take off the lid and stir in salsa or taco sauce, olives and pimentos, and parsley. Turn off heat and let stand 5 minutes. Serve hot Mexican rice in bowls placed on dinner plates and garnish plates with chips and leftover salsa or taco sauce for dipping. ★

These are like the giant stuffed pizzas you sometimes see at restaurants and pizzerias, but you can make these spicy individual tortilla pizzas a whole lot faster! Chorizo and linguiça are like Spanish pepperoni for your pizzas, but you can use pepperoni too, if you prefer.

✪ ✪ ✪ ✪
MAKES 6 SERVINGS

Quesadilla Pizzas

For ages 7 and up, with a Grown-up Helper

8 large (10-inch) flour tortillas

2 & 1/2 cups shredded cheddar cheese (one 10-ounce sack; preshredded is available on dairy aisle)

1 cup salsa, red or green, mild or hot

3/4 pound brick smoked cheddar or pepper Jack cheese

1/2 cup chopped green olives and pimentos, drained

3 scallions, cut up with kitchen scissors or chopped into small pieces

8 ounces chorizo or linguiça sausage (available near kielbasa in meat department), thinly sliced or diced

Have your GH (Grown-Up Helper) preheat oven to 400°F.

Take out 2 nonstick cookie sheets. Place 2 tortillas on each cookie sheet, one next to the other. Top each tortilla with lots of cheddar cheese. Place another tortilla on top of each cheese-covered tortilla. Put the tortillas in the oven and bake 5 minutes.

Have your GH take them back out of the oven using pot holders. Press the tortillas down a bit with a spatula to set them in place with the melted cheese. Top each cheese quesadilla with some salsa, a sprinkle of smoked cheddar or pepper Jack cheese, olives, pimentos, scallions, and some thin slices of chorizo or linguiça. Put the pizzas in the oven and cook until edges are brown and crisp and cheese is melted on top, 5 or 6 minutes more. Have the GH take the pizzas out and transfer 1 whole pizza onto each dinner plate. Serve with a chunked vegetable salad on the side. ★

30-MINUTE MEALS
MENU

CHEESY STUFFED PIZZA

1
entree
QUESADILLA PIZZAS

2
side dish
CHUNKED VEGETABLE SALAD

✪ ✪ ✪ ✪
MAKES 4 SERVINGS

Crunchy Oven-Baked Chicken Toes

For ages 4 and up, with a Grown-up Helper

1 cup corn flakes cereal, any brand
1 cup plain bread crumbs
2 tablespoons brown sugar
1 teaspoon salt
1/2 teaspoon freshly ground black pepper
1/2 teaspoon allspice (the SECRET ingredient)
3 tablespoons vegetable oil
1/3 cup all-purpose flour
2 eggs, beaten
1 & 1/2 pounds chicken breast tenders (2 packages), cut into 2-inch pieces by GH (Grown-Up Helper)
1/4 cup honey mustard, such as Gulden's brand
1/4 cup barbecue sauce, any brand

Have your GH turn the oven on to 375°F.

Make the breading: Pour corn flakes into a pie pan or other large, shallow dish. Crush cereal up with your hands. Mix in bread crumbs, brown sugar, salt, pepper, and allspice (your SECRET ingredient; do not tell anybody what your secret ingredient is—ever!). Drizzle vegetable oil evenly over the breading. Have the GH pour the oil out slowly. A vegetable oil bottle has a big opening, so 3 tablespoons will pour out pretty quickly, probably by the time you can count to 5, so watch the GH closely and count really loudly! Toss and turn breading to mix the oil all through the bread crumbs and crushed-up corn flakes.

Pour flour into another shallow dish, and beaten eggs into a third. Turn chicken in flour, then eggs, and then in the special crunchy breading. Arrange the chicken toes on a nonstick baking sheet. You and your GH should go and wash your hands now.

Place the chicken toes in the oven and cook until crisp and brown all over, about 15 minutes. Work on the other stuff in this menu—the veggies and the apples and dip—while the toes are cooking.

When the toes come out of the oven, it's time to stir up the sauce for dipping them. Mix together honey mustard and barbecue sauce in a small bowl. Dip your hot chicken toes into your honey mustard barbecue sauce. ★

✪ ✪ ✪ ✪
MAKES 4 SERVINGS

Creamy Salsa Dip and Veggies

For ages 4 and up, with a Grown-up Helper

1 cup (8 ounces) mild salsa, any brand

1/2 cup sour cream

12 carrot sticks, store-bought or cut by your GH (Grown-Up Helper)

12 celery sticks, store-bought or cut by your GH

12 cherry or grape tomatoes

12 sugar snap peas

Make the dip: Stir together salsa and sour cream in a small bowl. Put the small bowl in the middle of a big plate. Arrange the veggies all around the dip and serve. ★

✪ ✪ ✪ ✪

MAKES 4 SERVINGS

Fuji Apples and Peanutbuttery Caramel Dip

For ages 4 and up, with a Grown-up Helper

24 wrapped caramel candies (1/2 of a 14-ounce bag), such as Kraft brand

2 Fuji apples

2 tablespoons freshly squeezed lemon juice (from about 1/4 lemon)

1 cup plus 1 tablespoon water

2 tablespoons creamy peanut butter

Pinch of cinnamon (this is your SECRET ingredient)

Unwrap candies and place in a bowl. While you are working on that, have your GH (Grown-Up Helper) cut apples into quarters then cut out the seeds. The GH should then slice apples into 8 pieces per apple. Count for them; you'll need 16 slices altogether. Squirt lemon juice into a bowl and add 1 cup water to it. Add the sliced apples to the water and turn them around in it, then drain them in a strainer or colander. Lemon juice is sour, but it's only a tiny bit on lots of apple slices. The apples will still taste sweet and really good. The lemon juice keeps the apple slices from turning brown.

Add 1 tablespoon water and the peanut butter to the caramel candies. Place candies into the microwave oven and cook them on high for 2 minutes. Stir up the dip with a rubber spatula. If the candy is not melted all the way, put it back in the microwave on high for another 20 seconds. Add a pinch of cinnamon to the sauce and stir. DO NOT TELL ANYONE ABOUT THE CINNAMON! Tell your GH not to tell, too. This is your secret ingredient.

To serve, place the drained, sliced apples next to the Peanutbuttery Caramel Dip and dip away! To reheat the dip, place it back in the microwave for 30 seconds. ★

30-MINUTE MEALS
MENU

NICE ITALIAN MENU

1

entree
CHICKEN CATCH-A-TORY RAVIOLI STEW

2

side dish
A NICE ITALIAN GIRL'S SALAD (BUT BOYS CAN MAKE IT TOO!)

MAKES 4 SERVINGS

Chicken Catch-a-tory Ravioli Stew

For ages 7 and up, with a Grown-up Helper

3 cloves garlic, skins on

2 tablespoons extra-virgin olive oil (evoo) (twice around the pan)

2 sprigs fresh rosemary

2 sprigs fresh thyme

1 cup presliced fresh mushrooms (about 1/3 pound) (available in produce section, or Grown-up Helper may slice for you)

Salt and freshly ground black pepper, to taste

1 can (15 ounces) stewed tomatoes with peppers, onions, and celery

2 roasted red peppers from a jar, drained

1 cup tomato sauce

1 package (10 ounces) chopped frozen spinach, defrosted in microwave and drained

6 cups chicken broth

3/4 to 1 pound (1 package) chicken breast tenders

1 pound fresh ravioli, any flavor

1 cup grated parmesan, Parmigiano Reggiano, or Romano cheese, to pass at table

Crusty Italian bread or rolls, to pass at table

Have your GH (Grown-Up Helper) heat a medium soup pot over medium-high heat. Place 3 cloves of garlic on a cutting board and WHACK each clove with a small heavy frying pan. Pick out the skins and chuck them in your garbage bowl. Have the GH add evoo, 2 turns of the pan, to the soup pot. Throw in the smashed garlic and the fresh rosemary and thyme. The leaves will fall off the stems and give a delicious flavor to your special stew. Add mushrooms, too, and help stir as the mushrooms cook, 3 to 5 minutes. Season the 'shrooms up with salt and pepper as they're cooking.

Next, you or your GH can open the can of stewed tomatoes and add them to the pot. Use a sharp, small knife to chop the roasted red bell peppers. Keep your fingers on the hand that is not holding the knife curled under so you don't chop off a whole finger! You just want to cut up those peppers into pieces as big as your mouth; that's what they call bite-size. Add the chopped-up roasted red peppers and add 1 cup tomato sauce to the soup pot.

Put defrosted chopped spinach in a kitchen towel. Gather towel up and twist it to get the water out of the spinach. Squeeze the spinach over your garbage bowl until it stops dripping. Separate spinach with your fingers and add it to the soup. Pour in chicken broth and stir the stew really slowly or it will slosh out of your pot! Have the GH cover the soup and raise the heat to high.

Have the GH cut up the chicken for you on a separate cutting board from the one you cut up the vegetables on. Tell them to use a plastic board. Cut the chicken tenders into 1-inch pieces, and add them to the stew. Tell the GH to go wash up right away with lots of soap and hot water—including the board—so that the raw chicken doesn't get on anything else in the kitchen or any other food. If you touched the raw chicken, you should wash up, too.

When the stew comes up to a boil again, add the ravioli and leave the lid off. Cook stew until the ravioli is almost done, about 5 minutes. Turn off the heat and let the stew cool down a little bit. Have your GH serve up the stew and pass cheese and bread at the table to go with it. ★

Cacciatore is the real way to spell the name of this stew. It's the Italian word for "hunter." Chicken cacciatore is made with wild mushrooms and strong flavors. It is hearty, so it would keep a hunter full for a long hunt. This stew uses some of the same flavors and ingredients of the original dish, but it's even easier to make! Everyone in my family really loves this recipe. I hope your family loves it, too!

✪ ✪ ✪ ✪
MAKES 4 SERVINGS

A Nice Italian Girl's Salad

For ages 7 and up, with a Grown-up Helper

1 sack (10 ounces) chopped romaine lettuce (available in the produce aisle)

1/2 cup black pitted olives (available in the fancy olive bins near the deli)

1 roasted red pepper from a jar, drained and sliced

12 grape tomatoes

24 slices pepperoni

ITALIAN BLENDER DRESSING

3 tablespoons red wine vinegar (about 3 splashes)

2 tablespoons chopped green salad olives with red pimientos and juice

6 fresh basil leaves, torn up

2 to 3 tablespoons fresh flat-leaf parsley leaves (a handful)

3 big spoonfuls grated parmesan, Parmigiano Reggiano, or Romano cheese

Freshly ground black pepper, to taste

1/2 cup extra-virgin olive oil (evoo), eyeball it

Wash your hands. Pour lettuce into a big salad bowl. Break up the olives a little with your fingers. Scatter the olives and the sliced red peppers around the salad. Add in the grape tomatoes and pepperoni slices, too.

Make the dressing: Pour the vinegar into a blender. Add the olives, basil, parsley, cheese, pepper, and evoo. Have the GH (Grown-up Helper) place the lid on the blender and blend the dressing until everything is all chopped up and mixed up together. Pour dressing over the salad and toss it up good. ★

This recipe was especially designed for Sabia Rose to make for Bill and Vicki, 'cause she's Daddy's AND Mommy's Little Girl—and a really good cook, too!

319

✪ ✪ ✪ ✪

MAKES 4 SERVINGS

Bite-Size Antipast-Salad

For ages 7 and up, with a Grown-up Helper

DRESSING
1 tablespoon balsamic vinegar
2 tablespoons extra-virgin olive oil (evoo)
Salt and freshly ground black pepper, to taste

SALAD
1/4-pound chunk provolone cheese, cut into pieces
1/2 pound bocconcini (bite-size fresh mozzarella pieces), pieces cut or snipped in half (available in fancy cheese section)
1 whole roasted red pepper, chopped or snipped into pieces (available in jars or at the deli counter)
1 can (15 ounces) quartered artichoke hearts in water, drained
12 slices pepperoni
1/4 pound salami, sliced, chopped into bite-size pieces
1/2 cup olives, pitted black or green (good quality, from bulk bins)
1/2 pint grape tomatoes
1 heart of romaine lettuce, chopped or torn into bite-size pieces
10 leaves fresh basil, torn or snipped into slivers

Make the dressing: Whisk vinegar and evoo together in a small bowl until combined. Add salt and pepper and whisk again.

Combine cheeses, red pepper, artichoke hearts, meat, olives, tomatoes, lettuce, and basil on a shallow platter. Pour dressing over. Season the salad with salt and pepper. ★

✪ ✪ ✪ ✪
MAKES 4 SERVINGS

Mini Shrimp Scampi and Angel Hair Pasta

For ages 7 and up, with a Grown-up Helper

Salt and freshly ground black pepper, to taste

1 pound angel hair pasta

4 cloves garlic

2 tablespoons extra-virgin olive oil (evoo) (twice around the pan)

3 tablespoons butter (tablespoons are marked on the wrapper), cut into small pieces

1 pound 300-count baby shrimp (that means there are 300 shrimp to a pound)

1 cup chicken broth

4 to 5 blades chives, snipped with scissors (2 tablespoons)

A handful of fresh flat-leaf parsley leaves, chopped or snipped

Have your GH (Grown-Up Helper) put a large pot of water over high heat and bring to a boil; add salt. Cook pasta according to package directions, to al dente.

Meanwhile, smash garlic cloves with a small pan; separate out the skins and throw them away.

Have your GH heat a large skillet over medium heat. Add evoo and butter. When butter has melted into oil, add crushed garlic and cook 2 minutes. Add shrimp; add salt and pepper. Cook shrimp until heated through, 2 or 3 minutes; add broth and increase heat to bring to a boil. When liquid boils, remove pan from heat and have the GH drain pasta and add to the pan. Toss pasta with shrimp, sauce, and herbs. Adjust seasonings and serve. ★

For the salad, instead of making your own dressing, you can also use bottled Caesar dressing. I recommend Ken's brand Caesar dressing.

30-MINUTE MEALS
MENU

CHICK ON A
STICK

1

entree
CHICKEN
STICK-ENS

2

suggested side
CHUNKED
VEGETABLE
SALAD

✪ ✪ ✪ ✪

MAKES 18 TO 20 CHICKEN SKEWERS

Chicken Stick-ens

For ages 4 and up, with a Grown-up Helper

18 to 20 bamboo skewers (8 inches long)
2 packages chicken tenders, 1 to 1 & 1/3 pounds total (18 to 20 pieces)
3 to 4 tablespoons (a couple good scoops) hoisin sauce (found on Asian foods aisle)
3 tablespoons low-sodium soy sauce (3 splashes)
2 tablespoons honey (a big drizzle from the honey bear)
2 tablespoons sesame oil (twice around the bowl)
A couple shakes ground ginger (about 1/2 teaspoon)
A meat mallet
Waxed paper

Soak the skewers in a shallow dish of water.

Cover a work surface with a sheet of waxed paper and place the chicken tenders in a single layer across the surface. Top with a second sheet of waxed paper. Here comes the fun part: Kids can take turns whacking the chicken with a meat mallet to flatten the strips out. (Those of you in Little League or Tee-ball, watch it! Don't whack the chicken so hard that it dents the counter, okay?)

Now, pull back the top layer of waxed paper and thread the chicken onto the skewers one at a time, very carefully—skewers hurt when you poke them into your fingers, trust me. Poke the skewers in and out of the chicken meat until you get to the end of the tender. Helpers, keep your eyes peeled and your hands free to shadow small kids while they perform this step.

Wash up before you do another thing and do not touch anything or anyone until you do. Thank you.

Mix hoisin sauce, soy sauce, honey, sesame oil, and ginger in a small bowl.

Place the chicken sticks in a baking dish or shallow platter and pour the sauce over them. Turn the skewers all around to coat the chicken evenly in the sauce.

Wash up again.

Helpers, heat a big skillet or nonstick griddle pan over high heat. Using tongs to turn, cook skewers 3 minutes on each side in a single layer, half a batch at a time. If the pan smokes a lot, reduce heat a little.

Allow the chicken sticks to cool to room temperature before little hands pick them up. Serve with a chunked vegetable salad. ★

✪ ✪ ✪ ✪

MAKES 6 SERVINGS

Meatza Pizza Balls

For ages 4 and up, with a Grown-up Helper

1 pound 93% lean ground beef
1/4 pound pepperoni, chopped by Grown-Up Helper (GH) into small bits
1 egg
1/2 cup Italian bread crumbs (a couple of grown-up handfuls)
1/4 cup grated Parmigiano or Romano cheese (a grown-up handful)
2 shakes fresh or dried oregano (about 1/4 teaspoon)
3 shakes garlic powder (about 1/2 teaspoon)
A couple pinches coarse salt (plus 1 to throw over your shoulder for luck)
Vegetable oil cooking spray or olive oil
1 can (14 ounces) prepared pizza sauce or tomato sauce
Toothpicks, for dipping

GH, preheat oven to 425°F.

Kids, wash up, and roll up your sleeves. Combine beef, pepperoni, egg, bread crumbs, cheese, oregano, garlic powder, and salt in a big bowl. Squish everything up with your hands, really mixing all the spices and special ingredients into the meat.

Wash up. Thank you.

GH, place a nonstick cookie sheet or a baking sheet coated with cooking spray or brushed with olive oil in the center of the work space. Have a bowl of warm water ready for dampening small hands before they roll meatballs.

Kids, dip your hands into the bowl of warm water. Now, grab a small lump of meat and roll it between the palms of your hands to make a ball, then drop it onto the cookie sheet. GH, guide little hands and keep an eye out to make sure the balls are fairly consistent in size, about 1 inch in diameter, so that the cooking time will be the same for all of the meatballs.

When all the balls are rolled, wash up again.

GH, place the cookie sheet on the middle rack of the oven and bake until balls are evenly browned, 10 to 12 minutes. Loosen balls with a spatula about midway through baking if you are not using a nonstick cookie sheet. Break 1 ball open to test and make sure there is no pink left in the meat before removing from oven.

While balls are in oven, warm pizza or tomato sauce on stovetop. Transfer to a small bowl and place in the middle of a serving platter. Scatter balls all around the dip and place a small glass filled with toothpicks alongside for dipping. Celery and carrot sticks make a nice accompaniment. ★

30-MINUTE MEALS

MENU

HAVE A BALL!

1
entree
MEATZA PIZZA BALLS

2
suggested side
CELERY AND CARROT STICKS

30-MINUTE MEALS
MENU

MEGA COMFORT FOOD MENU

1

entree
MEAT LOAF MUFFINS WITH BARBECUE SAUCE
- - -

2

side dishes
SMASHED POTATOES AND CREAM CHEESE
- - -

MICRO-WAY-COOL GREEN BEANS AND BACON
- - -

✪ ✪ ✪ ✪

MAKES 6 SERVINGS

Meat Loaf Muffins with Barbecue Sauce

For ages 7 and up, with a Grown-up Helper

Vegetable oil or extra-virgin olive oil (evoo), for pan

1 & 1/2 pounds ground sirloin

1 small yellow onion, cut into quarters

1 small green bell pepper

A splash of milk

1 large egg, beaten

1 cup plain bread crumbs

2 tablespoons grill seasoning, such as Montreal Steak Seasoning by McCormick

1 cup smoky barbecue sauce

1/2 cup tomato salsa

1 tablespoon Worcestershire sauce

Have your GH (Grown-Up Helper) preheat oven to 450°F. Brush a 6-muffin tin with vegetable oil or evoo.

Put ground beef into a big bowl. Put onions into a food processor. Cut the bell pepper in half and rip out the seeds and the white stuff and throw it away. Cut the pepper into a few pieces and add to the food processor. Pulse the processor to finely chop the onion and bell pepper. Add to the meat bowl. Whisk the milk into the beaten egg, and add to meat. Add bread crumbs and grill seasoning.

In a small bowl, mix together the barbecue sauce, salsa, and Worcestershire sauce. Pour half the sauce mixture into the bowl with the meat loaf mix. Mix the meat loaf together with your hands.

Wash your hands well. Thank you.

Use a large ice cream scoop to put the meat into muffin tin. Top each meat loaf muffin with a spoonful of reserved sauce. Bake about 15 minutes. Have a GH cut open one muffin to test if it's cooked through. While meat loaf muffins bake, make green beans in the microwave (see below). Serve meat loaf with smashed potatoes and green beans on the side. ★

Timing Tip: While the water boils and when the potatoes are cooking, you can be working on the meat loaf recipe.

✪ ✪ ✪ ✪
MAKES 6 SERVINGS

Smashed Potatoes and Cream Cheese

For ages 7 and up, with a Grown-up Helper

2 & 1/2 pounds small red-skinned potatoes or baby Yukon gold potatoes
1/2 cup half-and-half or whole milk
8 ounces plain cream cheese or veggie cream cheese, cut into pieces
10 chives or 2 scallions, chopped or snipped with kitchen scissors
Salt and freshly ground black pepper, to taste

Place potatoes in a pot of water over high heat and boil until potatoes are tender, about 15 minutes. Have your GH (Grown-Up Helper) drain them and return them to the hot pot to let them dry out a bit. Mash potatoes with half-and-half or milk with a potato smasher. The GH can get the mash going for you if the going gets tough. Add in the cream cheese and smash until the cheese melts into the potatoes some, then add chives or scallions and season with salt and pepper. ★

✪ ✪ ✪ ✪
MAKES 4 SERVINGS

Micro-way-cool Green Beans and Bacon

For ages 7 and up, with a Grown-up Helper

6 slices microwave ready-crisp bacon
1 bag (16 ounces) frozen green beans
Extra-virgin olive oil (evoo), for drizzling
Salt and freshly ground black pepper, to taste

Place bacon between paper towels and microwave 60 seconds on high. Cool bacon and chop or crumble it up.

Place green beans in a bowl and drizzle with evoo; add salt and pepper. Cover the bowl loosely with plastic wrap and microwave green beans on high for 5 minutes, stir and cook 5 minutes more. Remove wrap and top green beans with crumbled bacon. ★

30-MINUTE MEALS

MENU

BREAKFAST
OR
BREAKFAST
FOR DINNER

1

entree
MONTE CRISTO
AND ELVIS
FRENCH TOAST
SAMMIES

2

dessert
TROPICAL
YOGURT
PARFAITS

★ ★ ★ ★

MAKES 4 SERVINGS

Monte Cristo and Elvis French Toast Sammies

For ages 7 and up, with a Grown-up Helper

8 slices thin sandwich bread, such as Pepperidge Farm brand

4 slices deli Swiss cheese

2 slices deli turkey

2 slices deli ham

1/4 cup peanut butter

1 small banana, sliced

2 eggs, beaten

2 splashes milk

2 tablespoons butter (tablespoons are marked on the wrapper)

Maple syrup, for dipping

Make the Monte Cristos: On a slice of bread, stack 1 slice Swiss cheese, 1 slice turkey folded in half, 1 slice ham folded in half, another slice Swiss, and another slice bread. Repeat to make 2 Monte Cristo sandwiches total.

Make the Elvis sandwiches: Spread the remaining slices of bread with peanut butter. Cover 2 slices with pieces of banana and place sandwich tops in place, using the peanut butter as glue to hold the sandwiches together.

Have your GH (Grown-Up Helper) heat a nonstick skillet over medium heat. Mix together eggs and milk. Add a tablespoon of butter to the pan and melt it. Dip all 4 sandwiches into egg mixture then cook the French toast sammies in the skillet until golden, 3 or 4 minutes on each side (flip with a spatula, or have your GH do it). While sammies cook, warm maple syrup in the microwave on high for 30 seconds in a microwave-safe pitcher. Pour the warm syrup into small cups and serve with sammies. Cut each sammy from corner to corner and serve half an Elvis and half a Monte Cristo per person. ★

✪ ✪ ✪ ✪
MAKES 4 SERVINGS

Tropical Yogurt Parfait

For ages 7 and up, with a Grown-up Helper

2 cups custard-style vanilla yogurt (low-fat or nonfat)
1 small can mandarin oranges, drained
1 cup crispy rice breakfast cereal, any brand
1 small can (6 ounces) crushed pineapple

Put a couple of tablespoons of yogurt in the bottom of 4 juice glasses. Top with mandarin orange slices and a few spoonfuls each of crispy rice and crushed pineapple. Add more yogurt to fill up the glasses and top off with another layer of fruit and crispy rice. ★

Cool! These recipes work for your breakfast or your dinner!
If you like these sandwiches, why not try making peanut butter and jelly French toast sandwiches or peanut butter and bacon French toast sandwiches. Make them the same way you make the Elvis sammies, just change the fillings. The peanut butters acts as a glue to hold the sandwith together.

30-MINUTE MEALS

MENU

BREAKFAST
OR
BREAKFAST
FOR DINNER
AGAIN

1
entree
BACON-AND-
CHEESE MINI
QUICHES

2
side dish
POTATO-AND-
APPLE HOME
FRIES

✪ ✪ ✪ ✪
MAKES 4 SERVINGS

Potato-and-Apple Home Fries

For ages 7 and up, with a Grown-up Helper

3 tablespoons butter (tablespoons are marked on the wrapper)
1 sack (24 ounces) diced breakfast potatoes (available on the dairy aisle)
1/2 pound ham steak, diced
1 green apple, such as Granny Smith, chopped
1 tablespoon grill seasoning, such as Montreal Seasoning by McCormick
  or Mrs. Dash seasoning

Have your GH (Grown-Up Helper) place a nonstick skillet on the stove over medium-high heat. Add butter and melt it. Add potatoes, ham, and apples and season them with grill seasoning blend. Turn every 5 minutes or so, letting the potatoes brown up on all sides. Cook 20 minutes, then serve. While the potatoes cook, make the mini quiches below. ★

These mini quiches can be changed to suit your taste. Try making them with bits of chopped defrosted frozen broccoli and shredded cheddar cheese or chopped Canadian bacon and Swiss cheese.

✪ ✪ ✪ ✪
MAKES 4 SERVINGS, 6 MINI QUICHES EACH

Bacon-and-Cheese Mini Quiches

For ages 7 and up, with a Grown-up Helper

24 filo pastry cups (2 packages of 12; available in the frozen foods section)
4 slices ready-crisp bacon (fully cooked and microwave-ready bacon)
1 cup shredded cheddar cheese
2 eggs
A splash of milk
Salt and freshly ground black pepper, to taste

Have your GH (Grown-Up Helper) preheat oven to 375°F.

Arrange the pastry cups on a cookie sheet. Cut up bacon into thin pieces with kitchen scissors. Add a little bacon to each cup. Add a sprinkle of cheese to each cup, too. Beat eggs in a bowl with a splash of milk and some salt and pepper. Use a large spoon to add egg to each pastry cup to fill them up. Bake until golden, 10 to 12 minutes. Have your GH take them out of the oven for you. ★

Mini Quiches

30-MINUTE MEALS

MENU

ANOTHER
BREAKFAST
FOR DINNER

1

entree
EGG SCRAMBLES

2

side dish
FRUIT
BENEDICTS

Use some kid-safe scissors that you have just for the kitchen to make these super scrambles. Try these recipes for weekend brunch, too. Brunch is when you skip breakfast and have an early lunch. The two words (and meals) get mixed up to make up a brunch! The fruit benedicts make a great snack, too, or even a dessert!

✪ ✪ ✪ ✪

MAKES 4 SERVINGS

Fruit Benedicts and Egg Scrambles

For ages 4 and up, with a Grown-up Helper

FRUIT BENEDICTS
4 English muffins, split by your GH (Grown-Up Helper)
Creamy peanut butter
1 cup crushed pineapple
1 banana, sliced by your GH

SCRAMBLES
8 eggs
4 stems chives (long, thin, green herbs that taste like yummy sweet onions)
4 pinches salt
4 grinds black pepper
4 slices Canadian-style bacon (round thin slices of ham)
2 tablespoons butter (tablespoons are marked on the wrapper)
1 & 1/4 cups shredded cheddar cheese (half a 10-ounce sack; preshredded is available on the dairy aisle)

Make the fruit benedicts: Have the GH heat the broiler. Put English muffin pieces on a cookie sheet and have the GH toast them in the middle of the oven on both sides. While they are warm but not too hot to touch, spread each half with peanut butter. Put spoonfuls of pineapple on each muffin on top of the peanut butter and then put sliced bananas on top of the pineapple. Put the fruit benedicts on a platter to serve.

Make the scrambles: Have the GH heat a nonstick skillet over medium heat. Crack the eggs into a bowl (can you help crack them?). Use your kitchen scissors to snip the chives into the bowl with the eggs. Add salt and pepper and beat up the eggs with a whisk. If the yolks won't break, poke them with a fork. When the eggs are mixed, use your scissors again to chop up the ham slices into little pieces, and keep them on the cutting board. The GH should add butter to the hot skillet and when it melts, add the ham you cut up. Cook ham 2 minutes. The GH can add your eggs and chives now and stir until they are scrambled, cooked, and the ham is hot all through. Add cheese and stir into eggs to melt it. Serve eggs with fruit benedicts and eat. ★

✪ ✪ ✪ ✪
MAKES 6 SERVINGS

Meatball Patty Melts

For ages 4 and up, with a Grown-up Helper

1 pound meat loaf mix (ground beef, pork, and veal) or ground beef only
1 egg
1/2 cup Italian bread crumbs (a couple grown-up handfuls)
1/4 cup grated Parmigiano or Romano cheese (a grown-up handful)
A grown-up palmful chopped fresh flat-leaf parsley
2 cloves garlic, minced by Grown-Up Helper (GH)
1 small onion, finely chopped by GH
Olive oil or vegetable oil cooking spray
1 cup pizza or tomato sauce
6 slices sharp provolone cheese
6 sesame-seeded hard rolls

Kids, wash your hands and roll up your sleeves! In a BIG bowl, mix meat, egg, bread crumbs, cheese, parsley, garlic, and onion. Take turns with the mixing—this is the really fun part!

Next, kids can form meat mixture into 6 hamburger-shaped patties. If you have trouble making a patty, roll some meat up into a big ball. Put the ball on a plate or cutting board and squish it flat.

Wash your hands with soap. Thank you.

GH can heat a griddle or nonstick skillet lightly coated with a touch of olive oil or cooking spray over medium-high heat. Cook 3 patties at a time for 4 or 5 minutes on each side. Kids can do the flipping with a long-handled spatula. Top patties with a couple of spoonfuls of pizza or tomato sauce and 1 slice of cheese. Reduce heat to low. Cover with lid or a loose aluminum foil tent and let stand 3 to 5 minutes to melt cheese and warm sauce.

Split rolls and fill with meatball patty melts. Serve with a mixed green salad or a chunked vegetable salad. ★

30-MINUTE MEALS
MENU

MELT-AWAY HUNGER

1
entrees
MEATBALL
PATTY MELTS

2
suggested side
MIXED GREEN
OR CHUNKED
VEGETABLE
SALAD

30-MINUTE MEALS
MENU

MY FIRST
MENU

1

entree
SPINACH &
MUSHROOM
LASAGNA
ROLL-UPS WITH
GORGONZOLA
CREAM SAUCE

2

side dishes
STEAMED
LEMON-
SCENTED
ASPARAGUS

BROILED
TOMATOES

✪ ✪ ✪ ✪
MAKES 4 SERVINGS

Spinach & Mushroom Lasagna Roll-Ups with Gorgonzola Cream Sauce, Steamed Lemon-Scented Asparagus, and Broiled Tomatoes

For ages 12 and up

Salt and freshly ground black pepper, to taste

8 curly-edge lasagna noodles

1 & 1/2 pounds fresh asparagus

1 lemon

2 tablespoons extra-virgin olive oil (evoo) (twice around the pan), plus more for drizzling

16 crimini (baby portobello) mushroom caps, cleaned with a damp towel and finely chopped in food processor

1 small yellow onion, finely chopped

2 cloves garlic, minced

4 vine-ripe tomatoes

1 box (10 ounces) frozen chopped spinach, defrosted and squeezed dry in a clean towel

1/4 teaspoon ground nutmeg

2 cups ricotta cheese

1 cup chicken broth

1/2 cup heavy cream (3 turns of the pan)

8 ounces gorgonzola cheese, crumbled

Bring a large pot of water to a boil for the lasagna. You're going to put a colander over (not in!) the water to steam the asparagus in, so be sure to leave enough room at the top of the pot. When the water boils, add salt then noodles. Cook noodles to almost tender, or al dente, 12 to 14 minutes. Drain.

While pasta is cooking, prepare the asparagus: Hold a piece of asparagus at both ends and push the ends together, making the spear snap and break. Where the asparagus snaps becomes your guide for trimming off the tough ends of the rest of the asparagus. Trim the spears (discarding the ends) and place them in a small colander. Pull 2 big pieces of peel off the lemon and add them to the asparagus. At least 4 or 5 minutes before the pasta is done, place the colander over the boiling water in the pasta pot; place a lid on the colander and steam asparagus until the tips are just tender, about 4 minutes. Place the asparagus on a plate. Cut the lemon in half and squeeze the juice from 1/2 lemon over the asparagus (squeeze it right side up so the

Spinach and Mushroom Lasagna Roll-Ups

This is the first menu I made by myself. I made it for my mother for her birthday. I was 12. She liked it. She liked it a lot—and I got away with murder for a long time because of it!

seeds don't fall into the asparagus); add a little salt. Serve at room temperature.

In a medium skillet over medium heat, warm 2 tablespoons evoo then add mushrooms, onions, and garlic. Season with salt and pepper and cook until mushrooms give off their juices and darken and onions are tender, 7 or 8 minutes.

While the vegetables cook, prepare the tomatoes: Split tomatoes lengthwise and arrange on a small baking dish. Drizzle with evoo and season with salt and pepper. Place a rack in the top position in the oven and preheat the broiler.

Add chopped spinach to the pan with the mushrooms and heat through for 1 minute. Add salt, pepper, and nutmeg (your secret ingredient!). Add ricotta cheese and stir into mixture to heat cheese through, 1 minute. Remove pan from heat but leave mixture in the warm skillet.

Make the sauce: Heat chicken broth and cream in a small pot over medium heat until liquid bubbles, then melt gorgonzola cheese into the liquid and return it to a bubble. Simmer sauce on low heat.

Broil tomatoes, 2 minutes. Place on a serving plate.

Place cooked lasagna noodles on a large work surface or cutting board. Cool 1 minute to handle, but work while pasta is still warm. Spread each lasagna noodle with a layer of spinach-mushroom filling. Place half the cheese sauce into a serving dish. Roll up pasta and arrange the 8 bundles in the dish. Dot the bundles with remaining spoonfuls of the cheese sauce and serve. Serve with steamed asparagus and broiled tomatoes. ★

✪ ✪ ✪ ✪

MAKES 6 SERVINGS

Eggcellent Sandwiches

For ages 4 and up, with a Grown-up Helper

2 tablespoons butter

9 large eggs

1/3 pound smoked ham (from the deli counter, in thick slices), diced into small bits

6 sandwich-size English muffins

6 slices Muenster cheese (from deli)

Kids break 1 tablespoon butter into bits and take turns cracking eggs into bowl and whisking them together with butter bits.

Grown-Up Helper (GH) should dice ham for kids under 10 or supervise dicing, allowing kids to use serrated paring knives—anyone chopping anything needs to always keep their eyes on the board and their fingertips curled under. Place ham bits in a small dish near the stove.

Kids toast English muffins in toaster and place 6 halves on a cookie sheet; pile the tops on a plate.

GH heat a nonstick skillet over medium heat. Melt the remaining 1 tablespoon butter in pan and distribute by tilting pan. Add ham and cook for 2 minutes. Add eggs to pan and allow kids to stir gently with a wooden spoon until eggs are scrambled and beginning to firm up, 4 to 5 minutes. GH distributes the eggs onto the 6 muffin bottoms on a cookie sheet. Kids top each egg-piled muffin with 1 slice Muenster cheese. GH places cookie sheet under preheated broiler to just melt the cheese. Remove from oven. Top with muffin caps and serve warm with fresh fruit on the side. ★

30-MINUTE MEALS

MENU

CLASSIC KID FAVORITE

1

entree
EGGCELLENT
SANDWICHES

2

suggested side
FRESH FRUIT

✪ ✪ ✪ ✪

MAKES 4 SERVINGS, PLUS EXTRA RESERVED COMPOUND BUTTER

Grilled T-Bone Steaks with Chipotle-Chili Rub & Cilantro-Lime Compound Butter

For ages 12 and up

1 lime

1 cup (2 sticks) butter, cut into chunks

3 tablespoons finely chopped cilantro

4 T-bone steaks, 1 & 1/2 inch thick

2 tablespoons steak seasoning blend for the grill, such as Montreal
 Seasoning by McCormick

1 tablespoon chipotle (smoky) ground chili powder or dark chili powder

1 tablespoon sweet paprika

Preheat a two-burner grill pan over high heat or a tabletop electric grill to high, or preheat the outdoor grill.

Grate the zest of the lime (the green part of the skin—not the white part) on the small holes of a grater. Cut the lime in half crosswise and squeeze all the juice from the lime halves into a bowl.

Place butter in a microwave-safe bowl. Place bowl in microwave and cook on high for 15 seconds. Stir in cilantro and lime zest and juice using a rubber spatula. Transfer the butter onto a large piece of plastic wrap.

Gather the ends of the plastic wrap in one hand and use a straight edge, like a small cookie sheet, to push the butter back and away from your body making the butter take on a log shape. Gently roll the log wrapped in plastic back and forth on the countertop to evenly round out the shape. Twist up the extra wrap on the ends and place the compound butter log into the freezer to make the butter cold enough to slice again.

Remove the steaks from the refrigerator and unwrap. Combine the steak seasoning blend with ground chipotle (smoked jalapeño powder) and sweet paprika. A tablespoon is about a palmful of powdered or ground seasonings. Rub the seasoning blend into the steaks, distributing the spices evenly among them. Go wash your hands. Using tongs, place steaks on screaming-hot grill, carefully place the thin tip of one steak facing the wide end of the next so that all 4 steaks fit onto the grill at the same time. Cook steaks 6 to 7 minutes on each side for medium doneness. Remove steaks and let them rest so that the juices can redistribute, 5 minutes.

When ready to serve, top steaks with disks of sliced compound butter, and serve with the cheesy smashed potatoes and sautéed veggies.★

30-MINUTE MEALS

MENU

MEAT AND POTATOES MENU FOR THE NEXT GREAT CHEF

1

entree
GRILLED T-BONE STEAKS WITH CHIPOTLE-CHILI RUB & CILANTRO-LIME COMPOUND BUTTER

▬ ▬ ▬ ▬

2

side dishes
CHEESY SMASHED POTATOES

SAUTÉED VEGGIES FOR STEAK

I designed this menu for my friend Harry who is just starting high school this year. He grew up in a gourmet market. I worked with his mom and dad. Harry is too cool. He plays the electric guitar, he's really cute, and he loves to cook! Look out girls! Harry might be the first rock star chef, so I thought I would write a menu that rocked, too. It's full of info and tricks-of-the-trade, so he'll know a thing or two ahead of time if he goes to culinary school one day.

✪ ✪ ✪ ✪
MAKES 4 SERVINGS

Cheesy Smashed Potatoes

For ages 12 and up

2 to 2 & 1/4 pounds baby Yukon gold potatoes
Salt and freshly ground black pepper, to taste
1/4 cup sour cream
2 cups shredded cheddar cheese
3 tablespoons chopped or snipped chives

Cut potatoes in half and place in a pot. Cover potatoes with water and bring to a boil. Work on other dishes while you are waiting for the water to boil.

When water boils, add 2 big pinches salt; boil potatoes 10 minutes or until tender. Go work on other stuff again.

Drain potatoes and return them to the hot pot. Mash potatoes with sour cream and cheese. When cheese melts into potatoes, add chives, salt, and pepper, and re-smash. Taste the potatoes and adjust seasonings. ★

✪ ✪ ✪ ✪
MAKES 4 BIG VEGGIE SERVINGS

Sautéed Veggies for Steak

For ages 12 and up

2 tablespoons extra-virgin olive oil (evoo) (twice around the pan)
1 pound large white mushrooms, sliced
1 red bell pepper
1 yellow bell pepper
1/2 large red onion
Salt and freshly ground black pepper, to taste
2 tablespoons cilantro-lime compound butter (recipe above)

Heat a large skillet over medium-high heat. Add evoo. Add sliced mushrooms and let them brown. While they cook, cut the peppers in half and pull out the seeds and connective membranes and throw them away. Cut peppers into quarters lengthwise, then slice across. Cut onion in half lengthwise and peel it. Wrap half and save it for another use. Cut off ends and cut the half onion lengthwise in half again. Then slice the onions across. Add peppers and onions to mushrooms and season with salt and pepper. Cook another 3 to 5 minutes, stirring often, until they're just tender but still have a little crunch left to them and lots of bright color. Remove veggies from the heat and add cilantro-lime butter. Toss veggies to melt butter, then serve. ★

This meal is a FEAST, and it's super fast: The sauce cooks in just one minute—really! And it's made with ingredients most of us have in the house: butter, half-and-half, and grated cheese.

✪ ✪ ✪ ✪
MAKES 4 SERVINGS

Green Noodles and Ham

For ages 7 and up, with a Grown-up Helper

Salt and freshly ground black pepper, to taste

1 box (12 to 14 ounces) spinach fettuccine pasta

1/4 pound prosciutto (Italian ham)

3 tablespoons butter (tablespoons are marked on the wrapper), cut into small pieces

1 cup cream or half-and-half

1 to 1 & 1/2 cups grated Romano or Parmigiano Reggiano cheese

1 cup frozen green peas

Bring a big pot of water to a boil and add a spoonful of salt to the water to season the pasta as it cooks. When it boils, add pasta to the water and cook according to package directions to al dente (done, but with a bite to it).

While the pasta cooks, you or your GH (Grown-Up Helper) can cut prosciutto into thin, short, ribbonlike pieces using kitchen scissors. Separate ham ribbons, loosely pile them up, and set aside.

Have your GH preheat a large skillet over medium heat. Place butter in pan to melt. Add 1 cup cream or half-and-half. Stirring constantly, add 1 cup cheese and cook sauce 1 minute, seasoning with pepper and a pinch of salt.

Turn off heat under sauce and have a GH drain pasta for you. Add pasta and peas to the skillet. Toss pasta until sauce coats the noodles evenly. Add prosciutto ribbons and toss to evenly distribute them. Taste the pasta and, if you think it needs it, melt in even more cheese, up to 1/2 cup. When the pasta tastes just perfect, start serving it up! Mangia! (That means "eat" in Italian.) Wow! Spinach green noodles are even yummier than white ones when you eat them with ham! For a complete meal, serve with a green salad on the side. ★

MANGIA!

1
entree
GREEN NOODLES AND HAM

2
suggested side
GREEN SALAD

✪ ✪ ✪ ✪
MAKES 4 SERVINGS

The Filiacis' Famous Banana-Nut Chocolate-Chip Bread

For ages 4 and up, with a Grown-up Helper

4 tablespoons (1/2 stick) butter, softened (tablespoons are marked on the wrapper), plus more for pan

3/4 cup sugar

2 large eggs

2 large or 3 small ripe bananas, mashed

2 cups all-purpose unbleached flour

2 teaspoons baking powder

1/2 teaspoon salt

1/4 teaspoon baking soda

1 cup semisweet chocolate chips

1 cup chopped walnuts

Have your GH (Grown-Up Helper) preheat oven to 350°F. Lightly grease a 9x5x3-inch loaf pan.

Cream sugar, butter, and eggs together until fluffy. Fold in mashed bananas with a spoon. Sift flour, baking powder, salt, and baking soda into a large mixing bowl. Add banana mixture, chocolate chips, and walnuts to the dry ingredients and stir until smooth. Pour batter into the loaf pan and bake until a toothpick inserted in the center comes out clean, about 55 minutes. Let cool before removing from pan. Serve thick slices with ice cold milk. ★

✪ ✪ ✪ ✪

MAKES 60 COOKIES

The Ultimate Peanut Butter Kiss Cookies

For ages 4 and up, with a Grown-up Helper

60 chocolate kisses (2 bags)
Vegetable oil cooking spray or softened butter, for pans
1 cup chunky peanut butter
1 cup sugar
1 large egg
1 teaspoon baking soda (this one you have to really measure)

Kids, unwrap all the chocolate kisses and pile them up on a plate. Try not to sneak'n-eat too many, or you won't have enough for the cookies.

GH, preheat oven to 350°F and lightly grease 2 cookie sheets with cooking spray or softened butter.

Kids, beat peanut butter and sugar in a big bowl on medium speed until the sugar is all mixed into the peanut butter. Beat an egg and baking soda in a smaller bowl and pour into peanut butter mixture. Beat again on medium speed until the egg is all combined into the peanut butter.

Kids, scoop out dough a teaspoonful at a time and roll it into a small ball. Place the balls at least 1 inch apart on cookie sheet and squish a kiss down on top of each ball, nesting it into the dough. Place no more than 30 cookies on each cookie sheet.

Wash your hands!

Bake 10 minutes. Remove and transfer to a cooling rack with a metal spatula, being careful not to stick your fingers in the kisses—the chocolate will be too soft. Let cookies cool completely before gobbling, and serve with ice cold milk. ★

My mom found this recipe in a magazine and made them even better by putting a chocolate kiss on top—her cookies are really cool.
I have to give you one serious warning though: Peanut butter cups will never taste as good as they used to once you eat these cookies.